New World of
INDIGENOUS RESISTANCE

NOAM CHOMSKY and Voices from
North, South, and Central America

Edited by
Lois Meyer and Benjamín Maldonado Alvarado

City Lights Books | Open Media Series

Cover design by Pollen.

Cover photograph by Mara Kaufman, February 14, 2006, on the Zapatista journey of the Other Campaign; Cerro de Semilla Nueva, Ixtepec, Puebla, Mexico.

All royalties from this book will benefit the indigenous educational efforts of the Coalition of Indigenous Teachers and Promoters of Oaxaca (CMPIO) and the National Congress of Indigenous Intercultural Education in Mexico.

The Open Media Series is edited by Greg Ruggiero and archived by the Tamiment Library, New York University.

"Resistance and Hope: The Future of *Comunalidad* in a Globalized World" interview with Noam Chomsky on February 20, 2004, was first published in Spanish as "Resistencia y esperanza: El futuro de la *comunalidad* en un mundo globalizado," in Meyer, L., Maldonado, B., Ortiz, R. & García, V. (2004). *Entre la normatividad y la comunalidad: Experiencias educativas innovadoras del Oaxaca Indígena actual.* Oaxaca, Mexico: IEEPO

"Video Message to the Second National Congress of Indigenous & Intercultural Education" and "The Imperial State and Hope from Inside Indigenous America" interview with Noam Chomsky on October 4, 2007, were first published in Spanish as "Saludo de Noam Chomsky" and "Entrevista a Noam Chomsky," in the Memoria/Proceedings of the Second National Congress of Indigenous and Intercultural Education, Vol. 1 and 2. (2009). *Mexico: Segundo Congreso Nacional de Educación Indígena e Intercultural.*

Library of Congress Cataloging-in-Publication Data
New world of indigenous resistance : Noam Chomsky and Voices from North, South, and Central America / edited by Lois Meyer and Benjamin Maldonado ; [interviews with] Noam Chomsky ; and voices from North, South, and Central America.
    p. cm. — (Open media series)
ISBN 978-0-87286-533-4
1. Chomsky, Noam—Interviews. 2. Chomsky, Noam—Critcism and interpretation.
3. Indigenous peoples—America—Politics and government. 4. Indigenous
peoples—America—Government relations. 5. Government, Resistance to—
America—History. I. Meyer, Lois. II. Maldonado Alvarado, Benjamín. III. Title. IV.
Series.

P85.C47N48 2010
323.17—dc22

                                    2010001368

City Lights Books are published at the City Lights Bookstore,
261 Columbus Avenue, San Francisco, CA 94133.
www.citylights.com

CONTENTS

V. CONCLUSION

Introduction

A Hemispheric Conversation among Equals

By Lois Meyer

Applied linguist, associate professor in the Department of Language, Literacy & Sociocultural Studies at the University of New Mexico in Albuquerque, U.S.A., and close collaborator with the Coalition of Indigenous Teachers and Promoters of Oaxaca (CMPIO). Email: lsmeyer@unm.edu

THIS BOOK INCLUDES THREE interviews with Noam Chomsky about indigenous resistance to globalization and cultural homogenization in the American hemisphere, but it offers even more than that. Gathered here for the first time in virtual conversation with the preeminent linguist and critical analyst of American foreign policy are voices from the indigenous Americas (South, Central and North), who speak to, with, and at times against, Chomsky's views. To our knowledge, this book is the first of its kind. It moves beyond interviews where Noam Chomsky's voice predominates, into a more textured and nuanced intellectual and political exchange in which Chomsky dialogues with more than twenty voices from the New World of indigenous resistance. We are deeply grateful to Dr. Chomsky for granting this series of interviews and especially appreciative that he opened his thoughts to analysis and comment by renowned activists, educators and scholars from the indigenous Americas. Together these voices participate in an unusual, and long overdue, hemispheric conversation among equals.

The perspective on equality and expertise that motivates the title of this chapter and the selection of participants in this conversation deserves comment. All of our commentators chose to join this hemispheric conversation not because of close personal or professional ties with Benjamín Maldonado or myself (many of them we have yet to meet personally), but because of their respect for Noam Chomsky and their desire to dialogue with him through text. Obvious differences exist among the commentators in terms of their participation in intellectual, educational, and political resistance efforts and movements in their local, regional, national, or international spheres of influence. Some of their commentaries on Chomsky's interviews include scholarly footnotes and bibliographic citations, while others narrate autobiographical accounts of oppression and resistance in specific communities or throughout their personal life histories. Both of these are important and valid paths to expertise, although they are differentially valued in Western and indigenous thought.

The commentators in this volume were selected to reflect and honor both scholarship and direct action as equal and necessary paths to wisdom. According to Grimaldo Rengifo Vásquez (this volume), "In local indigenous thinking, living is what gives knowledge, not gathering up a lot of *a priori* facts about the nature of things. As they say, 'To know, you have to live.'" While many of the commentators recognize Western knowledge to be important and strategically necessary for indigenous communities, they decry the relentless academic bias in Western thought and the consequences this bias has wreaked on oral indigenous cultures, alienating indigenous education from culturally authentic ways of learning, knowing, and remembering. Commentators in this volume emphasize that authentic ways of learning, in life and through communal action, are holistic, ecological, spiritual, and healing. It is this very form of learning and knowing that the indigenous movement seeks to revitalize, value, honor, and embed into schools and other sites of learning, not only for the benefit of their own children, but for the healing of the entire world.

We refer to this as a hemispheric conversation, for geographically the participants span the American continents, both North and South. We acknowledge, however, that the topics addressed here range beyond the so-called New World, encompassing profound struggles over political, economic, social, and educational power and ideology worldwide. The analyses in this volume dissect the yawning ideological divide between the communal priorities and practices of indigenous peoples throughout the Americas, and the priorities, practices, and power of global corporate capitalism, whose centers lie both in and beyond our geographic hemisphere. All of the contributing voices here come from the "New World" of indigenous resistance in the Americas, where they contest the hegemonic state policies and capitalist values emanating from Bogota, Rio de Janeiro, Lima and Mexico City, as well as from Washington, D.C., London, or Tokyo.

In this introduction and in many of the commentaries to follow, as well as in Noam Chomsky's interviews, this ideological divide is described in shorthand as the struggle between "Western" power and ideology and indigenous communalism, often termed the "Other." Given our complex hemispheric context, what do we mean by "Western"? We do not use this term to refer to a geographic direction on a compass or map, nor do we wish to reinforce the U.S. geographer's biased perspective where "West" implies a contrast with "Middle East" or "Far East," as if all physical directions were universally marked from a territorial center within this dominant world power. In today's convoluted and interconnected planetary geography, "Western" ideology permeates the farthest reaches of the global north, south, east, and west. Indigenous communalism, often slighted as the "Other," coexists with and resists "Western" domination inside the boundaries of virtually all nation-states of the Americas, which have been inhabited for centuries by non-Western cultures and communities. Our use of the term "Western" refers to the hegemonic values, beliefs, and policies which undergird global neoliberal capitalism. While these developed first in Europe and the United States, they now pervade elite classes and power structures worldwide. There is no place in our hemisphere (understood here in contrast to Europe, Africa, or the Asian-Pacific region) where indigenous resistance to Western domination and in defense of communal practices and priorities does not have its history and impact.

Our commentators denounce the marginalization, exclusion, and repression of indigenous peoples as it is evidenced in references to the "Other." When any alternative ideology and lifeway can be dismissed by those in power as the "Other," Western ideological hegemony flaunts its linguistic and conceptual impunity. Interestingly, this dismissive terminology has been taken up as a strategy of indigenous struggle—the Zapatista National Liberation Army in Mexico has declared its struggle of resistance to be the "Other Campaign" and its educational vision to be the "Other Education." We celebrate their defiance by featuring a photo from the "Other Campaign" on our cover.

As will be seen, "hemisphere," "Western," and the "Other" are only three of several terms whose meanings will be clarified and also complexified in the course of the multivoiced conversation documented here.

THE FIRST CHOMSKY INTERVIEW

As with any conversation of substance and significance, this one has a history. The first interview with Noam Chomsky took place in February 2004. At that time, Benjamín Maldonado and I were collaborating with others in Oaxaca, Mexico, on a book of case studies detailing innovative educational experiences in contemporary indigenous Oaxaca.[1] Each case study was followed by comments by both a prominent Mexican researcher and an international researcher. The book additionally included essays by Mexican and international figures. The book's goal was to document creative and ground-breaking educational projects in Oaxaca that walk the fine line between national education standards and communal ways of life—known in Oaxaca as *comunalidad*[2]—and to introduce these Oaxacan experiences into the international literature concerning educational globalization and communal resistance. Given the international focus of that earlier volume, I asked the Oaxacans which international figure they would most want to have as a contributing essayist. Their response was immediate and overwhelming—Noam Chomsky.

Their choice astonished me, for it reached far beyond my expectations. Still, I could not disappoint my Oaxacan colleagues, many of whom were taking great risks as participants in projects affiliated with or even dependent upon the educational bureaucracy by permitting us to publish in our book revealing accounts of their communal commitments and struggles. The responsibility fell to me as the only English speaker to communicate with Noam Chomsky and invite his participation. We had no idea whether he would even consider our invitation.

He responded immediately and agreed to participate through the format of an interview. On February 20, 2004, Noam made room in his intense schedule for our first conversation. Once transcribed and translated into Spanish, it was published in our book, then later reprinted in a Oaxacan education journal.[3] Now, for the first time, the interview appears in English in this volume.

Several major themes that reoccur throughout the present book are introduced in this first interview; they are then expanded, detailed further, and clarified in the second and third conversations. These themes include the brutal process of nation-state formation and its consequences: neoliberal economic policies, suppression of cultural and linguistic diversity, educational standardization, indigenous resistance, and also hope for the preservation and viability of communal ways of life.

In order to understand cultural suppression and indigenous resistance, Chomsky contends, one must understand the "very brutal, harsh process of driving people into homogenous national states" to serve the political and economic interests of imperial powers. Spread around the world by colonizing powers, this process of nation-state formation is centuries old, involving suppression, homogenization, and control, which "are the leading themes of state policy in the powerful countries," especially today in the United States. Britain and the United States gained their world dominance by employing protectionist strategies in their own national interest, the same strategies which capitalist financial entities such as the World Bank, the International Monetary Fund, and the World Trade Organization deny to developing countries today. In this view, successful competing models (Chomsky's example is Cuba) must be stopped and dismantled. As he says, "[s]uccessful models, what is called by the rulers 'successful defiance,'—meaning independent efforts of independent action—are very frightening. And efforts to stamp them out take all sorts of forms, violent forms like military coups, or less violent forms like educational homogenization."

Very early in this interview, Chomsky identified the role that educational homogenization plays in the destructive, worldwide process of state formation and its relentless defense. "State formation, by force mostly, has tried to impose national education standards in order to turn people into similar individuals." Educational standardization aims to level not only diverse cultures, but people, as well. "The educational system is intended to level people, make them passive, disciplined, obedient." Alternative educational efforts that seek to break this regimented mold in order to celebrate creativity and support cultural and linguistic diversity and communal ways, efforts such as bilingual or intercultural education, must be fiercely opposed and dismantled, or co-opted.

Still, Chomsky asserts, the process of cultural homogenization has been resisted throughout history. He names many examples, such as Spain, Wales, Bolivia, Mexico, and areas of Europe experiencing cultural revival which he calls the "Europe of the regions." In all these places, sustained popular resistance is now showing notable success: "In many respects you cannot undo history, but things are going back to something like the structure that existed before the violent process of state formation was created."

How can indigenous and minoritized communities[4] resist, when the homogenizing pressures are so pervasive, and the power of communities to define their own paths is manipulated and constrained by systems and powers beyond their control? There is no formula, Chomsky reiterates over and over. "It depends on the nature of the community, how integrated they are, how committed they are to retaining their own identity, what kinds of external pressures they are under, straight economic issues."

Significantly, Chomsky in this interview expresses what might be called "sober hope" for the future of communal ways of life in our increasingly standardized, homogenized, globalized world. Examples abound, he says, wherever there is courage and commitment: the Landless Workers Movement in Brazil, the efforts of Via Campesina to designate seeds as a basic human right and part of the patrimony of humanity;[5] the beginnings of native seed banks in rural schools of Oaxaca, and many others. These communal efforts in defiance of homogenization and in defense of *comunalidad* are important and impressive, but they must join together in solidarity in order to magnify their impact on the centers of power. Chomsky stresses that their power lies in international solidarity. "The opportunities for success are, I think, greater now than they have been in the past because this is the first time, ever, that there has been an international movement of solidarity on these issues. I mean, it is not yet powerful enough to change the basic institutions, but it exists."

THE SECOND CHOMSKY INTERVIEW

Initially, a second interview with Noam Chomsky was not contemplated, and three years passed before it would occur in October 2007. During these years, Oaxaca experienced heightened political and educational tensions, as well as economic and agricultural crises exacerbated by the North American Free Trade Agreement (NAFTA). Rural regions were depopulated by widespread migration to urban centers, northern Mexican states, and to the United

States, where laborers bartered their labor for basic survival. In May 2006, the state teachers' union of Oaxaca, Section 22 of the National Union of Educational Workers, demanded attention to its list of educational, social, and political grievances. When negotiations with the state of Oaxaca broke down, 70,000 teachers went on strike, occupying fifty square blocks of the center of the capital city, also called Oaxaca, in a massive encampment.

Before dawn on June 14, 2006, civic unrest exploded into armed conflict as state police, by order of Oaxaca´s governor, Ulises Ruíz Ortiz, moved with guns, attack dogs, helicopters and tear gas against the sleeping teachers. Within days, the Popular Assembly of the Peoples of Oaxaca (APPO) formed, demanded removal of the governor, and declared itself to be the de facto governing body of Oaxaca.[6] In late October, after months of popular control in rural communities and city neighborhoods, President Vicente Fox ordered Federal Preventive Police to forcibly enter Oaxaca, and political repression against protesters and union and APPO leaders intensified.[7]

By January, 2007, civil observers from the International Commission for Human Rights (CCIODH) had documented twenty-three deaths, scores of cases of persons disappeared, and hundreds of protesters and movement leaders beaten, tortured, and incarcerated, with over 140 flown to maximum security prisons in distant Mexican states. In their final report, the CCIODH called for immediate transparency and legal action on behalf of those killed, disappeared, arrested, and tortured. They warned, however, that the polarization in the state would not be resolved until the root causes of the conflict were attended to, which they identified as "structural problems of poverty, local rule by strong-armed chieftains, unequal access to resources, lack of educational and health supports, disrespect for historical memory and indigenous identity, abuse of democratic procedures and disrespect toward real access to channels of participation."[8]

In the summer of 2007, with Oaxaca still tense and heavily

militarized, the Promotion Committee of the Mexican National Congress of Indigenous and Intercultural Education (CNEII)[9] voted to hold its Second National Congress in Oaxaca as a show of support for the activist teachers of Section 22 and the APPO. Members of the committee asked if I would approach Noam Chomsky again and invite him to speak at the Congress. He responded quickly and graciously that this would be impossible, due to the grave illness of his wife. However, he expressed his respect and support for the popular resistance in Oaxaca. After pondering his response, the committee asked if I would inquire about conducting a second interview with him in Boston. Again, he generously made time in his schedule for this encounter.[10]

The second interview was conducted and videotaped at Mass. Institute of Technology on October 4, 2007, and included a special greeting to attendees at the Second National Congress.[11] The videotape was express-mailed to Oaxaca, where editing and Spanish subtitling of the special greeting began immediately. Three weeks later, on October 25, Noam Chomsky's message of admiration and encouragement to the 787 Congress attendees from seventeen Mexican states and ten foreign nations, representing speakers of thirty indigenous languages and language dialects, was projected at the plenary session which inaugurated the Second National Congress.

In his greeting, Noam Chomsky commended the Second Congress for supporting "the courageous teachers in Oaxaca," whose struggle "of enormous significance" he connected with a global struggle of resistance. Latin America, where the struggle is "particularly dramatic," has become "the most exciting part of the world for the first time in its modern history." The countries of Latin America are moving toward a significant level of integration, without which, he stressed, independence and self-determination are impossible. They also are attempting to close the yawning gap between the enormous wealth of the elite and the poverty of the masses. He remarked on the pivotal role of indigenous peoples in this hemispheric struggle; their mobilizations, demands, and achievements are "reversing 500 years of miserable and ugly history, revitalizing the languages, the cultures, technical resources, developing forms of social organization that come out of their own traditions but are adapted to the modern world. These are tremendously exciting developments."

This very personal message, projected onto a massive screen at the Second Congress and later distributed widely to Mexican news services, deeply inspired all who witnessed it.

The more extensive October 2007 interview which serves as the second "turn of talk" in our virtual hemispheric conversation was transcribed, translated into Spanish, and published in Mexico, along with Dr. Chomsky's special greeting, in the Proceedings of the Second Congress.[12] This second interview, like the first, has never before been published in English.

While broad themes from the first interview appear again in the second, the focus of analysis in this conversation is quite different. Perhaps due to the recent violence and continuing repression in Oaxaca, Chomsky lays out in stark detail the mechanisms of state domination at the hands of governing elites. While applicable more broadly to Mexico and governments throughout the hemisphere, most of his examples are drawn from the recent history of the United States. Other vital topics that emerge in the discussion—neoliberalism, democracy, education and schooling, cultural and linguistic homogenization, NAFTA, indigenous resistance and comunalidad, international solidarity—are all analyzed in relation to this focus.

As in 2004, Chomsky identifies state power in the hands of the ruling classes to be both the means and the end of the political oppression and cultural suppression that are imposed on indigenous communities. "The ruling elite are extremely dedicated to maintaining state sovereignty and power. They cannot do it everywhere, but where they can, they do. And that is independent of neoliberalism." Do not be fooled by neoliberalism, Chomsky advises; it is simply another mechanism of state domination and elite control. "[O]ne of its aspects is to use state power for the benefit of the concentrations of economic power." The term "neoliberal" is a misnomer, for it is neither liberal in the traditional sense, nor new. The neoliberal framework contains "elements of serious fraud," Chomsky states. So-called multinational corporations are always state-based and they use state power for their own purposes: to provide labor, resources, and protection. Though neoliberals claim to believe in markets, market rules are "rammed down the throats of weak people but the powerful do not accept [them] for themselves." The United States again is his chief example.

Democracy, too, is a casualty of neoliberalism and state control. "One of the effects of neoliberalism, and it is well understood, is to reduce democracy." Citing documents from the Carter administration (1976–1980), Chomsky describes two responses to the political activism of the 1960s which were initiated by U.S. administrations to reinforce control, or in their words, "to moderate democracy." First, neoliberal economic policies were instituted: "the free flow of capital, [so] governments are not going to be able to carry out social democratic policies." Freeing up capital movements, he emphasizes, is a "direct attack on democracy." And second, state control of education was increased.

Mexico became the target of U.S. political concern in the 1990s, when it was feared that a possible "democracy opening" might lead the country to move in an independent direction rather than continuing to acquiesce to U.S. control. The answer to that, says Chomsky, was NAFTA.

One of the main goals of NAFTA, and it was stated pretty openly, and I am quoting, is "to lock Mexico into" what are called "the reforms," meaning the neoliberal rules. You can lock Mexico into those rules by treaty, so even if there is a "democracy opening," that dangerous thing, it is not going to be able to do much because they are locked in. The so-called free trade agreements are not about "free" trade at all; they are a form of domination.

Education, or what passes for it in the modern state, is as fraudulent as neoliberalism, according to Chomsky. Rather than truly educating, state school systems are organized to discipline, pacify, and level. Educational policies like No Child Left Behind (NCLB) in the United States or the Alliance for Educational Quality (ACE) in Mexico make this transparent by reducing education to test taking and market-driven competencies. Chomsky is clear that this is not education, but control. Education means "being able to think, to create, to explore, and so on, to be imaginative. This is the opposite." Still, it should come as no surprise that schools are organized to serve the homogenizing, disciplinary ends of the state, he adds. Thirty years ago, the Carter administration said that U.S. schools, the public institutions responsible for, in their words, "the indoctrination of the young," were not doing their job. Schools needed to introduce more obedience, control, subordination, so students would not "run around thinking for themselves." Far from bolstering democratic values and processes, Chomsky views today's education policies and practices as offshoots of that earlier regime of control.

To really see democracy in action, Chomsky points to the election that swept Evo Morales into office in 2005 as the first indigenous president of Bolivia. The level of popular civic involvement displayed in that election would be "unimaginable in the West." In his opinion, what has been accomplished in Bolivia and in other areas of Latin America is truly a remarkable achievement. "But for the U.S., it is losing its capacity to control the region. This control is based on essentially two factors. One was violence, and the other was the weakness, disintegration of the countries themselves. Well, both are changing."

Chomsky stresses that imperial powers do not intend to give up their hegemonic control without a fight. In the face of growing indigenous resistance and evident shifts in the hemispheric power balance, the powerful states will fight back that is, indigenous resistance will be met with state counter-resistance. Cooptation of indigenous resistance efforts, wherever possible, is one strategy. Still, Chomsky sees many hopeful signs: the revival of native languages; the protection of native seeds; the passage of the U.N. Declaration on the Rights of Indigenous Peoples after decades of organizational effort; and the international solidarity movement both "inside the imperial state" and "inside the suppressed communities." All of these run counter to the effort to homogenize the world, Chomsky says, "meaning to control it and dominate it and subordinate it." And they all provide grounds for hope.

A METHODOLOGY OF "COMUNALIDAD"

With the completion of the second interview in 2007, Benjamín Maldonado and I agreed that the themes and topics discussed in the two conversations with Noam Chomsky were significant and deserved a wider readership. For reasons already described, my questions in the interviews had focused on Mexico; however, Dr. Chomsky's responses encompass all of Latin America, Canada, even Europe and the Middle East. And of course, his analysis of United States policies and actions is particularly pointed and incriminating. Given the scope of his topics, the varied examples on which he draws, and his many expressions of admiration, particularly for resistance efforts in indigenous South America as well as Mexico, we felt that a broad Latin American focus was a priority.

Early on, Dr. Chomsky had given us permission to publish the interviews in both Spanish and English, yet they had never appeared in English. Therefore, in the summer of 2008, Benjamín and I seriously began to conceptualize this book as an English edition. We always thought of it as a book, not as the publication of two Chomsky interviews, either singly or as a pair. The reason for this was our desire to honor and model our publication on a central theme of the interviews themselves, the communal principle and daily practices of *comunalidad* that provide indigenous communities with their cohesion and strength of identity to survive and resist. For this reason, we designed a format that goes beyond the Chomsky interviews to include a gathering of voices to discuss, deliberate, debate, and negotiate meanings and consider common strategies, much as community members do in their communal assemblies in indigenous Oaxaca. The volume we published in Mexico in 2004 was our first attempt at designing a book format to reflect the values and multi-voiced processes of *comunalidad*:[13]

> By this we mean that one of our goals in compiling this collection of materials is to display within the format of an academic publication several of the valued practices found in *asambleas generales* in Oaxacan indigenous communities: the expression and patient consideration of many disparate points of view, collective and critical discussion, and consensual decision-making. Our goal is that these communal practices might find a valued place in classrooms and other contexts of learning where this book is read and discussed.[14]

The present book continues the pursuit of a methodology of *comunalidad*, employing the interviews of Noam Chomsky as a source and spark of collective reflection, discussion, and negotiation of meaning.

The assembly of voices we have gathered here includes twenty-seven participants: Noam Chomsky, twenty-two conversational partners from indigenous North, South, and Central America who comment on the Chomsky interviews, graduate students Erin Tooher and Julianna Kirwin, Benjamín and myself. Our process of assembling and orchestrating this virtual hemispheric conversation deserves comment.

In order to secure a diversity of viewpoints, we purposely invited a richly varied group of commentators. Eight women and fifteen men, almost half of whom are indigenous, authored the commentaries included here. Geographically, they represent nine countries across the hemisphere (South America—Argentina, Bolivia, Ecuador, Peru, Uruguay; Central America—Guatemala, Panama; North America—Mexico, United States).[15] While some of the commentators focus their efforts primarily and intensively on their own region, state, or ethnolinguistic area, others have broad experience in several countries of the Americas and also in international agencies such as the United Nations. They represent an impressive array of professions and academic fields. Included here are sociolinguists, anthropologists, journalists, language researchers, bilingual educators, political and cultural activists, applied linguists, language policy experts, agronomists, lawyers, agrarian engineers, historians, classroom teachers, teacher educators, and curriculum developers. Virtually all are bilingual or multilingual; a list (probably not exhaustive) of their languages includes Quechua/Quichua/Kichwa, Aymara, Maya Achi, Zapotec, Triqui, Kuna, Tiwa, French, German, English, and Spanish. Some of the commentators are renowned writers whose works in Spanish are widely published and cited, a smaller number have published in English, while others are quite new to the world of publishing in either language. Still, all are respected activists, committed educators, or acknowledged intellectual leaders of cultural and political resistance efforts and movements in their particular world of indigenous struggle somewhere in the Americas. This variety of experiences and paths deepens the theme and enriches the content of this book.

The decision to publish this volume in English influenced our selection of commentators. Many of our authors are well-known in Latin America for their important resistance work. Still, readers in the English-speaking world, even Chomsky himself, know little about these commentators' views *in their own words*. This editorial and intellectual silence is one consequence of a significant journalistic "language divide": it is far easier to find scholarship by Western, English-speaking authors that has been translated into Spanish (bookstores in Latin America are filled

with such translated editions), than it is to find English translations of the research and perspectives of Latin American authors,
however respected they may be in their own continental context.
Only a few of our Latin American commentators speak or write
fluent English; consequently, their scholarship and achievements
are known minimally if at all by English speaking readers.

This disparity in global language power and media access
between Spanish-speaking Latin American and English-speaking North American indigenous resistance efforts, along with
pragmatic editorial constraints, led us to maximize participation by Latin American commentators and limit participation
by English-speaking North American commentators. Struggles
against globalization and cultural homogenization, both historic
and contemporary, by Native American and First Nations activists are well documented and extensively cited in academic
literature, partly due to their access to English-language media.
To provide an adequate representation of these many struggles
by many tribes across North America, along with those in Latin
America, is beyond the scope of this book. Consequently, we
limited ourselves to one contribution, the commentary by Glenabah Martinez, Taos Pueblo, New Mexico, as an important indigenous perspective to accompany the other U.S. contributors
to this volume—Noam Chomsky, of course, Erin Tooher, Julianna Kirwin, and myself. Our hope is that many thought-provoking discussions and responses will be sparked among Native
American and Canadian First Nations readers as they consider
the Latin American indigenous views and voices made accessible
to them here in English.

All of our commentators respond to the same source documents, the 2004 and 2007 interviews with Noam Chomsky. In
addition, for his closing commentary Benjamín Maldonado had
unique access to the third interview, conducted in 2009. We invited
the commentators to read these interviews in English or Spanish
and to identify the topic or topics they found most significant and

interesting, or problematic and troubling, and which have greatest relevance to their own community or region and experience of struggle. At no time were they asked to agree with Chomsky's views, or with the perspectives expressed by any other commentator. We did not share drafts of the commentaries among the authors as these were being developed; in fact, the publication of this book will be the first time that commentators will read each others' texts.[16] As will be seen in the pages ahead, while there are often points of convergence in their ideas, there are also obvious, at times heated, differences. The collective conversation becomes deeper, more nuanced, and also more honest, because of these disparate views.

It is impossible to adequately summarize the array of topics and perspectives—surprising, emotional, erudite, critical, profound—which surface in this collection of twenty-two commentaries, all sparked by Noam Chomsky's interviews. Nor will I "speak for" the commentators, which would contradict the very purpose for which we conceived and created this hemispheric conversation among equals. Suffice it to say that Noam Chomsky himself commented to me that he found the range and depth of the discussion "fascinating." Here I will only provide an illustrative glimpse into this conversation.

Three recurring topics, only highlighted here, resonate deeply with me as a U.S. bilingual educator and applied linguist:

1. Indigenous *comunalidad* reaches far beyond Western ideas of cooperation, collectivization, or social concern for the other, addressing the philosophical, moral, even spiritual, question: what, or who, is the very ground of existence, both human and cosmic? Taken seriously, the question tears down the barriers we construct between academic disciplines, ecosystems, galaxies, mind and body, sacred and profane, and conceptions of space and time. As Jaime Martínez Luna writes in his commentary in this volume:

"*Comunalidad* is a way of understanding life as being permeated with spirituality, symbolism, and a greater integration with nature. It is one way of understanding that Man is not the center, but simply a part of this great natural world. It is here that we can distinguish the enormous difference between Western and indigenous thought. Who is at the center—only one, or all? The individual, or everyone?"

In his commentary, Grimaldo Rengifo Vásquez writes:

"From the Andean point of view, community is understood as *ayllu*, a collectivity made up of human beings but also of the world beyond humans, that is, nature and the deities. Given this, human decisions are not only human, but also they are based on a consensus achieved with the world that is beyond human. The entire project of modernity, and especially that which is guided by the school, has been destined to destroy this relationship and mold it according to the interests of human beings living in society, that is, according to the interests of each individual who makes up the totality of society."[17]

2. If the learning and teaching implications of indigenous *comunalidad* (or Andean *ayllu*) were taken seriously, they would outstrip anything we have yet conceived of as progressive, alternative education. Indigenous America itself is searching and experimenting to discover what schooling, or non-schooled teaching and learning, might look like if the Western vise of entrenched individualism and industrial standardization were broken, and the teaching-learning process were returned to its communal roots.[18] Is it possible for indigenous notions of nurture, equality, and communal teaching-learning, to be actualized? If so, how? Grimaldo Rengifo Vásquez writes:

"The survival of these communities—*ayllus*—in the Andes and their relationship with institutions and with the entire global conglomerate have been marked by the notion of nurture (*crianza*). Nurture is a relationship of affective caring among the beings that make up the *ayllu*. It involves bringing up and being brought up in a relationship of equality that includes all entities that inhabit the cosmos."

Jaime Martínez Luna writes:

"A fundamental principle is to liberate the exercise of knowledge . . . I am not bothered by the idea of knocking down schools and suppressing teachers because, essentially, we are all teachers. Teachers are not the ones, despite their intelligence, who should determine what we must know. They must understand that it is EACH AND EVERY ONE OF US who has to open the door to knowledge. The collective task does not come from the outside; it has always been within us, and also the need."

3. Languages have been and continue to be weapons of state domination. Western knowledge, says Guillermo Chen Morales in this volume, cannot or will not comprehend or respect that an indigenous language "preserves in every word the essence of the community." Indigenous peoples have come to recognize, however, that their languages are powerful tools of personal and communal resistance and liberation. Carlos Mamani Condori writes:

"During the first half of the twentieth century in Bolivia, the struggle was carried out under the banner of equality, which included access to the Spanish language. Then, during the second half of the century, appreciation of the native languages and cultures was the goal, and struggles for language preservation were important. With this, the indigenist policies of assimilation were denounced as ethnocidal, another form of genocide. Education has become a battlefield between those groups that seek to preserve the privileges of the colonizer language and indigenous peoples who push toward policies of *interculturalidad*[19] and dialogues between civilizations, between systems of knowledge, etc."

María Yolanda Terán writes:

"The use of other languages to present our ideas is critically important. I have to use English, Spanish, Kichwa, or Portuguese, depending on the situation. On several occasions, I have had to translate for my friends when no translator was available or due to a poor translation. Of course, this has caused conflict within some agencies because "speaking so many languages has given me power," which is true in a sense, because we are no longer acting blindly or failing to understand in international gatherings."

TRANSLATING TEXTS, CONTEXTS, AND SUBTEXTS

A project of this complexity, bringing together multiple authors, some indigenous and others not, from widely dispersed geographic locations and educational contexts in the Americas, writing in two major world languages, has demanded complex decisions about the translation of *texts*, *contexts*, and *subtexts*. That is, we have wrestled with how to maintain through several rounds of back-and-forth translation the meanings intended by the authors, through our selection of words and phrases that preserve their broader frames of reference and their implicit as well as explicit meanings.

The interviews with Noam Chomsky that serve as the core of this book were conducted at his request in English to enable easier, deeper communication.[20] Each interview was carefully transcribed, the transcription approved by him, and any revisions incorporated, and then it was translated into Spanish. The Spanish translation was again reviewed in detail against the original English transcription to assure accuracy.

However, before the interviews were disseminated to the commentators, we felt that they required translation not only of their English *texts*, that is, the words Chomsky and I had actually spoken, but also of their broader North American cultural and academic *contexts*. We could not assume that Latin American commentators were personally familiar with the cultural, political, and historical references to which he alluded in our conversations. For this reason, and with Chomsky's approval, I attempted to facilitate understanding of the contexts influencing our exchanges by adding footnoted explanations of certain references that might otherwise be confusing. Since I, too, participate in the North American academic environment, but I also have spent more than a decade deeply involved in indigenous educational efforts in Oaxaca and Mexico, my hope is that the footnotes serve as a useful bridge to the contextual meanings behind the English text, not only for our Latin American commentators, but for readers worldwide. The four other texts included here that were originally written in English, especially this introduction, are also presented with explanatory footnoting for these same reasons.

There was never any question as to the language in which the invited commentators would submit their texts. It went without saying that each participant would write in his or her language of choice, Spanish or English. Twenty-one texts were submitted initially in Spanish and only four (those of Glenabah Martinez, Stefano Varese, this introduction, and the co-authored conclusion) in English. All original texts were reviewed by both Benjamín and me, and any uncertainties were clarified with the authors. On several occasions, we encouraged the writers to enrich their account with specific examples and concrete details from the experiences of struggle about which they wrote.

The texts submitted in Spanish, which were the vast majority, went through two rounds of English translation. A first translation draft was produced,[21] which I then carefully reviewed against the Spanish original in a second round of translation, in an attempt to assure accuracy, eloquence, and contextual meaningfulness. Alerted to problematic passages by the hopefully sensitive barometer of my own confusion as an English reader, either the authors or I added explanatory footnotes to these early versions to increase their comprehensibility for readers unfamiliar with the specific Latin American context in which the text was embedded. Given that these specific contexts span nine countries and multiple professional fields, even readers knowledgeable about certain regions or disciplines may benefit from consulting the footnotes to better grasp the contextual meaning of a commentator.

In our process of two-way translation, we have attempted to respect each author's perspective and voice. It is this level of personal meanings that we refer to as *subtext*. Across our many authors and national contexts, the use of certain key terms has varied considerably. Perhaps most noticeable are the array of adjectives used by these commentators to name communities as indigenous: *indígena*, *nativa*, and *originaria*. When this diversity did not impede reader comprehension, we tried to respect each author's preferred usage in our translation, believing that, as in oral conversation, shared meanings cannot be assumed or imposed on the participants in a conversation. Instead, meanings must be worked over, negotiated, explained, and clarified, in order for shared meanings to be constructed together across time and continued communication. This has meant that consistency of terminology throughout the book at times has been sacrificed in order to respect each author's individual, cultural, or ideological preferences.

The negotiation of meaning also accompanied, or dogged, our translation process. One case is our translation of the Spanish *pueblo* or *pueblos* as "people" or "peoples," in such terms as *pueblos indígenas* (indigenous peoples), *pueblos originarios* (original peoples),[22] or *pueblo Kichwa* (Kichwa People). We have been guided here by Benjamín Maldonado who writes in his commentary, "it is the greater community, the collective of communities belonging to the same culture which together form a people." Still, our decisions and definitions are open to question, as seen in the following concern raised by María Bertely Busquets, one of our commentators, in a personal communication:

> I am concerned about the translation of the notion of "pueblos indígenas" as "peoples," because the notion of "pueblo" is fundamental in the legal and political debate in Mexico and Chiapas, with respect to the indigenous movement and its struggle for autonomy and self-determination inside the Mexican state. Let me know if "peoples" and "pueblos" allude to the same thing: a legal entity or subject.

Decisions about appropriate punctuation, especially capitalization (such as of the term "indigenous peoples") were equally complex. In this matter, we have followed standard dictionary practice which is to leave these and related terms uncapitalized. It should be noted that capitalization of these terms was consistently employed by some, but relatively few, of our commentators in their original texts.

We have conferred, worried, and poured over these translations right to the moment of submitting the final manuscript for publication. Whatever their ultimate strengths or limitations, if María Bertely Busquets' thought-provoking concern is indicative of the constructive dialogue that this volume will spark, it will indeed serve to construct, and also correct, complex meanings and understandings across cultural, political and linguistic divides.

"THE TRANSLATION OF UNTRANSLATABLE WORDS"
Another caution is relevant to this complex translation effort, one which the anthropologist Malinowski described almost seventy-five years ago in his accounts of extensive field work in the

Trobriand Islands of Oceania. He cautioned ethnographers about "the translation of untranslatable words":[23] "In brief, every language has words which are not translatable, because they fit into its culture and into that only; into the physical setting, the institutions, the material apparatus and the manners and values of a people."[24]

While we might wish to believe that such untranslatable words are "but freaks or peculiarities," Malinowski assures us this is not the case; words such as numerals, parts of the body, prepositions, "words as ordinary as bread and butter," will never be used in exactly the same linguistic contexts with exactly the same meanings in any two languages on earth, no matter how closely related those languages may be. True translation of words or texts across any two languages depends upon "a unification of cultural contexts," claims Malinowski. For real understanding to occur across languages, this unification process is always a "difficult, laborious and delicate" one, even when two cultures have much in common. But when two cultures differ profoundly, "when the beliefs, scientific views, social organization, morality and material outfit are completely different, most of the words in one language cannot be even remotely paralleled in the other."[25]

It remains to be seen whether our English translations, supported by an abundance of explanatory footnotes, succeed in "unifying the cultural contexts" of an array of Latin American settings with those cultural settings familiar to English-speaking readers. Humbled by Malinowski's warnings, we nevertheless hope that this is the case, at least to some degree. But there are two Spanish words/concepts used repeatedly throughout the Latin American commentaries that we found it impossible to translate fully into English: *comunalidad* and *interculturalidad*.

We acknowledge their status as "untranslatable words" by leaving them in Spanish, marked by italics, throughout our book. The term *comunalidad* has already been employed several times in this chapter, defined in shorthand as the principle and practices of communal life and the source of indigenous identity and resistance. The term itself comes from the Oaxacan indigenous context and is described in considerable detail in this volume by two of its foremost expositors, Jaime Martínez Luna and Benjamín Maldonado. Several commentators from Central and South America appear to misinterpret *comunalidad* as referring to the more limited meaning of "community" (*comunidad*).[26] At least two other terms which seem, at least superficially, to convey the deeper meaning of *comunalidad* have surfaced in these commentaries: *minga* from Ecuador and *ayllu* from the Aymaras in Bolivia. However, without extensive fieldwork or at least expert corroboration, we will not rush to the assumption that these terms have the "same meaning" within their respective indigenous contexts. We are even less willing to risk the English translation of "communitarianism" or any of its derivatives, each of which is burdened with sociopolitical history and meanings in U.S. and other Western contexts. For all of these reasons, we have left the term *comunalidad* (and the other terms italicized in this paragraph) untranslated, allowing each author to provide the meaning appropriate to their text and context.

The term/concept *interculturalidad*, which also appears frequently across the commentaries, we have deemed equally "untranslatable," but for somewhat different reasons. To our knowledge, a term such as "interculturalism" or "interculturality" has no meaning in English; indeed, we would be forced to invent both the term and its meaning, which provides no solution in the translation task. The familiar English term "multiculturalism" is entirely inadequate as a translation for *interculturalidad*. Multiculturalism has its cognate in Spanish, *multiculturalidad*, but the contextual meanings of this term in Latin America imply a status-quo, non-critical "appreciation of other cultures" approach to diversity; in contrast, the term *interculturalidad* has evolved precisely to recognize and challenge the disparities of power and status between cultural groups in society. Despite its more political, critical intentions, several of our contributors (for example, Marcela Tovar Gómez and Grimaldo Rengifo Vásquez) suggest that the term *interculturalidad* in the official rhetoric of Latin America has been so co-opted and gutted of meaning that it now functions as a tool or mask of continued patronization and cultural subordination. To avoid facing Western readers with a long list of "untranslated" Spanish words embedded in English text, in some cases we have created an "English translated form" of derivative terms (such as "intercultural education" and "intercultural teachers"), though it would be difficult to explain an author's meaning of these in an English cultural context. However, we consistently leave the base terms, *interculturalidad* and *comunalidad*, in their original Spanish to mark these words and cultural concepts as "untranslatable."

A third term, *cosmovisión*, is perhaps equally untranslatable. However, here we have taken another tack; we rejected "world view," the translation provided in several Spanish-English dictionaries, in favor of creating our own literal, Anglicized translation, "cosmovision," implying a philosophical or spiritual perspective that attempts to account for or include a way of understanding the entire cosmos and humanity's place in it. We feel this suggests the possibility of envisioning multiple worlds, not just one, and approximates both the expansiveness and the unity conveyed by *cosmovisión* in indigenous thought.

AN OPEN-ENDED INVITATION

On June 17, 2009, Noam Chomsky and I engaged in a third conversation at the request of our editor, Greg Ruggiero of City Lights Publishers, in order to close this book with a "turn at talk" that responds to some of the commentaries. This interview, like the others, took place in Chomsky's office at MIT. On this occasion, Noam agreed to respond to the commentaries that we had received and translated into English at that early stage in our manuscript development.

I will not attempt to summarize this conversation before the reader has read the collection of commentaries from which our key discussion points were drawn. Suffice it to say that Noam Chomsky and I returned to and deepened some familiar topics, such as the nation-state system, democracy, *comunalidad*, and *interculturalidad*. Yet several significant new topics were sparked by thoughtful reflection on the commentaries we had read. If the second interview laid bare the mechanisms of state power and control, this third conversation centered on *comunalidad*, the real challenges it faces in the twenty-first century, but also its potential and actual appeal to many youth in our contemporary, technological world. As our discussion deepened, it moved to the holistic, ecological, and spiritual dimensions of *comunalidad*, as described in many of the commentaries, especially those by indigenous authors. Toward the end, Noam Chomsky provides surprising assessments of the fallibility of Western societies, especially that of the United States, and the hope, even the longing among many young people in Western ideology dominated societies, for a profound experience of *comunalidad*. There is much to comment on in this third interview, much that is new and perhaps quite surprising. Benjamín Maldonado includes an analysis of this conversation in his final commentary.

I will close by acknowledging another level of contribution by Noam Chomsky to this hemispheric conversation among equals—his transparent humility before the perspectives articulated by the other participants, and his apparent wish to keep the lines of communication open.

When I asked if he had comments he wished to make about the commentaries he read in anticipation of our interview, Chomsky acknowledged how much he had learned from reading them. More significantly, he admitted how much he still needed and wanted to learn about indigenous resilience and resistance in Latin America:

I found things that are interesting for me to think about [such as the emphasis on community, learning through doing, reshaping our notion of knowledge, studying and restoring the communitarian tradition], but I do not know if I have much that I can say about them. . . . Some of the notions I am sort of familiar with [such as progressive education]. . . . But in Latin America it obviously goes much further. And I do not entirely understand how it works.

He ended by expressing his wish to learn more and to learn differently, to be taught by and about indigenous America in order to more deeply understand *comunalidad* in education and in life. "I would like to understand better, get a better grasp of, the concept of restoring communal values in education and other aspects of life."

We offer this book as the next, but not the last, "turn at talk" in this hemispheric conversation about forms of being, educating and resisting that are ancient, yet still vital and viable. If engaged seriously, they may offer new hope for the future to all of us and to our endangered planet.

The author wishes to gratefully acknowledge the following colleagues who offered constructive suggestions on a first draft of this introduction: Courtney Cazden, Nancy Davies, Benjamín Maldonado, Richard Meyer, Carmichael Peters, George Salzman, Nelson Valdés.

NOTES

1. Lois Meyer, Benjamín Maldonado, Rosalba Ortiz & Victor García,. *Entre la normatividad y la comunalidad: Experiencias educativas innovadoras del Oaxaca Indígena actual* (Oaxaca: Fondo Editorial del Instituto Estatal de Educación Pública de Oaxaca, 2004).

2. The concept of *comunalidad* is referred to throughout this introductory chapter and throughout this book; it is described in detail in the commentaries by Martínez Luna and Maldonado.

3. Lois Meyer, "Resistencia y esperanza: el futuro de la comunalidad en un mundo globalizado. Entrevista a Noam Chomsky," *Identidades* 15 July-Sept. (Oaxaca: Fondo Editorial of the Oaxaca State Institute for Public Education (IEEPO), 2005), 4–15.

4. McCarty explains the use of the term "minoritized": "As a characterization of a people, 'minority' is stigmatizing and often numerically inaccurate. Navajos living within the Navajo Nation are, in fact, the numerical majority. 'Minoritized' more accurately conveys the power relations and processes by which certain groups are socially, economically, and politically marginalized within the larger society. This term also implies human agency." In Teresa McCarty, *A place to be Navajo: Rough Rock and the struggle for self-determination in indigenous schooling* (Mahwah, NJ: Lawrence Erlbaum Associates, 2002): xv, footnote 1.

5. The control and commercialization of seeds is an immense area of struggle between indigenous communities defending their use and control of native seeds, and multinational pharmaceutical companies attempting to control, capitalize, and impose genetically altered, reproductively infertile seeds. Beyond the issues of human rights and the patrimony of humanity mentioned here, this struggle has profound implications for the generative and adaptable evolutionary processes of life on our planet.

6. The Popular Assembly of the Peoples of Oaxaca (Asamblea Popular de los Pueblos de Oaxaca—APPO) was formed by representatives of more than 300 state regions and municipalities, unions, non-governmental organizations, social organizations, and cooperatives, the largest group being Section 22, the Oaxacan teachers' union.

7. For further information in English on the popular uprising and repression in Oaxaca in 2006, see Sorenson, L. (2007). On education in Oaxaca 2007, at www.goabroad.net/users/resourcefiles/2007/May/1601/admingroup/149e4c88e534fb1239730318.pdf, or Nancy Davies, *The People Decide: Oaxaca's Popular Assembly* (NY: Narco News Books, 2007). For information in Spanish, see the webpage of La Universidad Unitierra http://idescalzos.blogspot.com/ or Victor Martinez Vásquez, *Autoritarismo, Movimiento Popular y Crisis Política: Oaxaca 2006.* (Oaxaca: Co-publication of Universidad Autónoma "Benito Juarez" de Oaxaca; Instituto de Investigaciones Sociológicas; Centro de Apoyo al Movimiento Popular Oaxaqueño, A.C.; Servicios para la Educación Alternativa (EDUCA); Consorcio para el Diálogo Parlamentario y la Equidad, A.C., 2007).

8. Downloaded and translated on August 12, 2009, from http://cciodh.pangea.org/?q=es/node/94. See Soberanes in this volume for educational efforts of resistance growing out of this repression.

9. A grassroots national association of governmental and non-governmental organizations and institutions, cultural workers, teachers, parents, researchers and persons interested in developing indigenous and intercultural education in Mexico. In three regional conferences and two national congresses, the CNEII has worked in support of "one of the most important treasures of education in our country:

the existence of a great diversity of languages, cultures and Peoples." Downloaded on August 13, 2009, at www.cneii.org.

10. At the time of the second interview, Dr. Chomsky was restricting his engagements in order to participate in his wife's home care. Our third interview took place six months after Carol Chomsky's death in December 2008. Along with our condolences, we express deep gratitude for his willingness to continue participating in this conversation during such a difficult time of loss.

11. The special greeting is reprinted in this volume at the beginning of the second Chomsky interview.

12. Congreso Nacional de Educación Indígena e Intercultural (CNEII), *Memoria del Segundo Congreso Nacional de Educación Indígena e Intercultural.* (Mexico, D.F.: CNEII, 2009). The Proceedings of the Second Congress in Spanish will be available online at www.cneii.org.

13. For an explanation in Spanish of this methodological concept, see Lois Meyer, "Hacia una metodología de la comunalidad" In Meyer et. al., 2004: op. cit., 45–76.

14. Ibid., 50, translated by the author.

15. In addition, we attempted to include the perspectives of other commentators: a Miskito from Nicaragua, a Cree from Canada, a Mixe from Oaxaca, and a representative of the Zapatista Army for National Liberation (EZLN) in Chiapas, Mexico. With the generous assistance of Mariela Padilla in the Bolivian Vice President's Office, we invited commentaries from Bolivian President Evo Morales and Vice-President Alvaro García Linera. Vice-President García formally acknowledged our invitation, which due to other pressures he was unable to accept.

16. As many are literate in Spanish, not English, we are planning an early edition of this book in Spanish which they will be able to access.

17. For further analysis of the school's project to destroy Andean *ayllu*, see the discussion of Zibechi at the end of Maldonado's commentary.

18. *See* Zibechi, Soberanes, Chen, Bertely, and Esteva, this volume.

19. The meaning of this term is highly variable and will be considered in many of the commentaries. Mamani (this volume) links *interculturalidad* with "dialogues between civilizations and between systems of knowledge," and contrasts it with the effort "to preserve the privileges of the colonizer language," ways of thinking and being.

20. The request that our conversations be carried out in English, in addition to limitations on Chomsky's available time and our lack of travel funds or U.S. visas, resulted in my conducting the three interviews alone. Undoubtedly, the substance of the interviews would have been different had an indigenous Oaxacan colleague participated directly in these discussions. Noam Chomsky generously received a visit by two Oaxacans, Fernando Soberanes (commentator in this volume) and Beatríz Gutiérrez Luís, Ikootz (Huave) preschool teacher from the community of San Mateo del Mar, on October 8, 2008. In the hope that this conversation might

appear as an additional "interview" in this book, a professional translator, Ivanna Bergese, and a professional videographer, Jill Freidberg, generously assisted us. However, beyond the "text" of their talk, which was competently translated, their political and sociocultural "contexts" were so different as to limit greatly the depth, and at times even the comprehensibility, of the communication through translation between Dr. Chomsky and these Oaxacan teachers.

21. A team of colleagues and University of New Mexico graduate students provided invaluable service as first-round translators in this complex translation effort. We are grateful to the following individuals for producing the first translation drafts: Allison Borden, Daniel McCool, Shannon Reierson, Tenley Ruth, Andrés Sabogal, José Luís Santana, Erin Tooher, and Irene Welch-Mooney. We also acknowledge with gratitude the efforts of Ivette Buere and Sergio Perelló, Anselmo Torres Arizmendi, and Lucie W. Wacher Rodarte, who assisted us with the translation of the Chomsky interviews into Spanish.

22. From Benjamín Maldonado: "Several authors, including myself, prefer to use 'original peoples' rather than 'indigenous peoples.' To us, 'indigenous' refers to a condition of exploitation, domination and exclusion, while 'original' refers to antiquity and existence prior to nation-state formation. With this in mind, the terms can be considered synonymous."

23. Brosnislaw Malinowski "The language of magic and gardening," Vol. II. of *Coral gardens and their magic.* (NY: Dover Publications, 1978).

24. Ibid., 12.

25. Ibid., 14–15.

26. For example, see Macas and Rengifo (this volume).

I.
INTERVIEWS WITH NOAM CHOMSKY

Resistance and Hope

The Future of *Comunalidad* in a Globalized World

Interview with Noam Chomsky by Lois Meyer, February 20, 2004

Noam Chomsky is a renowned linguist whose contributions during his fifty-year academic career at the Massachusetts Institute of Technology (MIT) have revolutionized the study of linguistics, computer languages, and mathematics. In many places, including Latin America, he is perhaps even better known for his activism and outspoken criticism of United States policies, especially U.S. foreign policy. He is widely acknowledged to be the most often cited living author and one of the most respected and influential intellectuals in the world.

OUR BOOK[1] IS BUILT around ten cases of innovative educational projects in rural, indigenous Oaxaca. Some of the cases were initiated from within state educational institutions, others from non-governmental organizations. But all of them walk the line between state educational normative standards and indigenous *comunalidad*.

Dr. Chomsky, my Oaxacan colleagues seem to believe their major battle is maintaining *comunalidad* against the pressures of a Mexican educational bureaucracy with its uniform national education standards, rather than resisting the pressures brought to bear by other national and global movements. How do you see the relationship between state and national education standards and other broader global and national efforts to promote cultural homogenization and political conformity? Is there a causal relationship involved in either direction?

First of all, this is a process that has been going on for hundreds of years in Europe and the conquered areas of the world. Europe for the last several hundred years has been involved in a process of state formation that was very bloody and destructive. It is the reason why Europe was the most savage and murderous part of the globe for hundreds of years. The French and Germans were slaughtering each other for centuries over where the boundaries would be. Within each of the regions that ultimately became the nation-states, part of the process has been the suppression of local cultures, local languages, regional customs, and so on. And all this was done to try to turn themselves into national communities with boundaries that correspond to colors on the map.

And this is happening right up to this minute. If you take a language like Italian or German, or French, for that matter, and you go back a little bit, a generation or two, these were local dialects. People spoke their own languages. Right now, if you are an Italian, you may not be able to talk to your grandmother because she talks a different language. The imposition of a common language, a common culture, a common allegiance to a national entity, has been achieved through centuries of violence and destruction. And it is still continuing.

In fact, in Europe there is a reaction against it—the people are always struggling for their own rights. And it is very striking in Europe today. In Europe now there is a move toward even greater centralization—the European Union. But that is helping to incite a counter movement towards regionalization. So Europe today is sometimes called a Europe of the regions, not states, and, in fact, in some respects, that is going back to the circumstance that existed before the period of nation-state formation by force.

Take Spain, for instance. There is a degree of autonomy in Catalonia, the Basque country, and in Galicia, and increasingly in other areas. In England, there is a degree of autonomy developing in Scotland and Wales. Regional languages have been revived, cultures have been revived, and so on. In fact, this is happening all over Europe. In many respects you cannot undo history, but things are going back to something like the structure that existed before the violent process of state formation was created.

And the same is happening elsewhere. If you look around the world, the most violent, murderous wars that are going on trace in large part to the efforts of European imperialist powers, including the United States, to impose nation-state systems in regions where they just do not correspond at all to people's interests or concerns or relatives or anything else. And this does lead to violent conflict. Africa is torn by this, India and Pakistan are on the verge of nuclear war over it. Just about everywhere you look, the major conflicts have to do with that. Take Russia and Chechnya, and the United States and Mexico.

It is not a secret that the United States conquered half of Mexico. And there was a border which, like most borders, was and is completely artificial, the result of violence. Basically similar people lived on both sides of the border so it was quite porous. A lot of people moved up and back. And in fact, that continued pretty much up until NAFTA (North American Free Trade Agreement). The Clinton administration understood that the effect of NAFTA on Mexico was going to be an economic miracle for some small percentage of the population and for U.S. investors, but not for the people of Mexico. So, it was probably going to incite more movement to the North. And, therefore, you have to militarize the border to prevent that. So now hundreds of Mexicans are dying every year trying to get over a border that used to be relatively porous.

These things are happening right now, everywhere. The efforts of people to maintain their own culture, their own regional practices, their own languages, have been going on forever. Under the old Ottoman Empire—a lot of things were wrong with it, you do not want to reconstruct it—but there was something right about it. It mostly left people alone, which meant that if you were a Greek community in some town, you ran your affairs, your linguistic, religious, and other practices. The Armenian community in the other section of town ran theirs. And there were no borders, basically; you could go from one place to another in this huge Ottoman Empire without passing a border post. That corresponds to the nature of the region. In fact, it corresponds to the nature of just about everything in the world. The United States is one of the rare exceptions. But we know the reason for that: the English colonists were just genocidal. If you murder everybody else, then those who are left are homogeneous. But if you look at the country before it was colonized, there were hundreds of languages, radically different cultures, all sorts of diversity. The United States is institutionally homogenous now because of conquest and extermination.[2]

Could you relate what you are saying here to the issue of educational homogenization through a uniform set of national education standards?

Well, that's part of the process. State formation, by force mostly, has tried to impose national education standards in order to turn people into similar individuals. This happens everywhere. It is part of the same process that drives farmers off the land to become urban working class. In the United States, for example, public education as far back as the late nineteenth century was primarily socialization of independent farmers to turn them into a workforce of interchangeable parts. There was a lot of resistance to public education, not because people did not want to learn to read, but because of the way it was designed in order to socialize them. And what it was socializing them into was no big secret, either. If you are part of an industrial workforce, you are supposed to be a robot. In fact, this became professionalized under what is called "Taylorism."[3] The main core of contemporary industrial development essentially tries to convert people on the job in a factory, say, to become robots who carry out prescribed actions under tight managerial control and who do not think about what they are doing, or the fact that they do not have a decision over what they are doing. That requires a disciplined, passive, obedient workforce, which is not what independent farmers were.

In fact, the process of education actually destroyed individual culture. If you go back to the working-class literature of the mid-nineteenth century, right around here in Boston, for the Industrial Revolution took place approximately where we are, there was a very lively, independent, working-class press run by people in the mills. Some of them were what were called "factory girls," the young women from the farms who were brought into the urban environments to work in the mills as the farming communities were marginalized. Some were Irish immigrants living in miserable slums under hideous racist oppression in Boston. They would go out to the town of Lowell to work in a mill. And they ran their own press. It was very interesting. There are books about it; we can read about it. They bitterly condemned the industrial system for all sorts of reasons. They said that it was turning them into something much like slaves; they did not see much difference between wage labor and slavery. But part of their condemnation of the industrial system is that it was destroying their culture. An Irish artisan in Boston, let's say a shoemaker, if he could afford it would hire a young boy to read to him while he was working, and he might read contemporary literature. The young factory girls were accustomed to living in an independent culture, without much formal schooling, in which they read contemporary literature and the classics. It was just part of their very life. This was all being eliminated by national standards.

I can even remember some of this from childhood. My family happened to be first-generation immigrant working class, most of them. Many of them never went to school, perhaps no further than fourth grade. But they lived in a world of high culture—the Budapest String Quartet, debates about the latest performance of a Shakespeare play, Freud, Stekel, every possible form of political radicalism—in my life, it was the most lively intellectual culture I have ever been in, including the Harvard Faculty Club. But mostly these were barely educated, unemployed working-class people, seamstresses, shop boys, that sort of thing. And this was a large part of the culture of the people—I do not want to say "popular culture" because that makes us think of television sitcoms—but the culture really of the people, which was complex and rooted in their own traditions. The culture of the people absorbed a lot of world culture but also had its own independent roots and character. Well, all this gets leveled in educational homogenization. Now it is a very different popular culture.

But the conversion has been a process of careful control in all sorts of ways. Part of it has been the educational system, which is intended to level people, make them passive, disciplined, obedient. An awful lot of education is not teaching arithmetic and science. It is teaching obedience; it is teaching certain kinds of behavior. You are supposed to behave in a certain fashion when you are in a classroom. And you should not be too independent. You can raise your hand politely but do not display too much independent thinking; that is discouraged. In fact, if children do exhibit it anyway, they often become what are called "behavior problems." They have to be handled in some other fashion—with drugs, therapy, or maybe by kicking them out of school. Anyone who has observed schools in action is well familiar with this. It is part of the educational system, the socialization.

And this goes all the way to the top. Take the two U.S. presidential candidates running for election next November. Both come from rich families, attended Yale University, joined the same secret society. I have been through something sort of similar, as a graduate student at Harvard. I was not part of it, but I saw it. Those are processes of socialization. I do not know what they learned in their classes, if anything. But a large part of the education in places like Harvard and Yale and Princeton is initiation into the practices of the ruling class—how you talk to each other, what you drink, who your friends are. This kind of education has its consequences; it induces certain ways of behavior and of thought. Actually, Orwell once commented on this when he was discussing literary censorship in England, which comes out looking more or less the same as censorship in totalitarian societies, he wrote, even though it is free and there is no coercion. He said part of the reason is through a good education. In the best schools, you learn that there are certain things it "just wouldn't do to say"—you just do not say those things, and pretty soon, you do not think them. In this way you are embedded into your proper role in society. If it is Yale, Harvard and Princeton, you are prepared to be a manager—economic, political, doctrinal; if it is a community college,[4] you are prepared to be a nurse, policeman, factory worker, or something like that. We have fairly consciously designed these stratified systems of education to place people in certain social roles, and that requires eliminating individual differences, cultural differences, group identity, ethnic languages.

There is a big fight now to block bilingual education, and that is happening all over the world, it is happening in Europe. Not very long ago, maybe thirty years ago, my graduate students when they got their Ph.D.s would go to Europe to teach in universities. And being young, they would be given the lower rung positions. Many of them were teaching German to German students who did not know German—they knew the language where they grew up, which happened to be in Germany, but what was called German was not intelligible to them, so they had to be taught German as a second language. That is less true now because the process of homogenization has sharply increased through television and all sorts of other means. But that was happening not so long ago in Europe, right at the heart of things. It is not so true in the United States for the reason I mentioned—we have a unique history of elimination of the regional societies and cultures. It is not true in Australia, for the same reason. But in places where the indigenous societies remain, the problem is dealt with the same way it was in England or in the European countries, by trying to impose all kinds of standards, including educational standards. These certainly have their value—I have been at MIT for fifty years, and I don't denigrate educational standards. But a large part of it is, indeed, socialization and passivity and obedience and fitting into your social role. If you are in Skull & Bones[5] at Yale, you are prepared to be somebody who owns and runs the society; if it is community college, you are prepared to be somebody who quietly serves the owner, the elite and the powerful.

Several questions occur to me as I listen to you. One has to do with the consequences to indigenous communities if they try to resist this kind of homogenizing process in education. Is it even possible to resist? How would you imagine a community could effectively resist?

That depends very much on the society. The Mexican state happens to be quite violent. And you do face the problem of just straight state terror. There is less of that north of the border. Similar problems arise but you don't face state terror in the same way. Not that it is non-existent, but nothing like Mexico.

So how do you deal with it here? Well, my old friend and colleague who recently died, Kenneth Hale, one of the greatest linguists in the world, was a leading figure in the global movement of language and culture revitalization. He was working with indigenous communities all over to develop their own programs of cultural defense and revival and reconstruction, including language, but also everything else that goes with it. One of the ways that he did it, which took huge amounts of work, was to bring students from, for example, the Hopi reservation to MIT. He got them to go through a regular doctoral program. This was not easy because they did not have the background of our students, nothing remotely like it. They did not have the science, the math, they did not know how to behave in an academic environment—they did not have any of these things. So it required from him and a couple of others who helped him, maybe thirty hours of work per week for each student just to get them through. Some of them did extremely well, went back and wrote great Ph.D.s. For one thing, they were working on their own languages, so when they learned how to do linguistics, they could apply it to their own languages in a manner in which no outsider, no matter how great a linguist he was, could ever approximate. So they come up with very important material. Some of them succeeded very effectively to go back to their own communities in order to start up educational programs, language preservation and revival programs. Often these efforts extend well beyond language to other domains of the indigenous culture. And some of them are very successful. And some did not work.

But I do not think there are formulae for it. It depends on the nature of the community, how integrated they are, how committed they are to retaining their own identity, what kinds of external pressures they are under, straight economic issues. Most of the places where Native Americans have been driven are economically unviable, on purpose, which means either they kind of rot away or they have to drift out to the outside to survive. This causes all kinds of problems. And every one of those problems has to be overcome in its own way. I do not think there can be a formula.

As I say, this is happening everywhere. It is happening in Europe, right at the center of Western civilization. It just happens that the last couple of years I have spent some time in the Kurdish region, the southeast area of Turkey that has been under vicious repression for years. It is never discussed in the United States for a simple reason—the United States is responsible for the repression. It has been funding the Turkish army to drive millions of people out of their homes, and kill tens of thousands, and suppress the language and culture, and so on. So, it is a non-topic in the United States—you do not talk about your own crimes; it is one of the things you learn at Yale and Princeton and Harvard. Our crimes do not exist—but these things are happening. There are Kurdish efforts to resist, but it is very hard. Fortunately for them, they have the support of many Turks, including Turkish intellectuals, writers and artists and others. But it is mainly a problem of trying to survive a miserable repression. They do it with an awful lot of courage, a lot of dignity, and, often, in hideous conditions. And indeed, here is something in which the old Ottoman Empire basically did have the right idea. I mean, there should be Turkish or Kurdish autonomy, and not just in Turkey. The whole region should be integrated into a very large regional, federal system of some kind.

And again, those are things that are going on just about everywhere in the world. Mexico has its own specific characteristics. In the United States, it is different. One difference is that the native, indigenous communities in the United States were virtually decimated, while they still sustain themselves to a much larger extent in Mexico. So Mexico, in this respect, is perhaps more like Europe than like the United States. But every place is different.

Another thing that is said is that communal ways of life, indigenous *comunalidad*, are anachronistic and counterproductive and doomed to failure. According to this view, school systems exist to serve the needs of multinational corporate capitalism. What indigenous communities are really doing by their efforts to resist national educational norms is dooming themselves to poverty, illiteracy, linguistic annihilation, and cultural marginalization. Is it counterproductive in your mind for these communities to resist national standards (*normatividad*) in order to pursue and maintain *comunalidad*? Does this have to be a polarized choice? Is there something in between?

You know, there is a whole spectrum of choices, and the consequences depend on all kinds of factors. For example, it depends to a large extent on whether the specific form of international integration which is called globalization, meaning corporate-led globalization, is going to succeed, or not. There is tremendous resistance to it all over the world. In the industrial countries, and primarily in the South, in Latin America, there is very active resistance. Argentina is refusing to heed International Monetary Fund (IMF) orders, which is the first time that has happened. Venezuela is attempting to go in its own direction. From Venezuela to the Southern Cone there is large-scale resistance, much of it indigenous-based. I was in indigenous areas of Colombia last year. There, and in Bolivia recently, Peru and elsewhere, there is substantial resistance. And there are comparable things happening in Africa, India and the United States. It is not necessarily beautiful, it often takes ugly forms. There is large-scale resistance to these efforts to create a world society in which there is essentially uniform service to highly concentrated economic power.

Corporations, after all, are just tyrannies, basically totalitarian command economies largely unaccountable to the public, and with a huge link to one another, a link to powerful states. They are trying to impose an international system which will work in their interests—it has nothing to do with development. In fact, any serious economic historian knows that the World Trade Organization (WTO) rules essentially do what in the economic literature is called "kicking away the ladder"—they eliminate the options and opportunities that were used by the rich, developed countries to get to the point where they work. I mean, if the United States two centuries ago had been compelled to follow WTO rules, we would not be sitting in this room. Instead, you would be visiting me in my hut, where I am catching and trapping animals, or maybe fishing, or something like that. Because that was the comparative advantage of the United States, but it won its independence and so it violated all the rules, just as England had done before it. It violated all the rules, changed its comparative advantage—which is called development—by state intervention, by high protectionism, by stealing technology from England in a way which is now called piracy and nobody is allowed to do it. But in those days, it was just, you know, taking technology. There was nothing remotely like the extreme patent rules, the highly protectionist rules of the WTO, that are designed to make sure that the knowledge and technology of the future is retained by the private tyrannies of the industrial societies. None of this existed. If it had, the United States would not have developed.

In fact, England would not have, either. England had to set high tariffs and resort to large-scale state intervention to protect itself from superior products from India and Ireland. Not just textiles, but ships and all sorts of things. Without exception, this is the way countries have developed.

The WTO system is consciously denying these methods to everyone else. NAFTA, the Free Trade Area of the Americas, is just trying to extend it to that. It is beneficial in some ways; some sectors benefit from it. The neoliberal principles in Mexico have certainly benefited some people. In fact, the number of billionaires has increased about as fast as the poverty rate, and the same has been true throughout the whole history of colonialism. In every colonized society you look at, no matter how poor it is, colonialism has stratified the society. Central Africa has a sector of extreme wealth and privilege that is much better than I can imagine, in the midst of poverty and misery. It is the effect of those principles.

Will that work all over the world? Well, there is enormous resistance to it, and rightly. And alternatives certainly are conceivable and, in fact, may happen. You see examples now. Latin America is a striking case, where the resistance is becoming hard for the centers of power and privilege to deal with. And there is plenty of turmoil inside the industrial countries. So you do not know what direction it will go.

It is an undeniable fact that the struggles of indigenous peoples in Mexico, the Zapatista movement, have given inspiration to many of these international developments. The world is a compli-cated place. Resistance in one place can fuel activism in another. In fact, this is well understood by people in power.

Why, for example, is the United States so desperately com-mitted to stamp out any form of independent development in the regions of its control? Take, for example, Cuba. Why forty-five years of terror and economic strangulation to prevent Cuba from going on its own path? Well, we know the answer to that. This is a pretty free country. There is a huge documentary record of inter-nal planning available, which is a tribute to American democracy. But nobody knows about it, which is not a tribute to American de-mocracy. That is a tribute to American education, which prevents people from knowing what they ought to know. But you are not thrown into a torture chamber if you break those rules, so we can find out. And it is pretty straightforward.

Go back to the internal documents of the early 1960s and it is all explained. I am quoting now, the "very existence" of the Cas-tro regime is "successful defiance" of U.S. policies that go back 150 years to the Monroe Doctrine, and therefore it cannot be tolerated. And, furthermore, there is danger of "the spread of the Castro idea of taking matters into your own hands," which may be pretty meaningful to plenty of people in Latin America who are suffering under the same kinds of conditions. We have got to stop that.

And this is the main theme of modern U.S. policy, the tra-ditional imperial policy. You have to prevent successful defiance, stop the spread of the idea of taking matters into your own hands, dismantel the construction of models that others might want to pursue. These are the leading themes of state policy in the power-ful countries.

Going back to your question, yes, that is exactly the point. Successful models, what is called by the rulers "successful defi-ance," meaning independent efforts of independent action, are very frightening. And, efforts to stamp them out take all sorts of forms, violent forms like military coups, or less violent forms like educational homogenization.

But whether or not one decides to be defiant, or to be independent, is a complicated choice, just as it is in personal life. Suppose you are a student at a nice, suburban school in New Mexico, or wherever you live. You are a bright student, an imaginative student. You must face the problem every day in fourth grade and every other year up through Harvard graduate school, whether to accept the norms that are being imposed on you and be obedient, or not. If you do, you may go on to some appropriate position in the existing society. If you decide to follow your own path, almost always there is a personal cost. Maybe it is one you want to take, but those are choices in an individual's life. There are choices everywhere. Let us take a patriarchal family. Do you accept the dominance of the authority figure, or do you find your own independent way? There is no formula for that. There is usually a cost for independence, but there are tremendous gains that come from it. That is why we live in a better world than one with slavery and kings and so on.

Is it possible to reform these state education systems, these homogenizing school systems, such that they could possibly serve the purposes of promoting and protecting communal ways of life? Can communities make use of these systems for their own purposes? Or does the effort to protect and promote *comunalidad* have to come from civic society outside of the state system of education?

Again, there is no formula. I mean, take places where it has happened, for example, Wales. You walk through the streets of Wales today, in Cardiff, and listen to the kids coming out of school— they are talking Welsh. And that was not true twenty years ago. This developed; they were in conflict with the national state, but there was enough adjustment so that it developed peacefully, nonviolently. Now that was a large-scale change and a successful example, partially successful, at least. There are other cases where exactly the negative consequences you described have occurred—marginalization, poverty, hopelessness, despair, and everything in between. There just cannot be a formula for those things. It is a matter of carefully evaluating and calibrating the consequences of choices that you make.

It can be very successful. The opportunities for success are, I think, greater now than they have been in the past, because this is the first time, ever, that there has been an international movement of solidarity on these issues. It is not yet powerful enough to change the basic institutions, but it exists.

Go to the World Social Forum and you see people from all walks of life, all kinds of backgrounds, all kinds of interests. The last one I went to was in Porto Alegre a year ago. When I got off the plane, I did not even go to the World Social Forum meetings. A friend drove me directly to the Vía Campesina conference, which was a short distance away. The international peasant association was meeting in a Landless Workers Movement farm, and there were peasants from all over the place. What they were aiming at was very exciting. I just happened to get there toward the end and it was a celebration. Women were interchanging seeds and discussing how you use them. Most agriculture is done by women, of course.

The theme of the international meeting was to try to make seeds part of the patrimony of humanity—a little sexist residue in there. They want UNESCO to recognize this effort. In the same way they recognize Venice as a city that has to be preserved, they should also recognize that the right to seed is a basic human right. Most of the people in the world are farmers so they want the right to possess their own seed, to control it, to not be subjected to Monsanto[6] rules, and so on. This is just a core part of human existence. They want to preserve it. They are not anti-technological; they just want to control it. That is real globalization on the level of people. It has to reach the right scale, but things have to start with small germs, then they can grow. So sure, it can happen. And I think the programs in schools that you are describing make a lot of sense. Well, that is a really powerful movement, and it is no longer in isolation. For one thing, they interact with one another in ways they could never do before. Also, it is connected with substantial popular movements in the rich countries that have similar commitments and understandings and that can be supportive and provide the badly needed solidarity.

I do not want to exaggerate; it is by no means powerful enough to undermine the centers of power and authority. But it certainly is shaking them. They have to respond. The World Bank programs are different from what they were ten years ago. The IMF does have to back off in the face of Argentina. The World Economic Forum in Davos[7] have to take off their ties and pretend to be ordinary people because they know they are getting themselves very isolated from ongoing significant popular movements. How far that can go? I suppose that is up to us, really. Nobody knows.

Picking up on your comment about seeds, indigenous knowledge, and control of one's own knowledge. . . . The foundation of *comunalidad* is a whole structure, a social structure, a knowledge base, indigenous commitments to land, to reciprocity, to autonomy for communities and for their ways of being in the world. The question, then, becomes: can such values, such knowledge, such ways of being, be incorporated into schooling as it exists within state institutions? Is it possible to fold these deep values and commitments of *comunalidad* within the disciplinary structures and the subject matters of normative schooling? Or, do the values and educational commitments of *comunalidad* require setting up its own education system?

That depends. There cannot be one answer. It is technically conceivable to recreate the curriculum of state schools. There is no problem in laying out a curriculum in which communities would run their own schools with their own communal values and interests, and also introduce whatever they like from the outside—quantum physics, Shakespearean plays, or whatever happens to interest them. They could introduce it on their own terms, within their own cultural framework. My seamstress aunts did this sixty years ago. They kept their own culture, mostly imported from Eastern Europe, but absorbed on their own terms the parts of the broader culture that they wanted to include. It can be done in many different ways—locally run schools or regionally run schools are a perfect example. So in Catalonia, for instance, which is a big area, not a local community, schools are taught in Catalan. You learn Spanish as a second language.

One of the big differences I see with several examples you have given from European and U.S. contexts is that indigenous languages, including languages in Oaxaca, often do not have a literate tradition. Indigenous language traditions and practices are enormously different from Westernized traditions and practices. Mexican schools seek to impose the Spanish language and its traditions and thereby homogenize the Oaxacan linguistic landscape.

But first of all, a literate tradition—reading—is a very narrow part of human history. Most cultures have grown, survived, flourished, with a very small percentage, or maybe none, of the population literate. I mean, take the Bible—there was no written language for a thousand years, and the Bible was compiled far later from oral traditions that were handed down over centuries. That is why it is such a conglomerate of things out of Sumaria and Egypt, and what is now Israel-Palestine, and so forth. Oral traditions are extremely rich. They are preserved from generation to generation.

It is just like agriculture. I mean, peasant agriculture is highly sophisticated, very productive, and extremely efficient. When what is called "scientific agriculture" replaces it, it often leads to a reduction in productivity. Where is the knowledge of peasant agriculture? It is not in textbooks. It is in the heads of women who teach it to their daughters, and they teach it to their daughters. And it goes generation to generation, and it gets enriched and made more complicated. It is a very rich tradition, but very fragile. One year of chemical warfare in Colombia under the pretext of drug eradication is sufficient to destroy centuries of culture and scientific knowledge and tradition from the heads of the people, just as it destroys the land so that they cannot plant anything there. They are forced to move off into the urban slums, which is the main point.

So, yes, the systems are fragile, but very rich, very complex. In fact, the pharmaceutical companies are now all over the world, trying to mine that knowledge and steal it. Then they put patent constraints that will prevent the people themselves from using it.

And all of this knowledge has developed and survived without literacy. Literacy has its tremendous advantages, but there is no reason why it cannot be brought in to incorporate what has been achieved, just the way the biblical stories were finally written down, compiled from many centuries of oral tradition. The same is true of classical Greek literature and, in fact, much else. Actually, the same is true of contemporary American literature to the extent that it brings in what happens in the streets and in ordinary life. It is drawing from the richness and wealth of ordinary life and turning it into written literature.

You have expressed your deep appreciation of John Dewey, and I quote some words of his that you have quoted, "The ultimate aim of production is not production of goods but the production of free human beings, associated with one another on terms of equality." Now, basic to this concept of

democracy seems to be the individual who is free to associate, or not, with others. This raises a question about collectivized societies: how can this concept, which places freedom or voluntary affiliation of the individual at its center, accommodate for and respect communal values that ground the individual's being within the collective?

It has famously been said, "No man is an island." Every individual is part of some cultural, communal system, and heavily influenced by it, participating in it. But individuals should have a choice as to whether to participate or not. You should not be coerced into being part of your own community. But it certainly should be an obvious choice to make. I think when Dewey is talking about people freely associated, he does not have in mind individuals who are just randomly connected with one another, like a chat line on the Internet. Rather, I believe he means persons organically connected with one another in living communities and cultures and languages and practices, which can vary in all kinds of ways. And within those, individuals can make choices, which may extricate them from their communities. That is one of the choices. Or they may contribute to them by enriching them. These are among the free choices of freely associated individuals. That is what free association has always meant in the libertarian tradition. So, if you look at the movements for workers' control or worker self-management, they are systems of free association.

But they are also people working together, producing something, organizing themselves for commercial interaction, and so on. That is free association, but not in isolation. In fact, we now have a kind of free association of isolated individuals. A teenager in the U.S. talking on the Internet to somebody in Tibet, for example. That is an instance of isolated individuals, and it probably has pathological elements. In my view, it will probably be personally harmful and harmful to society. But it is about the first time in history that anything like that has existed, as a result of certain technologies. It is not healthy, in my view, but that is another question. Almost all of human history is individuals, in the best case freely associating, but within community. There is no other way.

But many of the authors of our cases describe two different kinds of normative standards—one is imposed by the state, the external state norms. But collectivized communities also have a pervasive sense of normative behavior, of what it means and what is expected if one wants to be considered part of the community. Does this in any way trouble your definition of individuals freely associating, when the community norms are very pervasive and defining of community membership?

Yes, if the norms are coercive, whether they are from the state or the community, then that is a negative aspect. Now, to some extent, norms are always coercive. There is something coercive about the fact that I am talking English instead of Swahili. English happened to be the language of my environment. But there are various degrees of coercion. There is disapproval that comes from departing from norms, which is a kind of coercion. And there is a whole range of modes of socializing people within communities, as well. But they should be as minimally coercive as possible to provide for optimal free choice, and rich enough and inventive and creative enough so that the free choice will commonly lead to participation in and enrichment of community life.

Norms from the state may conflict with this. Now we are back to the question of whether children in Wales, for example, should be brought up in schools that teach Welsh or teach English. And those are conflicts that have to be worked out differently in every case. Bilingual education right here in Boston is another case. And the indigenous communities in Mexico are still a different case. I just think it is a waste of effort to try to find some general formula. There is not one. It is highly dependent on particular circumstances and aspirations and commitments.

As I walk away from this interview, I believe I hear you saying that the time is more hopeful in some ways for indigenous communities than you have seen in the past. Is that correct?

Yes, and more hopeful than at any time I can think of in the past. I mean, this process of driving people into homogeneous national states has been a very brutal, harsh process. It goes back centuries in Europe to form the nation-state system, then spreads over the world as Europe attempted to impose similar systems elsewhere. The process also was evident in other imperial systems; for example, the Aztec system had similar characteristics. But it has been a harsh, brutal, violent system, and it has always been resisted.

This is really the first time when there is substantial international popular solidarity that draws from the experiences of regional communities. The effect of the Zapatistas is a classic case that did inspire much of the global justice movement. And it can also support this movement.

Take a state like Brazil, where popular will is suppressed by the force of international investors and lenders under the liberal system. I do not think Brazilians can break out of that on their own. But with the cooperation of people in the North who can relax those bonds, relax that stranglehold in the centers of power, they might break out of it. And the democratic possibilities that have been so dramatically realized could actually mean something. But those are long, hard battles for a huge country like Brazil, or for a little community somewhere in Mexico.

NOTES

1. Meyer, L., Maldonado, B., Ortiz, R. & García, V. (2004), *Entre la normatividad y la comunalidad: Experiencias educativas innovadoras del Oaxaca Indígena actual.* Oaxaca:

Fondo Editorial del Instituto Estatal de Educación Pública de Oaxaca (IEEPO). This earlier book was the occasion for the interview conducted in 2004.

2. When asked later how he could describe the United States as a "homogenous" country given the enormous diversity of its population, Dr. Chomsky clarified that he was not referring to cultural homogeneity:

> This is just a misunderstanding. The issue here is institutional homogeneity: one set of laws, one national language, etc. In these respects, the United States (like Australia, and to a large extent Canada, and partially New Zealand) are homogeneous, as distinct from Europe and most of Latin America, because the English colonists largely wiped out the indigenous populations, unlike most of Europe where nation-states were imposed on existing societies that were not simply exterminated.
>
> Of course, the U.S. itself is extremely heterogeneous in other ways. It's a nation of immigrants from all over, some of whom kept their own cultures and practices, sometimes even languages, for a long time. My parents, for example, were from the Jewish "pale of settlement" in Eastern Europe. They lived here in a kind of Jewish ghetto. My grandfather lived here for fifty years and never learned a word of English, or strayed very far from the house; I rather suspect he still thought he was in a Ukrainian village, and wondered why the peasants were black. But that's a different kind of heterogeneity, not the kind we were discussing. (personal communication, May 31, 2004)

3. Taylorism, named after F. W. Taylor (1856–1915), refers to an industrial process that focuses on scientific management and efficiency by breaking skilled labor down into a series of lower-skilled tasks and mechanizing them whenever possible.

4. Local two-year, post-secondary educational institution providing basic courses and job preparation not requiring a four-year university degree.

5. Secret student association at Yale University to which both George W. Bush and John Kerry, presidential candidates in 2004, belonged.

6. Monsanto advertises itself as "an agricultural company that applies innovation and technology to help farmers around the world produce more while conserving more." The aggressive efforts by this U.S. company—often successful—to patent genetically modified seeds worldwide has been widely contested by indigenous and other groups who seek to preserve the rights of local communities to control the use and distribution of native and un-modified seeds as the "preserve of humanity."

7. Davos refers to the annual meeting of the World Economic Forum in Davos, Switzerland, where international political leaders, top business leaders, and selected intellectuals and journalists come together to discuss and strategize responses to world issues.

Video Message to the Second National Congress of Indigenous & Intercultural Education[1]

Oaxaca, Mexico, October 25–27, 2007[2]

By Noam Chomsky

I AM SORRY THAT I cannot join you in person for this very important occasion. But I would like at least to say a few words to express my admiration for what you all are doing in your professional work in indigenous education and also for your support for the teachers—the courageous teachers in Oaxaca—who are fighting a struggle of enormous significance, not just there but part of a worldwide struggle which is particularly dramatic now all over Latin America, which has become, in my opinion, the most exciting part of the world for the first time in its modern history.

After half a millennium, the countries of Latin America are beginning to move toward a significant level of integration instead of being separated from one another and dominated by imperial powers. Integration is a prerequisite for independence and self-determination. And they are also beginning to move seriously toward overcoming what has been the real curse of Latin America, apart from outside domination—the curse of the huge gap, unprecedented in the world, between a tiny elite of enormous wealth and a huge mass of deeply impoverished people. It is a gap that also has a racial and ethnic correlate to it, as you all know. And there are steps towards trying to overcome that curse. Particularly dramatic has been the role of indigenous people, the most repressed and marginalized part of the population for centuries, even in countries where they are the majority. But they are finally organizing, demanding their rights, and making remarkable achievements, from the highlands of Bolivia to Chiapas and other places. That is a very dramatic and important development. It is reversing 500 years of miserable and ugly history, revitalizing the languages, the cultures, technical resources, developing forms of social organization that come out of their own traditions but are adapted to the modern world. These are tremendously exciting developments and people like you are right at the center of it.

This conference is at the core of the development and revitalization and defense and protection of indigenous rights, and with it, the rights of everyone. And I would take for granted that the people in the world who have any concern for justice and freedom would be very pleased to join me in offering the warmest hopes and expectations for the success of the endeavors that you are involved in.

NOTES

1. The Second National Congress of Indigenous & Intercultural Education (CNEII) convened in Oaxaca, Mexico, in October 2007, in support of the teachers' and civic uprising against the armed state repression of striking teachers in 2006.
2. Videotaped on October 4, 2007 at MIT, Cambridge, Massachusetts.

The Imperial State and Hope from inside Indigenous America

Interview with Noam Chomsky by Lois Meyer,
October 4, 2007

DURING OUR FIRST INTERVIEW almost four years ago, you spoke a great deal about the bloody, violent, historic process of state-making and its consequences in decimating local cultures and languages. Are those still the relevant processes today? Have they morphed somehow into neoliberal capitalism and globalization? And given the kind of global context we have now, is the idea of *interculturalidad* (the term used in Oaxaca), or multiculturalism, even possible across the huge disparities in the world today? Or is *interculturalidad* really just another strategy of neoliberal capitalism to oppress?

Any struggle for liberation will either succeed and gain its goals, or will be resisted. And one of the forms of resistance is co-optation. So you can just take for granted that any decent and honorable struggle will be adapted by those in power for their own purposes, whether it is women's rights, minority rights, democracy, whatever it is. People in power do not just give up and say, "Okay, fine, you win." They will resist, and one of the forms of resistance is to try to take over and distort and modify the efforts of liberation for their own purposes. So, yes, that can happen with multiculturalism and diversity. But it does not have to. Part of resistance is preventing that from happening.

You can see it all over. Let us take state formation. It is true that state formation has been an extremely violent and brutal process, and it remains so. And it continues. I mean, the so-called neoliberalism does not erode state power. It just uses it for definite purposes. So the United States is the center of neoliberalism, but the United States guards its sovereignty in an extreme fashion. It resists any infringement on its sovereignty. That is one of the reasons why the U.S. very rarely signs international conventions, and when it signs them, it adds reservations that make them inapplicable to the United States. So, here is the center of neoliberalism which also insists that it be a state that is relatively immune to international processes. Not because the American population wants it that way. The American population is opposed to that. So, for example, the population by an overwhelming majority thinks that in international crises, the United Nations ought to take the lead, not the United States. In fact, a majority of the population even believes, surprisingly, that the United States ought to give up the veto in the Security Council of the U.N. and follow the will of the majority even if we do not like it. Populations tend to be pacifist and internationalist, but governing elites are extremely dedicated to maintaining state sovereignty and power. They cannot do it everywhere, but where they can, they do. And that is independent of neoliberalism. Neoliberalism simply means, one of its aspects is to use state power for the benefit of the concentrations of economic power.

There are other elements of serious fraud in the neoliberal framework. Neoliberalism is supposed to involve a belief in markets. We happen to be sitting right now in an institution which is designed by the state to undermine markets. If you use computers and the Internet and microelectronics and telecommunications and so on, those things did not come out of markets. They came out of places like this, part of the state sector of the economy. Now, that is the dynamic sector for innovation and development. Corporations get the benefits but they play a relatively limited role in the hard work of research and development. It is the public that pays for that. So it is the exact opposite of this neoliberal doctrine. Neoliberal doctrine is to be rammed down the throats of weak people but the powerful do not accept it for themselves. And that goes back through history. The term "neoliberal" is a misnomer. First of all, it is not *liberal* in the traditional sense. It involves heavy reliance on state power. And it is not new. It goes back to the origins of the Industrial Revolution. The advanced industrial societies—England, the United States, Germany, France, and so on—got that way by violating those rules radically. And they still violate them, the United States maybe more than others. But they do ram those rules down the throats of the weak. That is the way to control and dominate them. That is what the so-called free trade agreements are about. They are not about free trade, but they are a form of domination. So they are not new and they are not liberal. We should not be misled by them. And state power remains. On the other hand, co-optation is going to take place.

Let me give you a concrete example. In my view, one of the healthiest developments in Europe is the rise of regional cultures and languages that had been oppressed for a long time, almost eliminated. So, take Spain. I have a daughter who lived in Spain in 1979. I visited her in Barcelona. I did not hear a word of Catalan. I did not see a sign in Catalan. In fact, there was no evidence that Catalan existed. It was suppressed by the Fascist government. You were not allowed to speak it. I went back a couple years later and all you heard was Catalan. All the signs were in Catalan. People were speaking Catalan, and so on. You lift the heavy hand of the dictatorship enough and the actual culture and society can revive—folkdances, everything.

On the other hand, it has its negative aspects. So, for example, one element of it is an extreme form of nationalism, like oppressing Spanish workers who live in Catalonia. These things can happen. There are all kinds of aspects to positive developments. You have to be cautious. You cannot generalize.

In terms of schooling, for decades Mexico and most of Latin

America have had a very centralized, homogenous school system. **And now, with the No Child Left Behind Act of 2001 (NCLB) in the United States, we have more federal involvement and intrusion in public schools than probably ever in our history.**[1] **Do you feel that state control of public education is a foregone conclusion in today's world? Is there any way that public schools can shake their institutional role of domination? And, is state control of public education a necessity of this kind of neoliberal agenda?**

We can think of different societies, more libertarian societies. But let us keep to ours. In our form of society, some kind of state involvement in the educational system is a good thing. So, for example, if you had no state involvement in the United States, you would have schools teaching racism, oppressing women, murdering immigrants, you know, doing anything they chose to do.

In fact, what you do actually have, and here is where there should be more state control, is powerful and wealthy institutions can take over segments of the curriculum. So, for example, there is something called the Objectivist Foundation which supports the ideas of Ayn Rand[2], to basically get everything for yourself and kick everyone else in the teeth. That is what it comes down to simply, though it is put in more complicated words. In Massachusetts, which is a liberal state, they teach that in the schools. The Foundation simply hands over to the schools a curriculum, including books of Ayn Rand, essays, lesson plans, prizes, and so on. Teachers accept that, you know, they do not have to think, they just take it over. The schools say, "Fine, we do not have to worry about planning anything." But the children—I've got grandchildren studying this stuff. It is shocking, you know. Here is a place where I think the community should not permit that to happen.

On the other hand, state control can be very harmful. Take No Child Left Behind. Like "neoliberalism," it is a misnomer. In fact, what it ought to be called is *Every Child Must Be Left Behind*.

No Child Left Behind is a system based on training children to join the Marine Corps. I mean, it is based on testing. Education is not about passing a test. It is being able to think, to create, to explore, and so on, to be imaginative. No Child Left Behind is the opposite. The children are trained—I can see it with my own grandchildren—to pass the test that is going to be given at a certain point. Well, when you are trained to pass a test, you can do it, and two days later you forget it.

I remember this from my own education. We had something like it when I was in high school. I was in an academic high school. All the kids were trying hard to get a scholarship to college because we did not have any money. So you were trained in the academic high school to pass the college entrance exams. You studied and worked, and you could pass them, and then forgot it. I had to pass an advanced placement exam in German, which I did not know anything about. So I sat for a couple of weeks and I memorized a 3,000-word dictionary. Okay, I passed the exam. How long do you think it stayed in my mind? That is not education, that is discipline, training for discipline, control, and obedience. Education is the opposite of that. It is offering opportunities to create, to inquire, to explore, to do what seems interesting to you. There has to be some structure to it, it is not anything goes. But it should be a laying out of opportunities that children can explore on their own, which is the opposite of No Child Left Behind. So instituting such a policy at a state level is understandable. That is a way of imposing discipline and control. But it is not education. In the science-based parts of the curriculum, let us say at MIT, you cannot imagine anything like that. The last thing you want to do is to run courses simply so that people will be able to pass an exam.

But that form of education is now included as a condition of the North American Free Trade Agreement and other trade agreements that are imposed on countries.[3]

That has a history. The 1960s were a period of a rise in activism of all kinds, which had a very civilizing effect on the society for human rights, minority rights, women's rights, concerns about the environment, opposition to oppression. Indigenous rights is a good example. Up until the 1960s, if you took a course in anthropology at a university in the United States, they would tell you that before Columbus came, there were, you know, some hunter-gatherers wandering around, or something like that. It was finally recognized, really in the 1960s, that there were rich, developed societies, and that something really happened here before the Spaniards.

In fact, think about Columbus Day, which is a couple of days from now. In my classes I used to tell the students, "We are not going to meet next week because of Genocide Day." And they did not know what I was talking about. But now everybody knows. In fact, they do not even call it Columbus Day anymore. They call it "What Used to Be Called Columbus Day." Okay, that is part of the civilizing effect of the 1960s.

Well, that frightened elites. They do not want the society to be civilized. They wanted it to be subordinated. And there was a very strong reaction against this, an elite reaction, across the spectrum. Not right wing, you know, liberals, too. In fact, there is an important book that should be read, called *The Crisis of Democracy*. This was the first publication of the Trilateral Commission, whose political complexion was liberal internationalists, the people who staffed the Carter administration. What was the crisis of democracy in the 1960s? The crisis of democracy was that there was too much democracy. There was an excess of democracy coming from all this activism. Parts of the population that are normally passive and obedient, what are called "special interests," like women, minorities, majorities, working people, farmers and other special interests, were all trying to enter the political arena to press their interests and concerns. And that was no good because we are supposed to run it, you know, we rich guys, and powerful guys, and those who work for us. So we have to have more moderation in democracy, and they discussed how to do it. And part of it had to do with schools. They had a phrase that they used to refer to the schools and the universities. They are the institutions responsible for "the indoctrination of the young." Now come on, that is the liberal internationalists talking, not the right wing. And they said the institutions responsible for the indoctrination of the young are not doing their job. They have to introduce more obedience, control, subordination, not having these kids running around thinking for themselves. What we are talking about is an offshoot of that.

In fact, neoliberalism is an offshoot of that. One of the effects of neoliberalism, and it is well understood, is to reduce democracy. Even just freeing financial flows. It was perfectly understood by the economists who designed the post–WWII economic system, John Maynard Keynes, for example, that if you have free financial movement, if you have no constraints on finance, on the free flow of capital, governments are not going to be able to carry out social democratic policies, for simple reasons. There is what is sometimes called in the economics literature a "virtual parliament," the investors and lenders that carry out a "moment-by-moment referendum" on government policies. And if they do not like those policies, they can destroy the economy by capital flight, by attacks on the currency, and so on. And, of course, the virtual parliament usually wins, even in rich countries. So you free up capital movements, as was done in the early 1970s, and you have a direct attack on democracy. That has happened, too. And there are many other aspects to it. But imposing discipline on the institutions responsible for the indoctrination of the young, to borrow the liberal rhetoric, is part of it.

In 2004 you also spoke to me a lot about state violence. My Oaxacan colleagues even questioned your comments about extreme state terrorism in Mexico. Certainly in the last

couple of years, no one is any longer questioning the presence of state terrorism in Mexico. At that time you commented that many people in the world would say the United States is the prime terrorist state in the world. I was recently reading the interview that *Democracy Now* conducted with Evo Morales[4], where he said that he was convinced that indigenous peoples are the moral reserve of humanity. Given this kind of a picture, in what ways do you feel indigenous communities, especially in Mexico and Latin America, but also in the United States, are fighting back against aggressive state militarism, and have perhaps unusual capacities for doing so?

It is going on, especially in South America. Central America was ravaged and devastated by Reaganite wars, and so on. South America had a bitter history—neo-Nazi dictatorships, Pinochet, the Brazilian generals, hideous plagues of repression, but it is beginning to emerge from it in interesting ways. And indigenous people are often in the lead.

Evo Morales is an example. I mean, they had an election in Bolivia of a kind that is unimaginable in the West. In fact, it is quite remarkable to compare the election in which Morales was elected in December 2005 with the election in the United States the year before. There is a striking comparison. Educated people can not see it, but think about it. In the United States you had two candidates, both of whom came from backgrounds of wealth and political power. They both went to the same elite university. They joined the same secret society which trains people to be part of the ruling class. They were able to run because they had similar programs and they were supported by the same corporate interests. And that is called a democratic election.

What happened in Bolivia? In Bolivia you had an election in which the majority of the population participated actively and knew what the issues were. In the United States few people knew the stands of the candidates, as shown by polls. In Bolivia, they knew what the issues were. In fact, they had been struggling, fighting for those issues for years. For example, control over water in Cochabamba, and all sorts of things. And the poor majority population elected someone from their own ranks. I mean, *that* is an election, *that* is a democratic election. Not the thing that they had here. But that is kind of unintelligible among Western elites. If I give talks and say, "You want to learn about democracy? Take a look at the Bolivian election." It is kind of like a haze, nobody knows what I am talking about. But if you think about it, it is true. And what they achieved is astonishing. For the imperial powers, mainly the United States, it is a real disaster. The continent is falling out of control.

Even the military bases are beginning to be driven out. When Rafael Correa was running for president in Ecuador, he was asked in the election campaign what he would do with the Manta Air Base that the United States has in Ecuador. It is one of the last big military bases. He had a good answer. He said that he would allow the United States to keep the military base if they allowed Ecuador to establish a military base near Miami. Okay, that is the right answer.

The United States is losing its capacity to control the region. It is the same with other imperial powers, but the United States is in the lead. This control is based on essentially two factors. One is violence, and the other is the weakness, disintegration of the countries themselves. Well, both are changing. You cannot use violence the way you used to. You cannot use economic controls the way you used to. Country after country is throwing out the International Monetary Fund (IMF) which is pretty much an offshoot of the U.S. Treasury Department, which was the main measure of control. Argentina, which was driven to disaster by IMF rules, threw them out. They paid off their debt with the help of Venezuela. Now Bolivia is doing the same. Brazil did it in a different way. In fact, the IMF is in trouble because it is not collecting from countries to which it used to lend. Well, that is one of the methods of economic control. As the countries become more unified and integrated, the barriers increase. And military control is nothing like it was. Take the election of Lula in Brazil. His program is not all that different from that of Goulart in the early 1960s. In that case, the Kennedy administration simply moved in, organized a military coup, and established the first of the major neo-Nazi regimes in Latin America, which had a big influence. Brazil is a powerful state. But we cannot do that now. In fact, now they have to regard Lula as the good guy, somehow, as opposed to the bad guy, Chavez. This requires the doctrinal system here to suppress a lot of facts. One of them, that when Lula was reelected, one of his first acts was to fly to Venezuela to support Chavez in his electoral campaign and dedicate a joint project, a bridge over the Orinoco River, and plan other projects. That is not supposed to happen. He is supposed to be a good guy. But the point is that the good guy is now the kind of government that the United States was overthrowing not long ago. The last time the United States tried a military coup in Latin America was in 2002 in Venezuela, and it was beaten back in days by a popular uprising and by outrage in Latin America, where democracy is taken more seriously than it is here. So that is resistance.

But what about Mexico? Speak about Mexico.

Mexico fell into deep recession because of the debt crisis. The United States raised interest rates very sharply under Volker and Reagan. That caused a tremendous debt crisis in Mexico. Now, they had a couple of ways out. One way out would have been the way Kirchner took in Argentina, or Morales is taking in Bolivia, by saying, "No, we are not going to pay the debt." I mean, the debt is illegitimate anyway. I do not have time to go into it, but it is not a legitimate debt, it does not mean anything. So, either restructure the debt, or do not pay it, or rid yourself of the IMF, or something. That would have been one direction to follow. The other direction to follow was to accept the structural adjustment, the neoliberal forms. Well, that led to a disaster in Mexico for the next decade.

But there was concern in the United States that Mexico might move in an independent direction. In fact, there was an important strategy conference at the Pentagon in 1990 or 1991, during which a lot of Latin American experts were discussing Latin America. They concluded that relations between the United States and Mexico were in pretty good shape. But there was a cloud on the horizon. They said there was a threat that what they called a "democracy opening" might take place in Mexico and lead the country to pursue its own interests instead of remaining under United States control. Well, there was an answer to that. The answer is called NAFTA.

One of the main goals of NAFTA, and it was stated pretty openly, and I am quoting, is "to lock Mexico into" what are called "the reforms," meaning the neoliberal rules. You can lock Mexico into those rules by treaty, so even if there is a "democracy opening," that dangerous thing, it is not going to be able to do much because they are locked in. That is the track that Mexico is in. They do not have to stay in it, but they are in it. And it was conscious, purposeful, and now Mexico is trapped in a way in which other countries are not. And it will have to extricate itself. It can. Like down in the Southern Cone, Argentina was able to rid itself of the IMF. And Mexico does not have to stay trapped in NAFTA. It was not an agreement among the *people* of North America. In fact, most of the *people* of North America were opposed to it. It was rammed down their throats, mostly in secret. And it has actually been harmful for the working people of all three countries, not surprisingly.

In fact, right now it is leading to a real crisis in Mexico having to do with corn, as the United States turns to ethanol production.

That is another example of the radical violation of neoliberal rules. The only way the United States can produce ethanol is by very high tariffs which keep out much cheaper and more efficient Brazilian ethanol, which is sugar-based, not corn-based. First, they have very high tariffs, and then a lot of government subsidies. Okay, that way you can get corn producers to turn to ethanol production. But that has an effect, and one of the effects is that food prices go up. Not just corn prices, but cattle, and everything. They used to interchange corn and soy beans to keep the soil fertile. Okay, now they do not do that, so soy bean prices go up. Well, it has an effect in Mexico. A lot of Mexicans live on tortillas. Tortilla prices have gone out of sight. They have had tortilla riots.

One of the goals of NAFTA was to drive people off the land. There is an abstract economic theory that says that Mexicans should not be producing corn. The place that invented corn should not be producing it. Why? Because highly subsidized United States agribusiness can produce it more cheaply. Therefore, Mexicans should go off into the cities and find jobs that are not there, and in fact, start coming across the border because there is no way for them to survive. That is part of NAFTA.

The National Congress of Indigenous & Intercultural Education has taken corn as one of its themes. And the Congress has been encouraging indigenous schools in Oaxaca and across the nation to actually cultivate corn, indigenous corn, native corn, study the process, start seed banks, etc. Do you feel that this kind of school-by-school resistance can impact something that seems as overwhelming as NAFTA?

It can. This kind of local resistance is not going to be easy, and it requires solidarity. It requires solidarity with people in the United States. There are popular forces in the United States that have come out of the dreaded 1960s, and they have become more civilized and are concerned about things like this. Sometimes these grassroots efforts are co-opted. They are co-opted into things like organic food crazes which can become just another way for corporations to make money. But they do not have to be. They can also be committed to fair trade, indigenous rights, food self-sufficiency, undermining state-supported agribusiness. They can be converted to that.

And one very, very important development that took place as kind of a long-term consequence of the 1960s, mainly in the 1980s, was the development of the solidarity movement in the United States. That was something new in the history of imperialism. Tens of thousands of Americans went down to Central America to try to help people, either literally to help people in poor communities, or just because their presence as a U.S. citizen could help protect people from state terror. That had never happened before. Nobody in France went to live in an Algerian village. Nobody in Belgium went to live in a Congolese village. Nobody in the United States went to live in a Vietnamese village. It was just not the kind of thing that was done. But it started being done in the 1980s.

And it was coming from right on Main Street, it was not the elite institutions. A lot of it was churches, in fact the evangelical churches, in places like Kansas and Arizona and rural Maryland, and so on. This is real mainstream America. And the commitment was very deep. It has now spread to an international solidarity movement, a lot of it religious-based. So you find Christian peacemakers in Hebron and places like that. But the connections with Central America, and now much of Latin America, were strong. That is part of the development of this sort of international solidarity that can really make a difference, inside the imperial state, inside the suppressed communities.

On September 13, the U.N. finally passed the International Declaration on the Rights of Indigenous Peoples. What do

you feel is the impact of this kind of declaration? Can you also speak to the fact that Mexico signed the declaration, while the United States, Australia, Canada and New Zealand did not?

That was very striking. Also very striking was the fact that it was barely reported here. What actually happened is that the four genocidal societies did not sign. The four societies which had been most involved in destruction of the indigenous populations refused to sign. New Zealand had made some accommodation with the indigenous population. In Australia the indigenous population was decimated. In the United States it was not totally destroyed, but went down by millions. It is not that the founding fathers did not know it. They talked quite openly about the extermination of the native populations, and so on. And Canada was a somewhat similar story, though more complex. So the four main societies that had come closest to genocide refused to sign, and there was very little discussion of it.

Now, if we had enough in the way of activist popular movements, they would have made a big issue about this. That requires organization, and education, and activism. There is a lot, but not enough. But it can be taken up. I mean, the Declaration is important, and the fact that these four countries did not sign it should be a big issue for activists inside those countries. What does it mean that we did not sign it?

Mexico is, after all, in a mixed position. The United States is sitting on half of Mexico. A lot of the wealth of the United States comes from Mexico. The Southwest, California, that is Mexico, conquered in a war of aggression. Not only did they take the riches of Mexico, they also took the culture. When Ronald Reagan straps on his cowboy boots and pretends to be John Wayne, he is taking over the Mexican cowboy culture which was picked up by Americans. That is where they learned about cattle and sheep, the customs and the culture, the mines and the wealth, and of course, the labor. So Mexico is sort of a mixed story: on the one hand, a serious victim of imperial aggression; on the other hand, there is a pretty brutal record internally. Well, they balanced the choices and signed.

But I think once the Declaration is in words, it can be used as a means of organizing and education, so it does mean something. And this is taking place. It is not coming out of the blue. It is taking place against a background in which somebody like Morales would be elected by the Indian majority. There are even calls for an Indian nation in South America, controlling their own resources. And the same thing is happening elsewhere in the world. It is out of that background that the Declaration could finally get through, after fifteen, twenty years of trying to get it through.

There has always been a close relationship between indigenous efforts for autonomy, experiences of self-determination, and use of a people's own language. Language has been a critical part of pulling those efforts together. What happens when indigenous languages are no longer the language of common communication in these regions? Can indigenous communities construct and maintain their own autonomy in Spanish in Mexico, or in English in the United States?

When you lose your language, it is not just words. Your language is a repository of cultural wealth, of tradition, of history, of social interaction, of oral literature, all sorts of things. So you are losing a large part of that, too. Can you retain it? Yes, but it is a lot harder. That is why you see a revival of native languages, sometimes pretty striking. Right here, on the very floor where we are sitting, something quite miraculous happened. One of our graduate students, Jessie Little Doe, is a Wampanoag Indian. That was one of the main languages spoken here before the colonists came. Now, that language has not been spoken for a century. But together with a really outstanding linguist here, Ken Hale, who died

recently, Jessie and some of the students managed to reconstruct
Wampanoag, using texts and comparative work with similar languages. And they have a fair reconstruction of it. Jessie learned it.
She has a daughter who is now about three. She is the first native
speaker of Wampanoag in a century! And it is arousing interest
among others. It is now being done with other languages.

There are a lot of things being done, astonishing things.
Take Spain again, or Europe. I mean, languages are dying out in
Europe at a very rapid rate. We do not pay much attention to it,
but it has been happening. They are being revived. Catalan was
always there in homes, but now it is *the* language of Catalonia, and
Basque is being revived. You go to Wales and you see kids coming
out of school talking Welsh. Things like that are extremely encouraging. They are running counter to the effort to homogenize
the world, meaning to control it and dominate it and subordinate
it. I think it would be hell to live in a world where everyone was
identical. Diversity is part of the richness of life.

And there is a reaction. It is political, like in Bolivia, and is
also cultural. In fact, Bolivia is quite interesting. I was in northern
Chile recently, and I met with the Aymara in northern Chile, who
are a very repressed community. And they are concerned that the
Aymara language might die. Right across the border in Bolivia,
Aymara is becoming the language of the country. But the disori-
entation of the countries, the separation between them has been
so enormous, there is almost no contact between the Aymara in
northern Chile and the Aymara in Bolivia, a couple of miles down
the road. That is a residue of imperial conflict. There was a war, a
Bolivia-Peru-Chile war, back in 1879. And the way it is described
in history books is that Chile won, but the real description is, Britain won. Britain wanted to control the mines in northern Chile,
so they intervened as an imperial power and made sure that Chile
won the war. Now Bolivia does not have an outlet to the sea, the
countries are in conflict, among the Indian population, too. But
that can be overcome.

In fact, there are steps towards overcoming it. The moves toward an Indian nation in South America are part of those steps. And similar things are happening elsewhere in the world. Now, how it is going to turn out, nobody can predict. There are conflicting forces. You put your energy into trying to make the better outcomes turn out.

Hegemony is not perfect. There are always cracks, spaces in which resistance is possible. In what ways does a kind of forced hegemonic alliance operate in the relationship between indigenous nations and states that have occupied aboriginal lands?

This issue, like the others, is in contention. It was not for a long time, but now it is very definitely in contention. In Canada, for example, the Inuit did get control of a substantial amount of land. They are under attack now, because with global warming that land is becoming valuable. The wealthy, dominant population wants it back. And there is going to be a battle about that. Similar things are happening in many places. Here again, there is cooptation. In the United States, many of the Indian tribes now have found that they are allowed to build casinos. That is not exactly a revival of indigenous cultures and rights. And it is leading to a lot of wealth and corruption, and so on. But these are things you have to struggle with. There is no simple answer.

Is there a final word about optimism that you would give? Last time you surprised me when you spoke so optimistically. I'm just wondering if you still feel that optimism.

The best remark about that is one that Gramsci made famous. He said we should live by *pessimism of the intellect and optimism of the will*. That is the right answer.

NOTES

1. NCLB, the U.S education policy passed by a bipartisan vote of Congress during the first Bush administration, offers states federal education funds in exchange for specific legislative actions, such as the creation of statewide education standards, mandatory testing of all students in specific grade levels, and mandatory public reporting of test scores by designated categories (e.g. race and ethnicity, English language proficiency, special needs, poverty). Prior to NCLB, federal funds for education were made available to states, school districts, and educational programs on a competitive basis. Regulations affecting schools statewide were by law the purview of a state's legislature, not the federal government, as long as federal laws protecting the civil rights of specific groups were respected.

2. Ayn Rand (1905–1982) was a Russian-American novelist whose "objectivist" philosophy professed, among other things, a belief that the moral purpose of one's life is to pursue one's own happiness or self-interest. She felt the only political system that supported her views of radical individual rights was pure laissez faire capitalism. The Objectivist Foundation promotes her views and writings, encouraging their use in classrooms.

3. The IMF, like the World Trade Organization (WTO) and the World Economic Forum (WEF), discourages government spending for social concerns like education, and actively promotes regional free trade agreements such as NAFTA. "National education budgets in most countries are determined by the Ministry of Finance based on the proposed budget presented by the Ministry of Education. Even where millions more children are enrolling in school and there is a clear need for more teachers to be employed, the key parameters of the education budget are determined behind closed doors in discussions between the Ministry of Finance and the International Monetary Fund (IMF). The IMF gives loans to most poor countries and in exchange for these loans they impose certain conditions, particularly relating to 'macro-economics.' In its discussions with Ministries of Finance the IMF shows little or no interest in national development goals or poverty reduction. Their central concern is macro-economic stability and to achieve this they focus most of all on setting low inflation targets and low deficit targets. This means that countries have to hold down public spending. As education is one of the largest items on which governments spend money, any limits put on public spending are felt very directly by the Ministry of Education. This recipe is a standardized one and is rarely adapted to the national context, even for countries in exceptional circumstances." Downloaded on 10/4/09 at http://www.right-to-education.org/node/584.

4. http://www.democracynow.org/2007/9/26/bolivian_president_evo_morales_on_indigenous.

II.
COMMENTARIES ON CHOMSKY
FROM THE INDIGENOUS AMERICAS

1.

The Fourth Principle

By *Jaime Martínez Luna, Mexico*

Zapotec anthropologist, early theorist of Oaxacan *comunalidad*, community member of San Pablo Guelatao, Oaxaca, and veteran community activist whose work has focused on the defense of communal forests and other natural resources, and more recently on traditional and activist music and the development and promotion of community radio. Email: tioyim@yahoo.com.mx

LOIS MEYER'S INTERVIEWS WITH Noam Chomsky spark a host of ideas that I discuss below. Above all, it is refreshing to see the common intellectual ground that I share with this sage who has achieved worldwide respect.

The history of Oaxaca has been interwoven with principles and values that display its deeply rooted *comunalidad*. For the Oaxacan people across many centuries, this has meant integrating a process of cultural, economic, and political resistance of great importance. Since the Spanish conquest—individualist and mercantilist as it was—Oaxaca has responded with a form and reason for being communal that has permitted it to survive even in the face of an asphyxiating globalizing process.

This historic and latent resistance is the basis for the achievement today of having the concept of *comunalidad* written into the State Education Act of 1995, as the fourth guiding principle of education. For its transcendence, this principle requires that it be integrally implemented so that in future generations, it becomes the foundational knowledge and the basis for constructing all other knowledge. This will guarantee its security and immediate identity within the current intercultural education process.

We have not the slightest doubt that *comunalidad* is the epistemological notion that sustains an ancestral, yet still new and unique, civilizing process, one which holds back the decrepit individualization of knowledge, power, and culture.

Based in the above, many of us as professionals who serve the interests of the form of education that Oaxacan communities demand consider it appropriate to lay out the set of criteria that undergird an integrated treatment of the concept of *comunalidad*, seen as the central concept in Oaxacan life.

A BRIEF HISTORY

The existence of a polytheism which sacralizes the natural world, the absence of private property, an economy oriented toward immediate satisfaction, and a political system supported by knowledge and work, led the original peoples to create a cosmovision originating from the "us," from the self-determining and action-oriented collective, and, along with this, to construct a communalist attitude which has been continually consolidating itself despite cultural and economic pressures from outside.

Meanwhile, the colonizers, who were educated in autocratic regimens with a monotheistic and individualizing religion, a market-oriented economy, and a concentrated, privatizing concept of nature, have forced original peoples to develop strategies of resistance based in the collective, in shared labor, and in respect for their community elders or wise men (or *señores naturales*, "natural gentlemen," as they were called in colonial law).

With independence and the creation of the nation-state, the encounter of these two visions did not erase their differences. The heirs of the colonial system, *criollos*[1] and *mestizos*,[2] set themselves up as the central power of the nascent republic, undergirded by Western values, such as liberty, equality, and fraternity, that were constructed in the glow of the French Revolution. The Constitution of 1857 reflects European and North American influences; it supports private property and declares that ecclesiastical property, and perhaps communal property, as well, though this is unclear, are no longer held in perpetuity. Resistance to these actions varied across the Republic. States with lands of interest to the market felt the effects of these laws the most; not so much Oaxaca, where flat lands appropriate for mercantilist agriculture are scarce, and the greatest capitalist use of plains and plateaus included livestock in the areas where private property today is prevalent, such as the coastal region and Tuxtepec. The same occurred in the political sphere. The majority of Oaxacan communities and municipalities retained their self-determination, inherited from their *cacicazcos*, or prehispanic forms of governance. These managed to maintain their authority with the strategic support of both the colonizers and the independents.

With the Mexican Revolution, there was not much change. The contradictions played out with greater intensity in the indigenous regions. Oaxaca stands out in its resistance, thanks to its topography. At present, it is the state with the greatest communal land ownership, the greatest number of municipalities, the most peoples with distinct languages and cultures, but at the same time, the least important state in the nation, according to government statistics, despite its illustrious native sons Benito Juárez, Flores Magón,[3] and Porfirio Díaz, in order of importance.

Presently, thanks to the ways of thinking and being of its people, Oaxaca boasts the best preserved natural regions. It stands out in terms of energy potential, which has made it an expansive region coveted by private interests as lucrative terrain for development. Globalization and privatization find in Oaxaca unlimited potential for profit-making. It follows, then, that Oaxaca has also provided many opportunities for resistance and a depth of knowledge to more clearly define this process. This is demonstrated in the *comunalidad* which displays itself in every dimension of life.

COMUNALIDAD—AXIS OF OAXACAN THOUGHT

The world is awakening from the illusion of a universal culture shaped by one hegemonic form of reasoning. Today it confronts the reality of diversity, multiculturalism, and the recognition of a daily intercultural process strengthened by increasing migration across the planet. The individualism which was imposed on the colonies, today nation-states, is reaching its limits in regard to the development of equality and democracy, as it confronts the truly vibrant epistemological proposal of *comunalidad*.

Comunalidad does not originate from a discourse devised in a cubicle, a classroom, or a laboratory. It emerges as a tacit display of social movements, which in the 1980s achieved their goal of controlling their own development by conceptualizing their actions.

The organizing mechanisms that sustain *comunalidad* are not visible outside of the social process; it is in this same social process that they become visible. In other words, *comunalidad* carries on independently of whether we conceive of it as such, or not. The actions are a demonstration of principles and values emanating from a historical reality, one that transcends the centuries and is being consolidated in a concrete struggle for the liberation of peoples, as well as their cultural reaffirmation.

Comunalidad is confronted by the individualism imposed as part of the logic of colonialism, privatization, and mercantilism, which are developed according to a philosophy centered in the individual as the axis of the universe. Neither Marxism nor nineteenth-century liberalism strays from this base. *Comunalidad* integrates diversity and reproduces it within collaborative forms of work and joint construction. In other words, we could say that predatory and now globalized individualism is confronted by an ancient "communalism" (which in the opinion of Marx, was surpassed by later modes of production). But in reality, *comunalidad* is an historical experience and a vibrant, present day set of behaviors, which is constantly renovated in the face of the social and economic contradictions generated by capitalist individualism.

In Oaxaca, the vitality of *comunalidad* as it presents itself witnesses to the integration of four basic elements: territory, governance, labor, and enjoyment (fiesta). The principles and values that articulate these elements are respect and reciprocity. *Comunalidad* and individualism overlap in Oaxacan thought. We are the unique result of our own culture, but we are also colonized. Everyone displays knowledge according to the context surrounding them; hence, contradictions are a daily occurrence, not only of individuals, but also of communities. This is why, due to the social processes that Oaxaca experiences, the study and reproduction of *comunalidad* in all dimensions of life is vitally necessary if we wish to transcend our prevalent socioeconomic contradictions.

COMUNALIDAD IN EDUCATION

In the 1980s, thanks to indigenous, peasant, and social movements in general, *comunalidad* was proposed as the explanatory concept of the organizational modalities of Oaxacan society. The teachers' insurgence, as well as the commitments of various Oaxacan and Mexican intellectuals, found in this concept a logical articulation of their mobilizations and their teaching. The outcome was that Oaxacan teachers managed to insert the concept of *comunalidad* as the fourth guiding principle—together with democracy, nationalism and humanism—in the State Education Act of 1995. That law was, of course, also a response to fears generated in government officials by the Zapatista uprising of 1994.

The communal vision of life transcends the labyrinth that presently entraps indigenous education. Community-controlled education starkly marks the boundaries that separate school-based, cloistered education from that which the community in its entirety provides.

Understanding the presence of *comunalidad* in education means understanding very specifically how to plant the seed of a civilizing process, one that investigates and proposes a concrete pedagogy that guarantees not only that the concept (and now guiding principle) of Oaxacan education is understood, but also that continuous mobilizations are undertaken for the liberation of knowledge.

Now that *comunalidad* is established as a principle in the State Education Act, spaces and opportunities must be opened up which are dedicated to developing the necessary knowledge and designing needed tools to make it a reality. This means incorporating this knowledge and these tools into the centrally planned state education which contradicts our realities and serves as an obstacle to our being able to express our own experiences. By expressing our experiences, we will be able to reproduce the principles and values that support the reaffirmation of our cultural diversity.

This line of reasoning can and must result in the achievement of our expectations. This leads us to the following conclusions:

It is necessary to integrate specific, local, and regional content in the education that is imparted throughout the territory of Oaxaca.

It is important to strengthen our ancestral knowledge using pedagogical agencies and tools appropriate to the task, in order to resist the ruinous individualization of knowledge.

It is imperative that we ground an epistemology in the everyday labor of society in order to shape a new conception of the universe. Thinking must not be the preserve or property of the academy. It must be the practice of all the world's inhabitants.

A NEW PEDAGOGY

What needs to be taught is nothing more than sharing—the sharing of anger, enchantment, routine, misfortune, pain, tenderness, joy. For teachers, all of these words are a familiar lingo. Paulo Freire called this *the pedagogy of the oppressed*, Makarenko referred to *the identity of others*, Summerhill saw it as constant hilarity; thus, everyone sees what they want to see. Everyone depends on his or her concept, context and text. In this sense, one cannot speak of one pedagogy, but rather an intellectual diversity that captures the world, that is not time-bound, but if given space, that defines character and emotion.

All pedagogical technologies depend on interests of all kinds: social interests, because they respond to the stimuli of relationships; acquired, and in many cases, imposed values; political interests, because they respond to governments set up by those who want to manage the lives of the inhabitants; and economic interests, because they respond to needs inserted from the outside, not only to those that are internal.

All of which leads us to understand that no one can teach anyone else, or all of us must teach each other, and with that we reproduce intentions and resolve needs. This is what we learn from *comunalidad*.

Noam Chomsky affirms that our peoples face challenges, in most cases historical challenges. Neoliberalism is neither *liberal* nor *new*, but it is a concentration of enormous power, and it also is collapsing. Edgar Morin shares the same view, believing that the communal is a very significant proposal, but it must be understood, valued and supported. The Mexican philosopher Luis Villoro is very enamored of this perspective and agrees with the communitarian view, though he will not be separated from his republican passion. The European philosopher Panikkar also agrees with communitarianism; however, his Western orientation keeps him from developing more detailed responses to this matter. González Casanova continues to be obsessed with democracy, a topic in need of debate in light of current realities.[4]

In education, that which is communitarian is a paradigmatic vision. A fundamental principle is to liberate the exercise of knowledge. It must be acknowledged to be the result of everyone's labor: the so-called university-educated, bricklayers, teachers, peasants, in the end, all of us who inhabit the natural world. I am not bothered by the idea of knocking down schools and suppressing teachers because, essentially, we are all teachers. Teachers are not the ones, despite their intelligence, who should determine what we must know. They must understand that it is *each and every one of us* who has to open the door to knowledge. The collective task does not come from the outside; it has always been within us, and also the need. Nature has obligated us to work together, and not for the politicized notion of mass labor embodied in the Industrial Revolution, if that is what you want to call it, but rather for the need to survive.

AN EXAMPLE TO HELP CLARIFY

As an 8-year-old boy, my mother enrolled me in a boarding school founded due to the initiative of Lázaro Cárdenas.[5] The students came from many communities, basically indigenous, a concept imposed on us thanks to Manuel Gamio[6] and his collection of anthropologist and bureaucrat followers. The tale is long but its importance centers on the the educational organization of the experience.

There was an assembly made up of all the students. Through a committee the students organized homework and chores; even the meting out of justice was decided in this representative way. The teachers were simply consultants; the students determined what was to be done.

There were workshops for agriculture, textile and shoe production, bread and food production, carpentry, ceramics, and music. The educational process was not centered on the teaching staff but rather in liberation and work. This is a long story, but we can understand and summarize it in the following manner:

a. An education founded in work.
b. An education based not in organization from above, but in the participation of all.
c. An educational method founded in respect for everyone´s knowledge, and fundamentally, respect for that which is our own.

The Fourth Principle

CONCEPTUAL CONTEXT OF THE IDEA

In 1856, Karl Marx wrote in his "Outlines of the Critique of Political Economy" or "Grundisse," about the existence of communalism, basing himself on the experiences of the Aztecs, the Iroquois, and the Asians, both Hindu and Chinese. He discovered in these sources distinct values and modes of organization. Yet his reflections were in a certain respect pessimistic. He thought that these were cultures destined to disappear. For him, industrial development made the worker into the subject responsible for social and economic transformation. However, in his reflections he provides elements that are consistent with an understanding of the communal within the relationship of human beings with territory.

This is the first reflection that I want to share with you. Communal beings, as Benjamín Maldonado affirms, make sense of themselves in terms of their relationship with the land. An indigenous person understands himself in relationship with the land. I want to clarify that I am not referring to the Zapatista or Magonista maxim of "Land and Liberty," but rather to a relationship with the land that is not mercantile, a relationship of sharing and caring. That is, humans are linked to the land not only for organic sustenance, but also for spiritual and symbolic sustenance. In other words, the land does not belong to those who work it, in my way of reasoning; rather, those who care for it, share it, and when necessary work it belong to the land, and not the other way around.

Obviously in a world ruled by the logic of the market, it is easier to appropriate everything from nature for ourselves rather than to grasp an entirely reverse conception of ourselves. The need to survive causes us to view everything from a materialistic perspective; on this subject Marx made an abundance of reflections of great importance. But here is where the difference from indigenous thinking springs forth. *Comunalidad* is a way of understanding life as being permeated with spirituality, symbolism, and a greater integration with nature. It is one way of understanding that human beings are not the center, but simply a part of this great natural world. It is here that we can distinguish the enormous difference between Western and indigenous thought. Who is at the center—only one, or all? The individual, or everyone? The market makes everything into a product, a thing, and with that nature is also commodified.

My second reflection is on organization. Marx respects the community as the nucleus that integrates families, that which makes of territory a space for social relationships appropriate for the exercise of a necessary social organization. This necessary organization is obligatory, not only for peaceful coexistence, but also for the defense of territorial, spiritual, symbolic, artistic, and intellectual values. The community is like a virtual gigantic family. Its organization stems initially and always from respect. Everything is done together, a practice obviously reinforced by the policy of the Spanish colonizers of concentrating populations. Still, it is a natural reaction, naturally linked up with the use of a common language.

The creation and functioning of the communal assembly perhaps was not necessary before the arrival of the Spaniards, but for the sake of defense it had to be developed. Once the population was concentrated, religious societies to attend the saints (*cofradías*), and community organizations to plan fiestas (*mayordomías*) developed, which were cells of social organization that strengthened the ethics of the assembly. Out of this, the communally appointed leadership roles (*cargos*) originated. Someone had to represent the group, but all this implied the need for greater consolidation for decision-making. The Spanish governors designed the details of the colonial organizational structure, but in one way or another over time all the new colonial roles simply were absorbed into already-established traditional roles and responsibilities. Centuries had to pass before the colonial *cargos* that were used to control the native population were diluted and leveled enough so that the *macehuales* (community members, now *comuneros*) could ascend the social pyramid, and the community could become a space of truly horizontal participation.

Today, as before, one does not receive a community *cargo* by empty talk, but rather because of one's labor, attitude, and respect for the responsibilities entrusted. Everyone knows this, having learned it even before the age of eighteen, perhaps at ten or fourteen years of age, when assigned the first *cargo*, that of community policeman (*topilillo*). This gives the *cargo* a profound moral value that has nothing to do with categories such as economic value, efficiency, profitability, or punctuality, but rather with respect for the responsibilities involved. This has created a truly complicated political spectrum in Oaxaca. We have 570 municipalities and more than 10,000 communities. Eighty percent of these continue to govern themselves by communal assemblies. Their representatives are named in the assembly. For this reason, the widespread civic uprising that occurred in 2006 in Oaxaca must be analyzed under more meticulous parameters, a topic that will not be addressed here.

The third reflection refers to communal work. Weber, as well as Keynes and Marx, analyzed productivity in terms of the individual. They found in individual labor a process of value production that they explained according to their theoretical frameworks. However, communal labor is a different matter. To begin with, communal labor does not respond to the drive for personal satisfaction, that is to say, it does not obey the logic of individual survival, but rather that of satisfying common needs, such as preparing a plot of land, repairing or building a road, constructing a community service hall, hospital, school, etc. This labor is voluntary, which implies that individual wages are not received. In the urban world, everything is money-driven; you pay your taxes and away you go. Curiously, it is said of Oaxaca that it is the subsidized state par excellence, while what is not taken into account is the value of communal work, which if calculated, would surpass all the fiscal supports that we are aware of. The value of this work can also be translated to the context of political representation. Ask yourself how many political representatives in the city would contribute their time if they were not paid for it!

Fifty percent of the cost involved in constructing any community service is the cost of labor, apart from the purchase of necessary materials. This wealth of local participation goes unnoticed by the state and federal governments. We could say that Oaxaca lives by its own resources without outside support, and this provides a wide degree of self-determination. It is not a coincidence that 418 municipalities are politically self-governed. I am referring here to what is called *usos y costumbres*,[7] a concept that for me is pejorative, yet there is no other state in the Republic of Mexico that enjoys this self determination. If we add to this all the communal labor, then the situation becomes even clearer.

It is important to point out a few details. Oaxaca is the state with the greatest number of municipalities (almost a quarter of the country's total). Almost 70 percent of its territory is in the category of collective ownership, and there are seventeen indigenous languages with thirty-seven variants of these.[8] It is the state with the two most biologically diverse areas in all of Mexico: the Chimalapas and the Sierra Norte. And something almost imperceptible but which marks the nature of Oaxaca—it is the geographical convergence of the two mountain ranges of Mexico: the Sierra Madre Oriental and the Sierra Madre Occidental. This makes Oaxaca a wrinkled landscape, or, as Father Gay[9] used to say, like a crumpled sheet of paper. It does not have plains to guarantee an elevated level of productivity, which also explains its motley pattern of communal organization. It was easier to produce the dye-generating cochineal insect than corn, first, because of the geography, and also partly because of the ease with which all of the inhabitants could participate, both adults and children.

Another reflection concerns the fiesta. In a neoliberal context, it is the market that establishes the rules, and it demands greater production of merchandise. In the community there is production, but it is for the fiesta. All year long every nuclear community cultivates its products: corn, beans, squash, fruit, chickens, pigs, turkeys, even cattle. For what? For the fiesta. Any urban dweller would say, what fools! They could sell them instead. But that is not how it works. Here is the root of the difference. The community member (*comunero*, or *comunario* as a Bolivian friend says), does not work to sell, but for the joy derived. The little money that she or he manages to gather is used to buy some skirts, trousers, fireworks. Many interpret this as ignorance; I call it a connection to the land, or spirituality.

I would like to share some brief conclusions with you.

1. The year 1994—the year of the Zapatista uprising—awakened new dreams, but in reality what it achieved was to pull away the blanket under which we were hidden. Now here we are, reclaiming our *comunalidad*.
2. The "isms" are aberrations that convert themselves into authorities that impose themselves and are not naturally born. I fear "communalism" because it sounds doctrinaire. And I believe that is what we least want for our own free self-determination.
3. Marx included in his writings a fountain of knowledge by which to understand our social longevity, but this was covered up by his focus on industry and the protagonist role of the worker. And we all know how that turned out.
4. We must find in the experience of our peoples the lessons necessary to create new conceptual frameworks. And we must not be afraid to construct new epistemological notions that will lead us to transcend even ourselves.

Thank you, Maestro Chomsky, for bringing refreshing ideas to this world of incessant devastation and resurgence, which is Oaxaca.

NOTES

1. Persons born in Latin America of Spanish descent.

2. Persons of mixed European and Indian descent; "half-breeds."

3. Ricardo Flores Magón (1873-1922) was a Oaxacan anarchist who began a revolution against the Mexican state ander the banner of "Land and Liberty." Exiled to the United States in 1904, he organized three armed uprisings (1906, 1908, 1911). He was the only revolutionary who was inspired by indigenous peoples, believing that their historic experience of communal life would be the foundation for reconstructing Mexican society after the revolution's triuph.

4. Edgar Morin is a French essayist who has influenced education through his proposals of transdisciplinarity and complex thought. See *Los siete saberes necesarios para la educación del futuro,* available on internet at http://www.scribd.com/doc/20275503/Morin-Edgar-Los-siete-saberes-necesarios-para-la-educacion-del-futuro-2000. Luis Villoro is one of Mexico's major contemporary social philosophers with significant contributions in the areas of epistemology and ethical reflections on the relationship of the nation-state with indigenous peoples. See *Saber, creer, conocer* (México: Siglo XXI Eds., 2008) and *Estado plural, pluralidad de culturas* (México: Ed, Paidós, 2002). Raimón Panikkar is a Hindu-Catalan philosopher who reflects on the vast distance between Western and other cultures. See: *¿Es occidental el concepto de los derechos humanos?* (Mexico, *Diógenes* 120, Winter 1982) and *Religión, filosofía y cultura* (2000) on the Internet at: http://www.raimonpanikkar.com/articles/religion_filosofia_y_cultura.htm. Pablo Gonzalez Casanova is a Mexican sociologist, affiliated closely with Zapatismo, who in the 1970s proposed the idea of internal colonization to explain the relationship of the Mexican state with indigenous peoples. See *La democracia en México* (México: Ed. Era, Serie Popular, 1978); also "El colonialismo interno," (2006) on the internet at: http://bibliotecavirtual.clacso.org.ar/ar/libros/secret/gonzalez/colonia.pdf.

5. Lázaro Cárdenas, the Marxist-oriented president of Mexico from 1934-1940, promoted socialist education policies and layed the foundation for indigenous assimilation (*indigenismo*) as public policy.

6. Manuel Gamio is considered to be the father of Mexican anthropology. He carried out important interdisciplinary studies and was a functionary in postrevolutionary governments.

7. A term used to refer to the traditional form of governance through a communal assembly that selects its community leaders in the form of *cargos*.

8. The number of languages and their variants spoken in Oaxaca is disputed. It is commonly reported that there are between fourteen and seventeen languages with between thirty to fifty variants, though some say the number of variants may be as many as ninety. A language such as Zapotec may more accurately be considered a language family, for its variants, such as Zapotec of the Tehuantepec Isthmus and Zapotec of the Sierra, are as different one from another as Spanish and Italian and Portuguese.

9. Fray Antonio Gay was an early Oaxacan historian whose work has served as the foundation of Oaxacan history. In reality, he pirated information from other sources and made unsubstantiated claims, such as that the Chatino people descended from Vikings.

2.

Noam Chomsky and Indigenous Education in Oaxaca, Mexico

By *Fernando Soberanes Bojórquez, Mexico*

Mexican agricultural engineer, coordinator of alternative projects for the Coalition of Indigenous Teachers and Promoters of Oaxaca (CMPIO) and the school district known as Plan Piloto, and co-founder of the Pedagogical Movement of the CMPIO and the National Congress of Indigenous and Intercultural Education. Email: cmpioac@yahoo.com.mx

IN THIS ERA OF globalization, original peoples find themselves at a crossroads. On the one hand, they can fight to strengthen their autonomy, defending their natural resources, their culture, and all to which they have rights. On the other hand, they can resign themselves to die off little by little, overrun by international integration policies controlled by multinational corporations which convert many local governments into one more link in the globalization chain.

What has been, what now is, and what could be the role of education in each of these two scenarios?

In Lois Meyer's interviews with Noam Chomsky about *comunalidad* and education, there are several extremely interesting aspects which permit us to understand what it is that has been happening with the languages, cultures, and education of original peoples to bring about the present situation. Also addressed are the future of these cultural elements, the role the state has played, and the forms of resistance generated by indigenous peoples. We will take up only a few of these aspects, looking at the education offered to original peoples by the state in Oaxaca, Mexico, and the efforts made by some public school teachers and indigenous peoples to construct alternative educational proposals.

STATE POLICY AND THE TRANSNATIONALS

Chomsky says in one of the interviews:

> The imposition of a common language, a common culture, a common allegiance to a national entity, has been achieved through centuries of violence and destruction. And it is still continuing. . . . But the homogenizing conversion has been a process of careful control in all sorts of ways. Part of it has been the education system, which is intended to level people, to make them passive, disciplined, obedient.

Mexico has been no exception. Although since 1992 the Constitution has recognized Mexico to be a pluricultural country, that diversity is not taken into consideration in the national curriculum and teachers' guides, nor in textbooks, nor has it been implemented in the preparation of teachers—not even those in indigenous education—a system of education which itself contributes to the extinction of the languages and cultures of original peoples.

To the above must be added the racism and discrimination against original peoples in society and its institutions, the lack of supports available to the countryside and consequently the poor agricultural production, the introduction of transgenic corn that has contaminated and put an end to native varieties, the reforms to Article 27 of the Constitution which legalized the plunder of peasant land parcels and permitted new concentrations of land, and the North American Free Trade Agreement which has further impoverished rural populations, forcing them to migrate to the cities, the agricultural fields of the northwest of the country, and to the United States. In other words, every attempt has been made to deprive original peoples of their natural resources, their organization, their knowledge, and all their forms of subsistence in order to weaken their resistance and finally make them disappear.

If this objective is achieved, the transnationals will have a free hand in implementing and operating their plans, such as the wind power project in the Isthmus of Tehuantepec, the construction of large dams such as Paso de la Reina on the Oaxacan coast, and more than thirty mining projects which will poison lands and water tables, as in the case of the Cuzcatlán Mining Company in San José del Progreso, Ocotlán, where people have been beaten and jailed for resisting.

But the education system is completely alienated from all of these problems and processes that are vital to the subsistence of communities. On one side is the life of the people and on the other is the life of children and youth in the schools. The community may be rich in natural resources, but in school one does not learn to conserve or take advantage of them. The children may be bilingual or monolingual in any one of the sixteen original languages that exist in Oaxaca, but they are taught and evaluated in Spanish, sometimes via national standardized examinations such as the ENLACE test, without taking into account their abilities or their linguistic and cultural rights. Chomsky refers to this when he says that "[t]here is a big fight now to block bilingual education . . . , by trying to impose all kinds of standards, including educational standards."

The Alliance for Educational Quality (ACE) is the most recent example of an education policy in which the linguistic and cultural diversity of Mexico are not recognized. And it is not that the policy speaks against diversity; rather, once again, original peoples are simply and completely forgotten. They are mentioned nowhere in the policy, despite the fact that the National Institute for Indigenous Languages (INALI) recognizes the existence in Mexico of 68 language groups and 364 language variants, and the state offers to part of this population what it has come to call bilingual and intercultural education.

Ever since the passage of the North American Free Trade Agreement and the refusal by the government to provide effective supports to the countryside, many rural population centers have become ghost towns, leaving the schools without children. The problem is so serious that some indigenous organizations in the Mixtec region of Oaxaca have mobilized to demand that the government reduce the minimum number of students per teacher so that their schools do not disappear. This has principally occurred in schools that, until the past few years, had several teachers but now are one-room schools, or where the school was started with one solitary teacher.

The teaching profession in Mexico no longer aligns itself with the policies promoted by the state. Today is very different from the Cárdenas period[1] when petroleum was nationalized and agrarian reform expropriated massive land holdings and distributed land parcels. During that time, the teacher played an important role in promoting those policies. Many teachers were assassinated by the landowners for promoting these government reforms while at the same time supporting the people. Today it is the complete opposite: the teacher is repressed and even assassinated for opposing the anti-popular policies of the rulers. In Oaxaca from May 1, 1980, the day on which the Democratic Teachers' Movement began, until before the intense period of teacher-popular uprising from May through November 2006, more than a hundred teachers had already been assassinated. Among these are Cenobio Fito López Reyes (1987), of the National Syndicate of Education Workers (SNTE), for opposing the gangster group, Revolutionary Vanguard; Paulino Martínez Delia (1990), Mario Ramírez Salinas (1991), and Crisanto Gabino Antonio (1995), for supporting the struggles of their respective peoples: Triqui, Chatino and Zapotec.

Speaking about the current education policy in the United States, Chomsky comments that like "neoliberalism," "No Child Left Behind" is a misnomer. He says, "what it ought to be called is

Every Child Must Be Left Behind. No Child Left Behind is a system based on training children to join the Marine Corps." In Mexico, the same is occurring with the Alliance for Quality in Education (ACE), which should be called "Alliance Against Quality in Education and For Its Privatization." The ACE consists of training children to forget all of the knowledge, abilities, and values that have enabled their peoples to endure for so many centuries. Instead, they enroll in the poorly paid labor market or integrate directly into the ranks of the millions of unemployed. They are prepared neither to live in their communities and take rational advantage of their natural resources, nor for worthwhile employment outside of their communities.

Following this path, how far can original peoples advance while they receive an education that takes no account of their knowledge, language, and culture in general? Where they have no supports for their productive activities and are constantly threatened with expropriation of their lands and water for megaprojects, and with repression if they protest? Where they suffer bio-piracy and geo-piracy, and bombardment by the mass communications media? Yet there are multiple forms of resistance, and, as in other parts of the hemisphere, Oaxaca is participating tenaciously in a variety of them.

RESISTANCE AND EDUCATIONAL PROPOSALS FROM BELOW

For many years, we teachers of indigenous education have been instruments of education policies that have tended toward the disappearance of original peoples by enabling their incorporation, assimilation, or integration into the dominant mestizo culture. Sometimes this occurred without our realizing it and at other times with our full awareness, but never did we have a clear idea of what to do so that the school system, instead of contributing to our self-destruction as peoples, would serve to strengthen us. Nevertheless, despite not knowing exactly what to do, there are many teachers who try to work differently, supported by the new discourse about bilingual, intercultural education, the Political Constitution of the Mexican State, the General Education Act, the State Education Act, and in international laws and treaties signed by Mexico, among other supports.

The creation in 1980 of the Democratic Movement within Section 22, our Oaxaca state branch of the National Syndicate of Education Workers (SNTE), along with other factors, led several years later to a recognition of the need to critically review the kind of education we were imparting. A transformation was badly needed in order to take into account the conditions and needs of the children and youth we worked with, as well as their context, and the contemporary and future needs of their peoples. Later, this very movement became an obstacle, or at least it was indifferent in the face of education policies promoted by the state.

Today, after the 2006 movement, and faced with the threat that the Alliance for Quality in Education (ACE) represents for teachers and the people of Mexico, a segment of the democratic teachers and their union local leaders are deepening the awareness of the need, not only to reject the educational policies of the state, but to propose, together with indigenous peoples, the construction of alternative educational proposals.

We will present here some of the most recent experiences that address some issues raised by Noam Chomsky in the interviews. We will speak about what we know best, which is the activities of the Pedagogical Movement of the Coalition of Indigenous Teachers and Promoters of Oaxaca (CMPIO) and its school-based structure, Plan Piloto. We will consider especially those specific efforts, not found in all 400 CMPIO–Plan Piloto schools, aimed at strengthening the languages and cultures of the original peoples, who participate alongside the teachers in all of these efforts.

Here we will mention several projects:

1. The Pedagogical Movement: In 1995, the CMPIO began its internal Pedagogical Movement for the purpose of constructing educational proposals appropriate to the needs and reality of original peoples. The government uses the rhetoric of Bilingual Intercultural Education for the Indigenous Population, although intercultural education should be for the entire population, but this rhetoric has never been concretized in teaching practice. This is because there are no teaching curricula and programs to implement such an education, teacher-training programs have no relevance to students' needs, and teachers lack the books and other relevant didactic materials that are indispensable to providing bilingual intercultural education. To guide our Pedagogical Movement, little by little we have developed its orienting principles, methodology, strategies, professional development, and the organization to promote it.

2. In the preparation and training aspect, we began by developing cultural and educational projects, reviewing different learning theories, and studying children's education and development, with the support of Juan Luis Hidalgo Guzmán of the Casa de la Cultura del Maestro Mexicano, A.C. (Mexican Teachers Cultural Center). We also carried out workshops on cultural dialogue, with the support of José Rendón Monzón, as a way of systematizing and defending the cultures of original peoples.

3. Subsequently, with the support of Lois Meyer of the University of New Mexico, we began to hold workshops such as "Our Word in Our Languages" to incorporate more theoretical and practical elements into our work toward bilingual education. Teacher-made books have been created in indigenous languages, and we have analyzed the teaching practices of our most advanced bilingual education teachers. Shortly afterwards, we collaborated on the Tequio Pedagógico[2] project with the participation of teachers, the community, parents,

and authorities, with the goal that the teachers participating in this project would become researchers of their own teaching practice.

4. With Benjamín Maldonado Alvarado we have continued the work begun with anthropologist Juan José Rendón, deepening our study and reflection on *comunalidad* among original peoples.

5. In all of these activities, the teachers, children and youth, parents, communal authorities, and the total community, play a very important role.

6. Community-based alternative middle schools: The Community Middle Schools for Original Peoples are the result of an agreement between teachers and the Chinanteco people in the linguistic conference of that linguistic area which took place in Ojitlán, Tuxtepec, Oaxaca, in the year 2001.

   In 2004, after formulating and negotiating the project for three years, the first five middle schools (there are now seven) began to function, with a different organizational and curricular structure than other existing government middle schools. These schools work with learning projects designed by students, teachers, and parents. They do not teach mathematics, Spanish, natural sciences, etc. as separate academic subjects, but instead embed the content of these courses in the learning projects.

   Two very important features of this project are that it recognizes and respects that the peoples themselves produce, recreate, and transmit knowledge, and that the communities participate actively in teaching and evaluating the students.

7. Alternative teacher preparation: "Communal Bilingual and Intercultural Preparation for Teachers of Original Peoples" is the name of an alternative professional development course for new teachers that attempted to integrate many theoretical and practical aspects. It focused on *comunalidad* and its relevance to first- and second-language pedagogy and

instructional strategies, without overlooking the political/union training of new teachers.

This preparation program was organized by CMPIO–Plan Piloto and the National Congress of Indigenous and Intercultural Education (CNEII).[3] It lasted one year, from July 2007 to July 2008. In its planning and implementation, the course took into account the expertise of experienced CMPIO–Plan Piloto teachers, and also considered the impact left on us by the teachers' and civic movement of 2006 in Oaxaca, organized and directed by two assemblies: the State Assembly of the Democratic Movement of Educational Workers, and the Popular Assembly of the Peoples of Oaxaca (APPO).[4]

After the great teacher and civic mobilization of 2006 and its brutal repression by the state and federal governments, the need to diversify our forms of peaceful struggle and resistance became clearer. One form of struggle is the immediate response by means of strikes, marches, and rallies in order to present demands and denunciations. Another form is medium and long term, through pre-service and in-service professional development, organization, and the reconstruction of our identity and conscience. This is where education truly lies; here is where we can make quality alternative education, from the peoples and for the peoples, into a strategy of struggle. This is the conceptual framework out of which we conceived our alternative teacher preparation course.

Fifty-three new teachers participated in the course, one from the state of Yucatán, another from Baja California, and the other fifty-one from Oaxaca, several of whom are children of teachers. Many in-service teachers recognized for their teaching practice collaborated as presenters and facilitators, as well as retired CMPIO–Plan Piloto teachers with a long history of working in communities, and also professionals and researchers from other institutions and organizations who are committed to social and educational transformation.

Some of the participants in this course may become valuable, groundbreaking teachers, capable of making reality the discourse about bilingual and intercultural education, but beginning from the *comunalidad* of original peoples, if and when their training in this area has continuity.

8. Initial education: In 2008, our growing concern about the government's assimilationist approaches to working with babies and toddlers and their parents in indigenous communities moved CMPIO–Plan Piloto to begin a reassessment of our efforts in initial education (birth to 3-years-old), from the perspective of indigenous *comunalidad*. Official approaches to the education of these very young children, which international funding agencies frequently encourage and support, focus on "retraining" indigenous parents, especially mothers, to abandon communal childrearing priorities and practices in order to adopt practices promoted by Western theories of child development. Individualism and the acquisition of the Spanish language are unquestioned assumptions and priority outcomes of these assimilationist official programs.

Our initial education project is still in its early stages. CMPIO–Plan Piloto teachers of initial education have met in several sessions with researchers, physicians, and experienced early education practitioners, to discuss the situation in their communities in order to determine a course of action. We are committed to allowing ourselves to be guided in this effort by the wisdom of the communities themselves. To do so, we have begun to interview childcare givers, usually mothers and grandmothers but also fathers and grandfathers, in communities of various original peoples of Oaxaca, to learn from them their hopes, values, and practices in raising their children. The interviews are videotaped in order to document the extensive and detailed information gathered, which includes both cultural and linguistic expectations and developmental indicators that are important to these caregivers. The interviews are conducted in the language that is most comfortable for the caregivers, usually the local indigenous language, by CMPIO–Plan Piloto teachers with whom they are comfortable and who speak their language. Once these interviews are transcribed, they will guide our development of new proposals for initial education that respect and promote *comunalidad*.

9. Language Nests: As a result of a history of official policies that denigrate original peoples and repress their cultures, in many communities only those over fifty years old still speak the indigenous language, and those between thirty and fifty years old understand but do not speak it. Those younger than thirty neither speak nor understand the language; they understand and speak only Spanish, despite the existence of indigenous schools, which supposedly are bilingual. While the age ranges may vary by community, the loss of the indigenous language among younger generations is a widespread, established fact.

Today we are trying to revitalize these original languages with the strategy called the language nest. We took this model of linguistic and cultural revival from the experience of the Maoris, an original people of New Zealand, without attempting to import it mechanically to Mexico. We are working together with the communities themselves on this project, basing ourselves in the *comunalidad* of our original peoples.

Initiating the first language nests in Mexico was one of the agreements of the Second National Congress of Indigenous and Intercultural Education (CNEII), which took place in Oaxaca in October of 2007. Since some of the communities where CMPIO–Plan Piloto works had already been discussing this idea, only four months after the Congress one of the Mixtec-speaking communities, Guadalupe Llano de Avispa, Tilantongo, Nochixtlán, created the first language nest in Oaxaca and in Mexico, and as far as we know, in Latin America.

Since that date, ten language nests have been created in Oaxaca. For this to happen, we have engaged in a process of reflection with the communities about the loss of their language and culture. This process has culminated in agreements by the communal assemblies to recover their language and culture via *tequio* (voluntary, unpaid labor) by grandparents and other adults who retain the language. The majority of the children in these ten nests are preschoolers who already speak Spanish as their first language, so they are learning their heritage indigenous language as a second language. Once these agreements are made, the communal authorities designate a space—a house, not a schoolroom—where the little children, preferably before they begin to talk, gather with their "guides" to spend time and participate together in everyday activities of the community, hearing from the guides only the language to be revitalized, never Spanish. This is possible if and when there is an agreement among the people to do so.[5]

Thus revitalization is possible, as in the case of the indigenous language of the Wampanoag, which Chomsky describes as having disappeared 100 years ago but today has been reconstructed with the help of linguists. Jessie Little Doe, an indigenous Wampanoag, learned the language, and her little daughter learned it as her first language. It is not possible for this child to recover all of the culture of her ancestors, however.

In Oaxaca today, it is still possible to revitalize the languages and cultures, but a widespread social movement is needed. Linguistic and cultural revitalization efforts require not just agreements and the work of some teachers and original peoples. Supportive public policies are necessary, backed by society and the state, without institutionalizing the language nests or taking leadership away from the peoples themselves, since this would lead to their degradation and disappearance.

This is part of what is being done in Oaxaca, from below, to resist and to promote another type of globalization *from the people*. It is not much, but as Chomsky has said: "Things have to start with small germs, and then they can grow."

NOTES

1. The period from 1934–40 when President Lázaro Cárdenas implemented many progressive policies.
2. The project name builds on the Oaxacan indigenous concept of *tequio* (unpaid labor by the community on behalf of the community), applying this concept to the shared work of analyzing and adapting teaching practices to meet the hopes and needs identified by the communities themselves.
3. The CNEII has its origin in a joint initiative of teachers and social organizations. See the introduction by Meyer, footnote 9, on page 35.
4. For more information on the Oaxaca uprising of 2006 and the APPO, see introduction by Meyer.
5. A Language Nest orientation booklet for communities and language guides is available in Spanish online at http://www.cneii.org/index.php?option=com_conte nt&view=article&id=10:nueva-publicacion.

3.

Beyond Education

By Gustavo Esteva, Mexico

Social activist, public intellectual, independent writer, and collaborator with various organizations in Oaxaca and México, primarily with the Centro de Encuentros y Diálogos Interculturales (Center of Intercultural Encounters and Dialogues) and the Universidad de la Tierra (University of the Land) in Oaxaca. Email: gustavoesteva@gmail.com

I HAVE THE IMPRESSION that the admirable Dr. Chomsky held back when he sketched out the historical relationship between education, on the one hand, and colonization and domination, on the other.

"In every step we have taken," our founding fathers said when presenting newly proclaimed Mexican citizens with their brand new constitution in 1824, "we have proposed as our model the happy republic of the United States to the North. . . in order to finally arrive at the temple of happiness, of glory, and of rest."[1] A little while later in Congress, a group of delegates proposed that Mexico also imitate the neighbors to the north in their solution to the "Indian problem." These delegates thought that Mexico could be as great as France or the United States if it weren't for the heavy burden of the Indians, which dragged them down like a dead weight. They had to be exterminated, just as the United States was successfully doing. Other delegates displayed reservations about the viability of this measure, because here there were too many Indians. Finally, the view of those who maintained that Indians should be educated won the debate. Instead of genocide, there would be "culturecide." It would be education for extinction:

they would cease being Indians in the process of conversion into "regular Mexicans."

This reality persists today. When President Salinas was asked if the intention of his project was to incorporate Mexico into North America, he responded immediately: "Exactly." There is no doubt about the obsessions of Zedillo, Fox, or Calderon. Far from being the path to "happiness, glory and rest," this maniacal commitment to destroy the cultural and historical foundations of the nation has been the road to catastrophes, plunderings, and humiliations.

When it was pointed out at the Indigenous State Forum of Oaxaca in 1997 that the school had been the principle instrument of the state for exterminating Indian peoples, and that the revolutionary union of teachers had been an accomplice of the state in this task, a historical truth was being publicly recognized. From the very beginning, ever since those decisions of the fledgling Congress in the first years of Mexico's independence and up to today, the educational system has had as one of its central purposes to dispossess Indian peoples of their own culture, of their way of seeing and experiencing the world, of their cosmovision, in order to "Westernize" them, which in Mexico generally means taking on the U.S. version of that project. And the educational system, which continues to fail in its explicit purpose of preparing people for life and for work, in good measure has accomplished that Westernizing intention more or less covertly. For this reason, for this kind of pyrrhic success, the country has managed to have presidents like Salinas, Zedillo, Fox, and Calderon.

It is almost impossible for a person to maintain their indigenousness, their own culture, upon finishing their university studies: every one of the pillars that sustain their culture will have been demolished along the way. It is inevitable to think that that which is Indian persists in Mexico only to the degree that the educational system has been incapable of including the majority of the population and because only one in a thousand indigenous youth is able to obtain a university degree. Because of these factors and the notable resistance of these peoples, indigenousness persists—not only among officially recognized indigenous peoples, but also in the majority who, according to Guillermo Bonfil, make up "Deep Mexico," the Mexico of those who do not share in, or they share in some other way, the "norms, aspirations, and purposes of Western civilization," blindly adopted by the imaginary Mexico, the Mexico of those who "embody and promote the dominant project in our country."[2]

The homogenization that all educational systems of the world seek, constructed as they are for purposes of domination by those who lead the nation-states, in Mexico has a very precise meaning: to dissolve the Indian way of being and thinking, in order to install in its place another civilization that is considered superior.

INSTITUTIONAL OR CULTURAL HOMOGENEITY?

Dr. Chomsky distinguishes between institutional homogeneity—a code of laws, a national language, etc.—and cultural homogeneity. The United States, he says "is institutionally homogeneous now because of conquest and extermination." It seems to him that that contrasts with Europe and the majority of Latin America because "the English colonists largely wiped out the indigenous populations, unlike most of Europe where nation-states were imposed on existing societies that were not simply exterminated. He thinks that his country is heterogeneous in other ways: "It's a nation of immigrants from all over, some of whom kept their own cultures and practices, sometimes even languages, for a long time."

It is not clear what he is referring to in that vague and imprecise distinction, and, much less, what the nature is of the contrast he is establishing.

It is difficult to conceive of a greater scale of extermination than that which occurred in the first century of the colony, when nine of every ten inhabitants of New Spain died. The survivors had to suffer under a double stigma: that of not being accepted for what they were, and that of not having had the dignity to die when their gods died. And in every case, the institutional homogenization that Dr. Chomsky mentions was established quickly and remains to this day: a code of laws, a national language, etc. Where is the difference?

It is true that nation-states were imposed in Europe "over existing societies that had not been exterminated," but always with the same sign of cultural dissolution, by means of education and the police—the two principle instruments for constructing nation-states. When Dr. Chomsky refers, rightly, to the present resurgence of the Europe of the regions in response to the creation of supranational entities, he recognizes the vitality of the regional cultures that each of the European states tried to dissolve.

This is the same phenomenon that was observed after the collapse of the Soviet Union, which supposedly had resolved the problem of the "small nationalities." The same thing will be observed in the United States when the brutal pressure of the "melting pot" is reduced, that kettle in which it has attempted to fuse, to dissolve, each one of the multiple immigrant cultures. In U.S. society one can already hear the clamor to adopt, as a unifying principle, the idea of the "salad bowl," referring to a form of society that recognizes and celebrates difference. This is the ideal suggested by the Zapatistas, that instead of the Western project of constructing one world, unified under the domination of the West, we would be able to construct *one world in which many worlds fit*,[3] a world in which difference is not only recognized but also celebrated. Tolerance is not enough. To tolerate is to insult, Goethe said. To tolerate is to say: "You are not as you should be: you do not have the appropriate skin color or god; but I am so generous that I am going to allow your presence. I tolerate you." Instead of tolerance, we need hospitality. We need to open our heads, hearts and arms to the radical otherness of the other, celebrating it with hospitality.

Culture, says Raimón Panikkar, is "the encompassing myth

of a society in a given time and space." And also myth, in this context, is "the horizon of intelligibility within which all of our perceptions of reality make sense." The myth offers the frame within which the cosmovision is inscribed; it is that which permits and conditions any interpretation of reality. It is not seeing something or believing something, but believing that one sees. It is that which gives meaning to meaning, without being contained within it. Like light, it permits us to see but we cannot see it. [4]

It is necessary to distinguish among the distinct planes of culture:

The morphological plane: entirely visible, like the folliage of a tree, made up of the traits that constitute the external manifestations of cultures: language, dress, food, etc.

The structural plane, partly visible and partly invisible, like the trunk of a tree, composed of the forms for organizing behaviors according to shared norms: medical or religious practices, governmental requirements, legal and social norms, etc.

The mythic plane, entirely invisible, like the roots of a tree, whose substance is the cosmovision, the notion of being, the perception of time, etc.

Our cultures are clearly affected in the morphological and structural planes. The Spanish language, cola drinks, and blue jeans dominate, as well as electoral practices and the school, even in the most isolated communities. But an exercise of prodigious resistance has permitted the survival, with surprising vitality, of the mythic plane of the negated civilizations, the very substance of Deep Mexico. With reason indigenous peoples say: "They wrenched off our fruits, they ripped off our branches, they burned our trunk, but they could not kill our roots." Those roots are now making possible an exercise in cultural regeneration that openly resists the processes of homogenization by trying to reorganize society from below.

All nation-states practice a continual effort to homogenize, using for this purpose the institutions and particularly education. In general, institutional homogenization in the way that Dr. Chomsky describes it prevails in all of them. But perhaps no institution has completely crystallized cultural homogenization. Everywhere so-called "subaltern cultures" are appearing.

IS LOCAL CONTROL ENOUGH?

With wisdom and good judgment, Dr. Chomsky resists offering general formulas. He recognizes that each situation is different. However, he has the clear impression that local control of the educational system, when culturally determined, will make it possible to avoid the destructive effects of the education that is imposed by national systems. For the same reason, he advocates for bilingual education. At the same time, however, in clear contradiction to this proposal, he opposes all forms of coercion. Coercive norms seem negative to him, "whether they come from the state or from the community." As he thinks that "to some degree norms are always coercive," he suggests that norms should be "as minimally coercive as possible to provide for optimal free choice," so that "free choice . . . will lead to participation in and enrichment of comunity life."

All schools, whether controlled nationally, locally, or by families, are coercive systems. Because of this, as Dr. Chomsky recognizes, they always generate resistance—not because people do not want to learn to read or count, but because of the form in which this learning and others are organized in school. In order to avoid coercion, the first thing you would need to abandon is the school itself, that is, education.

On the other hand, Dr. Chomsky's hierarchy of values merits serious reflection, in that he attributes priority to individual freedom of choice.

In indigenous communities, a normative system prevails still today that has a triple origin:

• Ontonomy—regulation from within one's own culture, from

tradition. Even the youngest children in every community know what the dominant norms are within that community.

- Autonomy—regulation provided by the current generation of community members, frequently modifying traditional norms. One of the best traditions of indigenous communities is that of changing tradition in a traditional manner. This provides historical continuity—communities continue being the same—but at the same time, they remain highly dynamic, which has ensured their survival and allows them to continuously update their norms. Autonomous regulation becomes ontonomy for the following generation.

- Heteronomy—regulation imposed by others, from outside the community. In contemporary societies, the market and the state, that is to say, capital and its administrators, establish norms that are coercively imposed on all citizens. To resist them, as is continually done in the communities, always has a high social, economic, and political price.

The individual condition is not something given, a feature of "human nature." It is a specific way of constituting and programming people. The social construction of the individual in the form of *homo economicus*—the possessive and needy individual who was born within a capitalist system and who constitutes a fundamental condition of its existence — is an entirely Western enterprise.

In indigenous tradition, people are knots in nets of real relationships, they are not individuals. There are indigenous languages that have no words for "I/me" and "you" referring to single individuals. Among all indigenous peoples, the condition of the strong "we" is expressed existentially and in the language itself, for this is the subject of *comunalidad*, the first layer of existence, formed by the interlocking of the networks of real relationships that make up each person. Contrary to external prejudice, in indigenous communities there are surprising margins of freedom and personal initiative, unknown or seriously limited in contemporary societies. But we are not talking about the individual freedom of choice to which Dr. Chomsky refers, which often appears in the very heart of the communities, arriving from the outside and installing itself in the school. Generally, it constitutes a factor in the dissolution of the community and the culture.

INDIGENOUS AND INTERCULTURAL EDUCATION?

These currently fashionable expressions were amply supported by Dr. Chomsky. He believes that the struggle for indigenous and intercultural education is part of the defense and protection of indigenous rights and of the struggle for justice and freedom.

In this way, Dr. Chomsky appears to share the general prejudice that education is a universal good and that it ought to be everyone's right. In reality, buying this merchandise could achieve the function of the Trojan Horse and be the instrument of recolonization. In truth, it reflects a pernicious form of colonialism, in which intimate enemies colonize us from the inside.

The expression "indigenous education" can be seen as an oxymoron, a contradiction in terms. Education is a strictly Western enterprise and it cannot be separated from the capitalist project. It is not an indigenous initiative. To place the adjective "indigenous" in the expression means, in the end, subordinating indigenousness to the educational plan and converting it into a marginal or secondary aspect. This is like saying: we are going to convert you into a good Mexican, fully Westernized, but we will permit you to wear your *huipil*[5] when you want to or include in your vocabulary some Zapotec words.

Dr. Chomsky says that "state formation, by force mostly, has tried to impose national education standards in order to turn people into similar individuals." This is true. As Tolstoy said, education is the conscious intention to transform someone into something. And that something, as Dr. Chomsky clearly says, is the construction of "passive, disciplined, and obedient individuals," who serve capitalist ends.

Educators have schooled us in the idea that education is as old as the hills and was born alongside man. But the thing we call education arose with capitalist society and from the beginning served as one of its main pillars. As Illich[6] has pointed out, the education of children is mentioned for the first time in France in a document from 1498, and the word "education" appeared for the first time in English in 1530. Even in 1632, that is, well into the seventeenth century, Lope de Vega referred to education as a novelty that had just appeared in Spain. In that year, the University of Lima celebrated its sixtieth anniversary. "Centers of learning existed before the term 'education' became part of everyday language. One 'reads' the classics or law, but one is not educated for life."[7]

Illich explains that in the seventeenth century the conviction became widespread that people lacked the competence to live in society unless they were educated. Education meant the opposite of vital competence. And that inherent incompetence, that new original sin, was the incompetence to live under the new forms imposed by capital: it was necessary to mold people in the way prescribed by capital, something that had not occurred naturally or spontaneously in pre-capitalist society. Before capitalism, one learned in order to live freely and to practice autonomous subsistence, not to submit oneself to the regimen of work and life imposed by capital.[8] In the material process of capitalist production, Marx warned, the worker is confronted constantly with the intellectual powers of the system of exploitation, which were unknown to him previously. Workers will not be able to adapt themselves to these mental powers unless they are taught to do so, that is, they must be educated to incorporate themselves into the work market, under conditions imposed by capital.

Neither local nor indigenous control of education has succeeded in re-forming these capitalist purposes. Why at this point in time should indigenous peoples adopt a tool that only serves the purposes of domination and control and which has failed everywhere in the world to achieve its explicit purposes of educating for life and work and providing equal opportunities for all?

A commitment to indigenous liberation, coming from indigenous peoples and their ways of seeing and experiencing the world, should not be negated by adopting—in education—a regimen that undermines and dissolves one's culture from the inside. One can turn again to one's own traditions and capacities to validate other ways of learning. As Dr. Chomsky says, what is important is "having the capacity to think, to create, to explore, and to be imaginative." Why call that education? As he himself explains, education which is associated more and more with test-taking skills is the opposite of all those conditions.

THE FREEDOM TO LEARN

Everywhere in the world, day by day, as part of an increasingly anti-capitalist liberatory commitment which is also stimulated by the present crisis, an effort is growing that goes far beyond schools and education, in fact leaving them behind. Many people continue to be entrapped in educational deceit and are willing to do anything so that their children have an "education." They demand better quality schools and make any kind of sacrifice so that their children can advance their studies. At the same time, a growing number of people and communities engage in initiatives that go beyond education.

Very important changes have occurred in the last half-century.

- For many years, everywhere there was intense opposition to school. Still in 1909, in Massachusetts, where Dr. Chomsky has spent the majority of his life, the government called in the National Guard to impose school on the people. In Mexico, during the 1930s, the army or the police surrounded rural and indigenous schools in order to prevent children, with the support of their parents, from escaping. In 1953, when the Alliance for Progress tried to promote development in Latin America and included education as one of its principle components, a group of UNESCO experts diagnosed that the major educational problem in the region was the indifference or open opposition of parents.

• Eleven years later, the same experts reached the conclusion that the problem had changed: not one state in Latin America could satisfy the demand for education that had been generated. The campaign that was initiated after the 1953 diagnosis had been successful: parents were appropriately educated in the idea that they should send their children to school, and they started to demand it. In this way, a demand for education was created at all levels that no Latin American government will be able to satisfy. This is an inability shared by all countries of the world. Not even the richest nations can satisfy the artificial demand for education that has been created. The present economic crisis will further increase this gap.

• During the last two decades, a new movement began. People started to free themselves from this educational obsession. They discovered what school really meant, and they began to look for alternatives for learning. Millions of people throughout the world have stopped sending their children to school, and alternative methods and spaces are multiplying, whose primary emphasis is the freedom to learn.

The present effort is not concerned with deschooling society, but rather with bypassing the educational system. The *need* for education was artificially created through force and propaganda. That "necessity" later became a *right*, and it has now become a kind of *social addiction*, reinforced by *bureaucratic imposition*. Bypassing the school means treating it the same way that many people treat bureaucratic requirements: when it is impossible to avoid them, comply without granting them the least intrinsic value. Parents recognize that diplomas have become a kind of passport to get around in modern society. Many don't want to run the risk of depriving their children of a credential, but recognizing that their children are not learning in school what they need for life, they try to find circumstances where this deficiency can be compensated for through autonomous learning opportunities.

Increasingly, people are saying, "No, thank you!" to various educational offerings, and instead taking actions to regenerate the art of free and autonomous learning. They are saying, "Enough!" to that specific form of oppression.

When the free act of learning is confined inside the walls of the school or its equivalents, this immediately produces scarcity: there aren't enough schools, teachers, or packets of knowledge for everyone. Learning has been economized. To remedy that situation, we need to break away from educational dependency—a noun—and regain our autonomous capacity to learn—a verb. In this way we can rediscover, as many people are beginning to do, a new kind of sufficiency, beyond economic scarcity. With our initiative, freely, with the resources we now have, all of us can have ample opportunities to learn what we really need and want to learn.

John Holt once pointed out: "Birds fly, fish swim, people learn. . . Learning is the experience of being alive, it is an expression of vitality. We only stop learning when we die."

Holt wrote a book called *Instead of Education* (New York: Dutton, 1976). When he was asked what word he used in place of education, he said there wasn't one. Forced by the interviewer, he said, "I would use the word 'living.'" To be alive—to live—means, precisely, to be learning. And to do it in this way, without dependence on education, we can live constructing a society that eradicates privilege and discrimination.

During the last decade, people started closing schools in some communities in various states. The experts soon took notice and, after some time, discovered, much to their surprise, that there was nothing better for the children. It was shown, for example, what UNESCO had long known: anybody can learn to read in a few weeks if he or she acquires that ability with another person, not in a group. In school, six years are sometimes insufficient for a child to learn to read well. And many who learn in school, leave hating to read.

In many places, in cities as well as in rural areas, many learning modes and spaces are being recreated from within groups, in the community. A practical problem is that many groups or communities have no one with the skills or knowledge to teach whatever it is that someone wants to learn. Perhaps for the first ten years of life this is not a problem: everything that a child needs and wants to learn can be learned alongside someone in his/her family or community. But, what happens later? What happens when someone is interested in topics or skills that can't be learned from anyone in the local community? The spaces and conditions multiply in which interested young people can become apprentices to those who practice what they want to learn, outside of their community. They work and even live with a carpenter, a geographer, an agrarian lawyer, or a specialist in free software, ultrasound, or community radio production. They learn by doing: philosophizing, making maps or chairs, resolving land disputes or speaking into a microphone. This way, among other things, one of the classic problems of the school is resolved: habitually, teachers are ones who don't practice what they teach. The teacher is not a mathematician, geographer, historian, or person of lettres. The teacher is a teacher. S/he teaches what s/he does not do. Now the thing is to learn with those who are doing things, so that the learner not only acquires specific skills and capacities, but also the ways these are applied in the real world. In this way, young people learn to do something useful for their communities or groups and, through this, they gain dignity, esteem, and income.

At the end of his book, Holt also recounts that he started to play the cello at the age of forty. He says that he was told that there would be a time when he would be learning to play the cello, and that after that preparation, he would be able to play the cello. He thought this was silly. He started to play from day one. By doing so with dedication and discipline, he came to play well. He tells us that a friend of his is the first-chair flutist in a symphonic orchestra. According to his friend, if he learns nothing one day, he realizes it; if he learns nothing for two days, the orchestra director realizes it; if he learns nothing for three days, the public realizes it. Great philosophers, athletes, and musicians continually learn, every day. If they stop learning, they stop being who they are. And learning means being what you learn.

This new attitude involves, above all, recognizing anew what it means to know: it is a relationship with others and with the world, not the consumption of a commodity, of packets of knowledge or information, or the ability to pass tests, as Dr. Chomsky says. To consume "knowledge" is, in the best of all cases, to obtain information *about* the world. And to know supposes learning *from* the world, by relating ourselves with it, with others or with nature, through experience.

It also involves recognizing that a good part of what is offered now as knowledge and information, inside and outside of school, is garbage. Just as we ought to know that certain products are junk food, that they are not nourishing, and that we ought to avoid being part of a wasteful civilization that is inundating us with garbage, it is important to recognize that a good part of what is handed out in school or on the Internet is nothing but garbage: it makes no sense to acquire it, much less to remember it.

The new attitude involves combating the premise of scarcity as a principle of social organization, which is a continuous source of inequality, oppression, and discrimination. It doesn't matter that the resources are allocated by the market or the state. They will never be enough to accomplish unlimited ends. If we recognize that ends are only the other side of means, they can't be unlimited. They always are the size of our means. If we increase our means, the ends will increase. If we enrich our means,

Beyond Education

capacities, and opportunities to learn, our learning purposes can be enriched. *The aim is to increase our capacity to learn* and to do, more than the capacity to buy or consume packets of knowledge, or anything else. Without doubt, this implies redefining personal responsibility in terms of what we need to do, and also recreating our being, as real persons, not as individuals, and in this way, also recreating our community spaces. We must go beyond education, the most modern form of enslaving and discriminating against the majority.

Resisting school and abandoning education as defined and imposed by the state implies substantially increasing the dignity of ordinary men and women and defying all existing political and economic systems. This is not an easy task. It imposes fundamental changes in the everyday lives of those who attempt it; furthermore, they will confront all manner of practical and institutional obstacles. Soon they realize that pursuing this effort involves beginning to seriously reorganize society from its base, beyond capitalism and representative democracy.

However, the main obstacle is not the practical difficulties of taking children out of school or starting to walk in a path of learning that one has set out for oneself. The most important challenge lies in the intimate enemy, in the way in which we have been colonized from within. Hundreds of millons of people, perhaps thousands of millions, remain convinced of the need for education and they will do anything to secure it for their children, confident that in this way they will improve their condition.

Political leaders and the media continually reinforce that manner of thinking. In his February 24, 2009, State of the Union message, President Obama used everyday examples to underscore the reality and pervasiveness of the economic recession, such as "the college acceptance letter your child had to put back in the envelope." He pointed out later, "And dropping out of high school is no longer an option. It's not just quitting on yourself; it's quitting on your country." For these reasons, he promised an

129

expansion of the educational system "to ensure that every child has access to a complete and competitive education, from the day they are born to the day they begin a career." Although it is mistakenly said that the United States is the most educated society on the planet and that this is the reason for its economic hegemony,[9] President Obama will not be able to carry out that promise. As of November 2008, only one-third of the American workforce had university diplomas. The majority will continue to be unable to climb to the last rung of the costly educational ladder. "Education for all," the main program of the World Bank for many years, continues to be the refrain of demogogues, in rich countries as well as poor ones.

The time has come for radical decolonization, the end of an era, because a type of society and civilization based on subjugation and exploitation of the majorities, through various means including education, has plunged into crisis.

We should all listen, with seriousness and rigor, to the words that Michel Foucault spoke to Dr. Chomsky at the end of their conversation about human nature. Foucault argued, refuting all universalist thought, that new concepts are needed in order to understand the new society that is in the process of construction. Using today's concepts makes little sense because:

> they are all ideas and concepts that have originated within our civilization, within our type of knowledge and within our type of philosophy. As a consequence, they form part of our classification system. And however unfortunate this may seem, we cannot use these same concepts to conceive and justify a struggle that should—and will, ultimately—overthrow the very bases of our society. I do not find an historic justification for this extrapolation.[10]

Beyond Education

NOTES

1. *Acta Constitutiva de la Federación*, 1824. Published by the Comisión Nacional para la Conmemoración del Sesquicentenario de la República Federal and by the Centenario de la Restauración del Senado, 1974, 63–64.

2. Bonfil, G. *México Profundo: Reclaiming A Civilization* (Austin: University of Texas Press, 1996), p.xvi

3. The translation of this slogan is difficult. It is often translated (also by other commentators in this volume) as "a world in which many worlds fit," which I do not like, as the force of the Spanish *"quepan"* is lost. I have often used my translation: "A world in which many worlds can be embraced," which reflects the sense of the Zapatista proposition. "A world with many worlds inside" is problematic because it still alludes to ONE world, an idea the phrase intends to eliminate. Editor's note: In other English publications, Zapatista leaders themselves have used the translation we use here.

4. http://www.barcelona2004.or/dialegs/dialeg4/s/panikkar/html.

5. Traditional top or blouse worn by indigenous women.

6. Ivan Illich (1926-2002) was an Austrian philosopher and Roman Catholic priest who used his prolific writings to critique the institutionalization of knowledge in contemporary Western culture. In *Deschooling Society* (1971) he argued that institutionalized education serves the capitalist system and destroys possibilities for true learning for life. Medicine, work, energy use, economic development, and Catholic theology became the focus of other of his scathing critiques. See also *Tools for Conviviality* (1973) and *Toward a History of Needs* (1978).

7. Illich, I. "In Lieu of Education," *Toward a History of Needs* (New York: Pantheon, 1978), 75.

8. This does not imply, by any means, an idealization of the societies that existed prior to capitalism, which sustained the most diverse forms of exploitation. I simply intend to show the difference in the content and applications of learning. Typically in a feudal society, for example, peasant communities were obligated to pay tribute and they endured all manner of extortions, but they subsisted by means of their own capacities and they learned in order to reproduce the forms of autonomous subsistence. That learning, combined with others, finally permitted the dismantling of the feudal system. The formal and very real subsumption of labor under capital creates conditions of subordination without historic precedent and constrains the activities engaged in by labor to forms that require specific training: education.

9. See, for example, C. Goldin and L. F. Katz, *The Race Between Education and Technology* (Cambridge, MA: Belknap Press/Harvard University Press, 2009).

10. Available at http://www.youtube.com/watch?v=hbUYsQR3Mes&feature=related.

131

4

Chomsky as Hope

By *Fausto Sandoval Cruz, Mexico*

Nánj Nï'ïn (Triqui) bilingual teacher since 1977, presently at the Emiliano Zapata Indigenous Bilingual Elementary School in Miguel Hidalgo Chicahuaxtla, Oaxaca, and author of the official government textbooks in the Nánj Nï'ïn language for grades 1 through 4 of Mexican indigenous elementary education; also school principal, supervisor, regional union representative, and participant in various events concerning indigenous education, both nationally and internationally. Email: faustoj_o@yahoo.com.mx

I HAD THE OPPORTUNITY to meet Noam Chomsky in October 2006, when I participated in the First International Congress of Indo-American Languages and Literatures and the XII Days of Mapuche Language and Literature, which were held in Temuco, Chile. At the inauguration of the Congress, Chomsky gave the plenary address, titled "Year 1514: Globalization for Whom?" At the end of the activities of the first day, there were wine and cheese for those who had arrived, and in addition to good Chilean wine and delicious hors d'oeuvres, we had the opportunity to at least see Dr. Chomsky close-up and shake his hand. I did this, of course, and cherish from this event a photograph in which I appear next to him, though I could barely greet him since I do not speak English and Chomsky does not speak Spanish.

As I observed this man of extraordinary simplicity and humble aspect, I remembered his public declarations about the attacks on his country in September 2001:

> It was an atrocious response to the atrocities of the United States. The horrendous attack of last Tuesday marks the

initiation of a new type of war that will benefit the "strong-men" of the United States and their terrorist counterparts abroad, while poor nations, in particular the Palestinians, will pay the price.[1]

I thought, "How can someone have such courage and dare to make a criticism like that in that place and at that moment?" "What consequences did he have to face for having said what he said? Or, is his moral stature such that he can express himself so freely?" I could feel only admiration and great respect for him. A year later, this time in Oaxaca, I once again encountered his words:

I would like at least to say a few words to express my admiration for what you all are doing in your professional work in indigenous education and also for your support for the teachers, the courageous teachers in Oaxaca, who are fighting a struggle of enormous significance . . . (Chomsky 2007, page 63 of this volume).

With these words Chomsky greeted the Second National Congress of Indigenous and Intercultural Education that took place in Oaxaca in October 2007. When I heard this message, a list of questions passed through my mind, questions that I would have liked to have asked him. For example, did he know of the atrocities committed by teachers of Section 22 of the National Union of Educational Workers (SNTE) against teachers who do not share their dominant positions regarding the union struggle? Did he know that many of the women teachers who were abused at the hands of the police during the armed attack on June 14, 2006, were in the strike encampment that morning with their children because they were required to be there by their union colleagues? Did he know that, though indigenous education in Oaxaca has been under the control of the teachers' movement for more than a decade, in the vast majority of schools the indigenous language and culture are still nowhere to be found? Did he know that many teachers of Section 22 and the Popular Assembly of the Peoples of Oaxaca (APPO)[2] are fanatical supporters of state education, the system which "by force mostly, has tried to impose national education standards in order to turn people into similar individuals"? Did he know that the teachers' movement is opposed to any form of social and community control of education? That in many communities the teachers have formed themselves into groups of strong-armed bullies that go so far as to wield strategies used inside the teachers' movement to force into office certain municipal authorities, in the process displacing the processes communities have developed for electing their own authorities? That the groups that control Section 22 aren't ashamed to commit electoral fraud against their own colleagues in order to stay in power? That they have systematically rejected direct democracy in the form of free, universal, and secret ballots for the election of union leaders, which means that in twenty-eight years of the movement for democracy, no union leadership committee really has been elected by the union rank and file, but instead by delegates who have done so in their name?

"[Resistance] often takes ugly forms, it is not necessarily beautiful," Chomsky comments in the first interview with Lois Meyer. Perhaps he would have responded in the same way to my questions. Still, should those ugly forms be criticized and denounced, or covered up because they are committed by social activists? Who really cares about them? Those who suffer the injustices, Chomsky would say. When the government commits an atrocity, I ask myself, why is there always a chorus of voices ready to complain and denounce, but when the atrocity is committed by social movements, communities, unions, or social organizations, that is, by the "good guys," why is there no such reaction? Why, I continue asking myself, were there no recommendations or pronouncements made by human rights organizations, governmental or not, international or local, when they received complaints of violations committed by teachers or by some of the organizations during the 2006 conflict? Could this be because, if voices had been raised, this would have weakened the social movement? Though, clearly, there were and will be honorable exceptions.

"It is because not all atrocities are the same," could be the response, and of course, an atrocity committed by someone with little power, that is, with few resources for causing damage, is not the same as an atrocity committed by someone who has "all the power of the state" at their disposal. Here, then, it would be good to ask oneself, how can a union, in this case Section 22, violate the labor and human rights of its own union members? Is it because it has the power of the state, or at least part of the state, that it can do so? The answer is "yes," Section 22 can engage in repression because it has at its disposition and control a part of the state. It is not a secret to anyone that the entire structure that operates the administration of Basic Education[3] (the directions and districts of the Department of Basic Education), the payroll offices, the supervision offices of school districts, the directors of the schools, the bureaucracy of the Institute of Public Education of Oaxaca, that is, the state education institutions, are in its hands. This means that if some teachers disagree with the union party line, do not participate in union actions, and also do not agree to pay the penalties that are imposed, they are declared a traitor to the teachers' and popular movement and are demolished, without the support of any union to defend them. With this part of the state in the hands of Section 22, these teachers will have problems being paid, or retiring, or receiving a work assignment. If one of their children earns a scholarship that the union has negotiated, it will be snatched away from them. They will no longer be given raises since their rights in terms of the pay schedule will be cancelled, and they will even have to confront the union mafia to fight for accreditation of their students' studies. Nor can they request the intervention of higher level functionaries, those whose jobs depend on the government, not the union, because these persons are always ready to support the decisions of those who were "named" by the "rank and file" teachers, so that their own heads won't roll. In the end, one group as much as the other is protected by the impunity of those who hold power. And, why does this union terrorism exist? I suppose its purpose is to suppress the individual independence of teachers so that they better serve the movement, somewhat like what occurs, though on a more massive scale, when nation-states are formed. As Chomsky comments: "The imposition of a common language, a common culture, a common allegiance to a national entity, has been achieved through centuries of violence and destruction. And it is still continuing."

"Almost all of human history is individuals, in the best case freely associating, but within community. There is no other way," Chomsky also says. The big question, then, is: are resistance movements obligated to achieve the free association of their members, or will we continue to be enticed to capitulate to the enchantments of corporatism and authoritarianism? I think it will depend to a large extent on our capacity to be self-critical. We can no longer do what we have done so often in the past, that is, criticize the atrocities of some and close our eyes to the atrocities of others.

As I write these words, I realize that as a teacher, I also hold in my hands a part of the state, that is, I have the tools with which to repress and impose. The closest potential victims are the children and my own community. What I most transmit with my teaching, even without realizing it, is not so much the contents of my curriculum, but rather "initiation into the practices of the ruling class—how you talk to each other, what you drink, who your friends are. This kind of education has its consequences; it induces certain ways of behavior and of thought," as Chomsky says. And indeed, behaviors in the school, which greatly resemble those in a factory or office, are very different from those in family or community life. It does not matter much if I address topics relating to our culture because the model of appropriate behavior in school promotes a foreign way of life.

"You don't talk about your own crimes; it is one of those things you learn at Yale and Princeton and Harvard. Our crimes do not exist—but these things are happening," says Noam, talking about the atrocities committed by the United States. But I have to admit that, day after day, my teaching practice hides an authoritarianism that is at times subtle but often direct, which I exercise in different ways, all protected by the state. If the children do not comply with my requirements, I have the power to retain them, and they will have the "opportunity" to attend yet another academic course until they yield. The imposition is more starkly apparent where the children are more strongly tied to their indigenous culture, especially because they are accustomed to learning through social practices and applying their knowledge in concrete activities, those that are important in daily life. In contrast, in school we submit them to activities that have little to do with social practices. In classrooms, all learning is controlled by the written word, both learning and displaying what has been learned. Knowing is not important anymore, what matters is being able to write down what you know. So if you do not acquire proficiency in the written language, what you have learned is of little worth at school. We now know that skill with written language is a product of its use in social contexts in the daily life of a culture, so those who come from oral cultures where writing has little practical use, such as indigenous and peasant cultures, will suffer for this. And if, in addition, what one must learn is written in a language one does not understand or understands very little, and the context in which it is taught is far removed from real life, then attending school becomes a real torture.

Self-criticism must lead to action, Chomsky proposes:

> There is no problem in laying out a curriculum in which
> communities would run their own schools with their
> own communal values and interests, and also introduce
> whatever they like from the outside—quantum physics,

Shakespearean plays, or whatever happens to interest them. They could introduce it on their own terms, within their own cultural framework . . . It can be done in many different ways—locally run schools or regionally run schools are a perfect example.

We should take these words very seriously. The authorities of the community where I work, the parents, the children, and I should reinvent the work in the school, with a very vigilant eye to my teaching practice. First, education should be returned to family and community control. We must find ways to give our students greater access to education itself. By this I am not so much talking about bringing the contents of community knowledge to the classroom, which in the end means submitting what is learned to the control of the school and the state. Rather, it means finding ways to recreate knowledge in the spaces, times and forms of communal life, with the idea that school learning complements community learning, that in school we teach what the community is not able or cannot manage to teach, and that this learning serves to increase the well-being both of the individual and the community. Hopefully we can do something, even in a small way, to help make the marvelous thought of Noam Chomsky a reality, for the good of ourselves and our future generations.

NOTES

1. Jim Cason & David Brooks, "Chomsky: fue una respuesta atroz a atrocidades de E.U.," *La Jornada*, September 15, 2001.
2. See Meyer's introductory chapter, footnote 6, in this volume.
3. In Mexico, Basic Education includes preschool and grades 1 through 9.

5.

Views from the Hemisphere of Resistance

By María Bertely Busquets, Mexico

Academic director of the Dirección Académica at the Centro de Investigaciones y Estudios Superiores de Antropología Social (CIESAS) in Mexico, and co-author of intercultural, bilingual educational materials with the Union of Teachers for a New Education for Mexico (UNEM), made up of Tseltal, Tsotsil, and Ch´ol educators from the state of Chiapas. bertely@ciesas.edu.mx

FROM THE OPENING GREETING sent by Noam Chomsky to the Second National Congress of Indigenous and Intercultural Education held in Oaxaca, Mexico, in October 2007, critical thoughts explode in the reader's mind and heart in response to his words, thoughts which, for this writer, are nurtured by personal experiences with the indigenous Tseltales, Tsotsiles, and Choles of the state of Chiapas, inhabitants of the hemisphere of resistance.

I concur with Chomsky's encouraging thoughts but, especially considering the ideological positions of our last four governments, I disagree as to the level of Mexico's integration into the fight against imperialism initiated once again by other Latin American countries. If, as Chomsky maintains, "integration is a prerequisite for independence and self determination," governments such as those of Brazil, Venezuela, and Bolivia, among others, are at the forefront in this hemisphere of resistance, whereas the current Mexican government, even well into the twenty-first century, lags behind the thinking even of the new president of the United States, Barack Obama.

The Mexican government insists on defending the small, wealthy elite that, through financial speculation and economic monopoly, promotes the globalization of poverty, according to John Gledhill (2004). It is an elite that ignores the fact that globalization implies interdependence, though the world's great majority is impoverished and, as Chomsky contends, they are taking "steps towards trying to overcome that curse."

Mexico's integration into the "Latin America of Resistance" occurs principally through indigenous movements such as the one that erupted in Chiapas in 1994, when the so-called "impoverished indigenous society" organized itself (in a manner in paradoxical contrast with the racist stereotypes that define it as "marginal" and "vulnerable"), displaying a strength and cultural richness lacking among ignorant elites. This cultural patrimony is derived from the integral unity of the indigenous peoples[1] with Mother Earth, wherein children, community members, and elders recreate and renew the ancient behaviors and values which lead them to demand recognition, no longer as a handout *from above*, but rather for rights they have exercised and which they continue to exercise today, consciously and actively, in their daily lives, *from below*. These rights they exercise not only *de facto*, but *de jure*.[2]

In Chiapas and other states of Mexico, the revitalization and development of languages, cultures, techniques, tools, and vital indigenous meanings begin to be controlled by these very communities. Faced with the failure of official state education and the abusive exercise of power by authoritarian official indigenous teachers, communities have begun selecting their most ethical and committed youth to devise and take charge of the *Other Education* for their daughters and sons. Autonomous education, as it is called, as well as other alternative and new forms of education in Chiapas, regardless of their diverse ways of negotiating with the government and the state educational system, enact a praxis of resistance characterized as *altermundista* (otherworldly). Two Zapatista slogans, "One world in which many worlds fit," and "Everything for everyone, nothing for us," capture this spirit, where the defense of world rights is directed toward the defense of everyone's rights.

Reflecting on my own country, Mexico, I find many paradoxes in the interview that Lois Meyer conducted with Chomsky in 2004, paradoxes that flow from Mexico's political and cultural history. On the one hand, the consolidation of the nation-state permitted the construction of a single political and legal community in a territory that had been socially fragmented and controlled by local strong-arm leaders (caciques) and popular leaders (caudillos)[3] in the nineteenth century. Treaties between Mexico and other nations achieved important advances in terms of guaranteeing fundamental human and citizenship rights in the twentieth century.

What is more, the constitutional and legal definitions *from above* of the relations between citizens and the state, and corporatist public policies, as well as national institutions that emanated from the social pact derived from the Mexican Revolution of 1910, helped to nurture the gradual appropriation *from below* of those rights granted by law but never fully exercised, as well as subsequent peasant, worker, and popular struggles, up to and including the Zapatista movement. The motto of the Zapatista Army for National Liberation (EZLN), "Never again a Mexico without us," alludes to the power that the state still wields within this movement.

On the other hand, in intercultural terms, the national community—as it has been imagined—has tried to impose, through education and through subjective as well as objective violence, "a common language, a common culture, a common allegiance to a national entity," as Chomsky says, via a series of devices designed to assimilate, incorporate, and integrate the indigenous peoples. The effect of "institutional homogeneity," as Chomsky calls it, on this population was a form of domination that occurred within consolidated nation-states.

The expressions of autonomy to which Chomsky alludes

are distinct from those actually occurring in Mexico, since the movements in Spain and Great Britain, among other European countries, are separatist in intent while the Zapatistas seek autonomy within the Mexican state. In all of these cases, however, as Chomsky says, "things are going back to something like the structure that existed before the violent process of State formation was created."

But, in what context has Zapatista autonomy developed, and how do Zapatistas understand autonomy? Let's not forget that on January 1, 1994, the EZLN rose up after Article 27 of the Constitution had been reformed. For the indigenous peoples of Southeastern Mexico, this reform affected their inalienable rights to the communal and *ejidal* (state-recognized communal) lands that they inhabit, by permitting and stimulating the commercialization, subdivision, and privatization of land. Since that time, the EZLN's struggle has focused on guaranteeing recognition of indigenous people's autonomy via reforms to the Mexican Constitution, as well as various modifications aimed at transforming the treatment of indigenous peoples from the status of *subjects of public interest*,[4] characterized by "institutionalized *indigenismo*,"[5] to a recognized status of *entities of public law*.[6]

The Mexican Government and the EZLN signed the Accords of San Andrés Larráinzar[7] in order to establish a new relationship between the indigenous peoples and the nation-state of Mexico. These treaties formulate a pluralistic judicial order composed of common norms for all Mexicans, respect for indigenous normative systems, as well as the autonomy of indigenous territories and regions, which are constituted as integral parts of the reformed state. In other words, it was agreed that these peoples have the right to free association, to coordinate actions in their own interest, and to participate in the different levels of government under the principles of relative majority and the redrawing of electoral districts.[8] Lastly, the Accords introduce the definition of the term *spatial, material, and personal spheres* within which indigenous peoples can exercise their rights, a *sphere for the distribution of responsibilities* (political, economic, social, cultural, educational, and legal) for the management of resources and environmental protections, as well as a *sphere of self-determination* in which the communities determine their own development programs and projects.

Although the Mexican government did not comply with the San Andrés Accords, nor with the terms of Convention 169 of the International Labor Organization (ILO),[9] the organized indigenous peoples in *active resistance* in the state of Chiapas have complied and started building their own autonomy *from below*, with the solidarity and support of men and women from France, Argentina, Greece, the United States, Barcelona, Japan, Australia, Slovenia, and Mexico, among other countries, as well as the legal protections in international law in favor of differentiated citizenship and pluralistic development, represented by such legal documents as Convention 169 of the ILO.

Eleven years later, having created the autonomous municipalities,[10] in the Sixth Declaration of the Lacandon Jungle, the EZLN called for a national anti-capitalist movement that would articulate with international non-party-affiliated leftist movements and with the poor and marginalized sectors of Mexico, including peasants, workers, teachers, homosexuals, and women. This declaration can be read as a strategy of active anti-electoral political resistance aimed at denouncing the bankrupt state of the liberal partisan political model. This strategy was justified when the partisan Left, represented by the Democratic Revolutionary Party (PRD), betrayed the historic struggle and the terms of the Accords by signing the Bill of Indigenous Rights[11] passed by the Mexican Congress.

The dismal social benefits achieved by the parliamentary system and its welfare policies demonstrate the injustices suffered by miners, factory workers, day laborers on wealthy ranches, as well as the poor in towns and urban ghettos and slums. The criticism that the autonomous Zapatista model represents for the democratic system and its institutions and practices of "bad government," is based on the lessons and values derived from their own experience of self-government, acquired by the autonomous authorities who make up the "*Caracoles*":[12] "we learned to govern ourselves and to resolve our own problems. The people are learning to govern and to supervise our work and we are learning to obey. The people are wise and they know when one makes a mistake or gets off track in their work. That is how we work."[13]

Why such appreciation for the community? In Mexico, as in many other parts of the world, imperialist power extended its damaging effects in various ways. The twentieth century, as Eric Hobsbawm (1993) maintains, has witnessed a transition from the optimism generated by the supposed social welfare, economic development and modernization to be derived from the indiscriminate exploitation of the planet's natural resources, towards a profound pessimism motivated by large and intermittent wars over the control of petroleum, water, and the production and commercialization of basic foods, as well as contamination, environmental instability, and generalized poverty around the globe.

In the second half of the twentieth century, the men and women of this part of the hemisphere of resistance found themselves submerged, either voluntarily or involuntarily, in desperation and disillusionment provoked not only by the false promises of the North American Free Trade Agreement and the opening of the markets, but also by the neoliberal politics that have sought the reduction of the state and the elimination of the protections of fundamental rights. A form of political nihilism overcame many Mexicans, caused by disillusionment brought about by the transition to a supposedly party-based democracy, where the "people's representatives" distance themselves more and more from the most pressing needs and interests of their constituents, and electoral fraud occurs with impunity.

Views from the Hemisphere of Resistance

In the so-called "Mexican demodernization" of Sergio Zer-meño (2005), the school also transitioned from a nationalist model to one of efficiency and productivity, focused on individual competencies that seek more flexible training outcomes. In this context, there appear to be two possible destinies for rural populations, peasants, and the indigenous who are educated. On the one hand, basic compensatory education creates an army of barely qualified laborers who are absorbed into the informal job market, or day laborers who participate in the massive migration to agrobusiness fields in the north of Mexico and in the United States. On the other hand, the professionalization of an indigenous and peasant minority enables limited social mobility, which, while far from improving the working conditions and lives of the communities, intensifies the social differences and conflicts inside these communities.

In those Latin American countries burdened with what Chomsky defines as the "homogenizing conversion," the effective exercise of citizenship and its relationship with an intercultural education constructed *from below* deserves particular attention. This concern contrasts starkly with the official educational focus, as our author indicates, of teaching obedience, political passivity and certain habits of behavior that serve as a hidden curriculum to reproduce a form of socialization intended to train for a more flexible job market. This form of education, even if it declares itself in favor of pluralism and the recognition of linguistic and sociocultural diversity, seems to favor a process that alienates man from nature and a process of citizenship that promotes individualism and the abandonment of those original territories inhabited by indigenous peoples. In addition, it stimulates national and international migration to the large urban and industrial centers in search of employment and material goods.

With the intention of designing an alternative global political project, the Tseltal, Tsotsil, and Chole educators who are the inspiration for this reflection have designed another model of citizenship education based in territorial control and rootedness, self-sustainable development, care of the environment, the exercise of reciprocity and solidarity, and the strengthening of communal organization and autochthonous languages and cultures, in compliance with the most advanced national and international legal agreements pertaining to indigenous rights. The *Other Citizenship* demands the construction of an alternative and more humane society, not only for indigenous peoples, but for all the population of the planet, all those interested in bringing to life the *Other Mexico*.

Noam Chomsky argues that the students of Harvard, Yale or Princeton acquire certain patterns of socialization, behavior and thinking that are characteristic of political, ideological, and business elites. As Chomsky states, "If you're in Skull & Bones at Yale,[14] you're prepared to be somebody who owns and runs the society; if it's community college, you're prepared to be somebody who quietly serves the owner, the elite and the powerful."

From my experience with the indigenous peoples of Chiapas, these patterns suggest not only the reproduction of a stratified system, but also the recreation of a dominant educational paradigm where postmodernity, artificial lifestyles, and urban attractions, among other cultural expressions, are erected on top of peasant rural life, which is perceived as inferior and backwards.

Those students belonging to Yale's Skull & Bones club are not only prepared to rule, but also to impose, at all costs, a model of dominant society where, particularly in universities, only a few educated indigenous youth return to their communities with projects and initiatives that improve their conditions of life. Faced with the agrarian crisis, those indigenous university students, as well as those of limited education, who come from "non-viable" economic regions where their only options—as Chomsky states—are either to fade away and die off "without options in their territories" or "resign themselves to leaving in order to survive," learn to conform. New generations consider these to be natural processes and, in general, opt to abandon their territory and migrate to urban spaces, where the dominant social model and its values are imposed.

While it is true that "there is no unique formula" for resisting these processes, in those regions marked most by poverty and structural, political, and social exclusion, the relationship between citizenship and intercultural education moves between two contrasting alternatives: contribute to the creation of compensatory policies designed from the *top down*, meant to adapt indigenous peoples to confront the demands of the global marketplace, or, on the contrary, to contribute to the construction *from the bottom up* of actively democratic and participatory models that prioritize solidarity. In this last case, the indigenous movement is fighting to have the state recognize the exercise of its self-determination and autonomy as a right, based in mandate, social control, and the most advanced national and international legislation in the field.

We are speaking of an active resistance that attempts to reveal, through the contrast between "ideal types" of societies—in the manner of Weber—the crimes and mechanisms of domination and repression exercised by *some*, and the values, the alternative forms of the "good life" and the subaltern practices of the *others*, placing at the center of this comparison the unity of society-nature. *The ones and the others* include everyone in the world, whether indigenous or not, from Guatemala, Colombia, Bolivia, Chile or Peru, from African communities, from India or any part of the world. The identification of *the ones and the others* depends on the consciousness or unconsciousness that one has of the global interdependence of man in regards to nature, as well as the reality of being—as are all living beings on this planet—rooted in this soil.

Those colonizers who ignore this rootedness and interdependence enrich themselves and form part of a "virtual parliament of investors and lenders" that, with its own stinginess, is digging its own grave. Essentially, the monopolization of wealth does not contribute to a productive, social circulation of capital and, least of all, to democratic life, as our author maintains in reference to the thought of John M. Keynes. The "abundance of turbulence," as Chomsky calls it, includes today these very same corporations. Even they are beginning to recognize that, in the interests of their own reproduction and survival, they should participate in social investment, promote citizen participation, distribute wealth more equitably, and contribute to new fields of scientific and technological development, particularly directed toward improving the environment and the use of alternative energies. The deep concern of the colonial power for its own survival can be perceived in the current policies and social projects of Barack Obama, as well as in the measures taken by some humanistic businessmen who value solidarity, and who are conscious of the threat implicit in the construction of alternatives, that is, *other social models*—such as the Cuban one in the past—and *other political cultures*, which, without the participation of the United States, permit successful confrontations with the global crisis.

The vision from Chiapas of the Tseltal, Tsotsil, and Chole educators who form the Union of Teachers for a New Education for Mexico (UNEM)[15] coincides, to a certain extent, with the "successful models" suggested by Chomsky:

> Successful models, what's called by the rulers "successful defiance," meaning independent efforts of independent action, are very frightening. And efforts to stamp them out take all sorts of forms, violent forms like military coups, or less violent forms like educational homogenization.

The success of independent models is measured more in terms of action, that is, praxis and its effects in daily life, rather than in terms of empty words. Similar to the Landless Workers Movement in Brazil, whose experiences the author relates, UNEM teachers who are part of the present Mayan world assume that the *men and women of corn* are the peasants, the indigenous, and even the urban-dwellers who—reminiscent of the

Popol Vuh[16] are "genuine people." They are genuine, in part, because they live *in* nature, in accordance with the times and cyclic rhythms that Mother Earth prescribes, in contrast to the "false" women and men, those made of artificial and urban images and materials which affect the social and environmental equilibrium of the planet.

The education promoted by UNEM seeks to prepare today's *men and women of corn* so that they learn to be, to do, and to develop themselves *in* their own territories and contexts. Such beings are capable of interchanging these learnings and possibilities with others, both indigenous and non-indigenous, and, in this way, they are ethically and technologically adept at strengthening the active and conscious relations of everyone on earth with the natural environment. Territorial control and attachment, then, are relevant not only to communal and peasant life; rather, there is a need to multiply across the planet genuine persons who—far from feeling alienated from nature, as occurs among city dwellers—perceive that, accept it or not, they are rooted in the land they inhabit, as are corn plants.

Assuming this position implies the existence of an intercultural and historical conflict between "genuine" and "false" persons. Official education has nurtured "false" persons by alienating women and men from their natural surroundings, either by teaching them that they must exploit and dominate nature in order to development themselves, or by motivating them to forget the land in order to improve their standard of living and overcome their poverty. "False" persons uproot themselves, migrate, and abandon their territories because they believe that Mother Earth is arid and dead, or because they are seduced by city life, the material commodities offered by modernity, and the promise that they will gain access to their basic rights via liberal democracy, represented by deputies, senators, the president of the republic, justices, and magistrates.

The right to seeds, as a basic human right defended by the

landless workers of Brazil, points to the control of a resource that should not be controlled by the rules of transnational corporations. The actions in the practical lives of these Mayan teachers of UNEM and others, and their discourse documented in the workbook *Los hombres y las mujeres del maíz: Democracia y derecho para el mundo* (Bertely, coord. 2008), rattle and undermine those power centers to which our author referred. A fragment is sufficient to provide a taste of their alternative vision of work and of life. Here, Andrés Hernández Díaz, a Tsotsil educator, discusses reaching agreements about the land (Xchapanel kosoltik):

> We Tsotsiles know how to resolve our differences by making agreements. We make many agreements but, concerning our collective lands, we are worried about the future of our territory.
>
> That's what happened when the authorities of *La Pimienta* called us to a communal General Assembly. We were 92 *ejidatarios* (collective farm members), 241 aspirants seeking to become *ejidatarios* or children of *ejidatarios*, and other members of the community. Though we come from different regions and political parties, in the assembly we spoke of our common problems: potable water, the highway, and matters related to our collective land (*ejido*). A government representative told us that if we accepted his program, he would give each of us the deed to our parcel, as well as credits and loans. . . . If we didn't accept, the three large properties that compose the 1766 hectares of La Pimienta Ejido would remain as one single property, which would be registered in the office of rural affairs and receive a certification of ownership that would have to be renewed every year.
>
> When we analyzed what the government agent had told us, we disagreed among ourselves. The majority of the *ejidatarios* did not accept the division of our *ejido* into individual parcels, but some said yes, that was what they

wanted. As there was disagreement, we drew a map of La
Pimienta and imagined the future of our *ejido*, both as a
single property and in parcels. . . . Pedro would no longer
allow anyone to pass through his coffee groves. Juan would
not be able to get to his pasture. Now Antonio wouldn't
be able to go and collect firewood on the parcel where the
woods are. If we accepted the government's program, we
would no longer be free in our own territory, or free to live
from our resources. The deer would no longer roam free
but would be penned up in Pascual's pasture. We would no
longer be able to collect and eat *sats'*.[17] We realized that if
we broke up our land into parcels, we would lose our freedom in our ejidal lands.

We went to consult with Sr. Antonio Díaz Díaz, our
wise elder, and asked for his advice. He advised us in this
way:

"I will tell you a little of the history of our community.
In the past we never asked for government support. We
lived free and we valued working the earth because all the
family participated and planted different crops in our fields:
corn, beans, bananas, tomato, chili, squash, *pij'*, *tsui*[18] and
other vegetables. We lived free and we valued our labor on
the land. Each member of the family carried out distinct
activities that benefitted everyone. The women . . . prepared
the tortillas and *pozole*, the men had various chores in the
fields, and the children always helped us in our work. . . .
And there's more. . . .

"Before, we were united and content cultivating our
fields. That was how we lived, poor but happier and in community. Now things are different! Every year life gets more
complicated, and if we lose our *ejido*, our community will
have no future, only many problems!

"You who live in the city, how do you live, and what
value does your work have for you?

"Why is it important that our families work united, helping one another?
"Do you work with joy, satisfaction and liberty?
"How do you resist selfishness and the power of individualism?
"Do you know how to work in community?
"How can we build a better future for our children?"
(102–107)

This recorded tale ends by mentioning the property and cultural rights of indigenous peoples and includes the selection of specific articles of Convention 169 of the ILO, the San Andrés Accords signed by the EZLN but with which the Mexican government has never complied, the Mexican Constitution and the Agrarian Law, in order to strengthen not only the ethical and territorial formation of the children, youth and community members who participate in the *Other Education* promoted by UNEM, but also their legal training from the perspective of the situational application of the law in local, national, and international contexts.

This material, despite being designed on the margins of the official education system and *from below*, was chosen by the Secretary of Public Education to be distributed in the secondary schools of Mexico, with a print run of 32,500 copies. This experience shows, as Chomsky mentions, that the centers of power are yielding; this is also visible, as he says, in the ideological changes taking place in the World Bank, the International Monetary Fund and the World Economic Summit. Even these powerful bodies are worried that they have marginalized the "common people" from their decisions.

In this case, the contribution of the UNEM to the assembly of voices convoked by Lois Meyer and Benjamin Maldonado is only one small example of curriculum designed and controlled by communities themselves. The variety of intercultural and bilingual materials that make up this curriculum is beginning to arrive in other parts of the country, such as Puebla, Oaxaca, and Michoacán, via the participation of both indigenous and non-indigenous peoples in shared learning experiences. As Noam Chomsky points out, in these workshops, peasant knowledge is not found in books or in the "scientific agriculture" that displaces and reduces their productivity. This knowledge is found as much in the "heads" of indigenous peoples as in the movements of their bodies and in their hearts, for it is embedded in the collective and practical activities undertaken in their territories and natural environments.

We agree with John Dewey—mentioned by Chomsky—that individual liberty is the basis not only of democracy, but of active and mutual democracy, which UNEM seeks to strengthen. Communitarian norms do not infringe on individual rights; on the contrary, they offer ways to channel disagreements and free choice, as shown in the example recounted above.

Those words communicate the *other world* and global values of Zapatismo. As discussed in another interview conducted by Lois Meyer with Chomsky in 2007, they exemplify that our words must not be emptied and distorted to neutralize their substantive connotation, as has occurred with the term *interculturalidad*, which—in contrast with multiculturalism—necessarily implies conflict. It also seems necessary to guarantee control of educational proposals *from below*—with significant participation by native educators—in contrast to the concentration of curricular evaluations and decision-making *from above*. None of this should be taken to suggest the renunciation by the Mexican government of its responsibility to "lead by obeying," and in the United States, the liberating activism displayed during the 1960s. As Lois Meyer reminds us in reference to the thought of Evo Morales: "indigenous peoples are the moral reserve of humanity."

REFERENCES

Bertely, M.,coord. 2004. *Tarjetas de autoaprendizaje*. México: CEIB-SEP, UNEM, OEI. Fondo León Portilla, Editorial Santillana.

——— coord.2008. *Los hombres y las mujeres del maíz: Democracia y derecho indígena para el mundo*. Libros del Rincón, Colección Espejo de Urania. México: UNEM, CIESAS, SEP.

——— coord. 2009. *Sembrando nuestra propia educación intercultural como derecho*. México: UNEM, ECIDEA, CIESAS, IIAP, Fundación Ford, OEI.

Gledhill, J. 2004. *La ciudadanía y la geografía social de la neoliberalización profunda*. *Relaciones* 100, Vol. XXV: 75–106. Universidad de Manchester.

Hobsbawm, E. 1993. Introduction: Inventing traditions. In *The invention of tradition*, eds. E.J. Hobsbawm & T. Ranger, 1–14. Cambridge: University Press.

UNEM. 1999. *Bachillerato pedagógico comunitario para la formación de docentes de educación primaria bilingüe intercultural. Plan y programas de estudios*. Chiapas, México: mecanuscrito.

Zermeño, S. 2005. *La desmodernidad mexicana y las alternativas a la violencia y a la exclusión en nuestros días*. México: Editorial Océano.

NOTES

1. The legal definition of "indigenous peoples" as collectivities ("pueblos") with rights and legal standing, not merely individuals with the same rights as all Mexican citizens, is fundamental to indigenous struggles in Chiapas and elsewhere, as will be described in detail in this commentary.
2. I refer here to the fact that autonomy—formerly exercised "de facto"—is exercised now "de jure," by law. This refers to the existence of constitutional reforms or international agreements which guarantee these rights, exercised by indigenous peoples "by law," despite national governments that ignore or fail to comply with them. One might talk about "de facto autonomy" when these legal supports did not yet exist.
3. In the world of rural Mexico, "caciques" are the powerful persons who are able to impose their will on the communal assembly, often by use of arms. "Caudillos" tend to be opinion leaders whose power is usually based on their power to sway public opinion more than on the use of violence.
4. By "subjects or entities of public interest" is meant that the indigenous are treated as if they were a "problem" that state institutions need to attend to and resolve. This means, for example, that the General Direction of indigenous Education or the National Commission of Indigenous Rights deals with the indigenous as subjects whose interests it is the responsibility of these public institutions to "attend to."

Views from the Hemisphere of Resistance

5. In the period following the Mexican Revolution of 1910, the treatment of the indigenous population as "subjects of public interest" led to the creation of official departments and institutions charged with the responsibility of attending to the necessities of this population. Because of this, at the end of the 1940s the Autonomous Department of Indigenous Matters (DAAI) was created, and in 1948, the National Indigenist Institute. Mexican anthropology participated in the definition of a public "indigenist" policy whose intent was to support a process of integrating local indigenous cultures within the Mexican nation.

6. When indigenous "peoples" are defined as "entities or subjects of public law," this means that they as peoples are responsible for effecting their rights to self-determination and autonomy as declared, for example, in Convention 169 of the International Labor Organization (ILO) and, in Mexico, in the San Andrés Accords, the legal agreement signed between the EZLN and the Mexican government in 1996. In this case, it is not public institutions that assure implementation of the rights of the indigenous, but rather the indigenous themselves, recognized as peoples, oversee compliance of their rights under the law.

7. On February 16, 1996, the Mexican government and the EZLN signed these accords, granting the Zapatistas autonomy and land. The Accords state, in part: "Autonomy is the concrete expression of the exercise of the right to self-determination, within the framework of membership in the National State. As a result, the indigenous peoples shall be able to decide their own form of internal government as well as decide their political, social, economic, and cultural organization."

8. In Mexico, only political parties can register candidates for municipal, state and federal elections; independent candidates are excluded. Also, only a portion of deputies elected to the federal Chamber of Deputies are elected by majority vote; others gain their positions by proportional representation. Granting indigenous peoples in Mexico "relative majority" breaks significantly with these practices, implying rights to free association and election by majority rule, and requires the redrawing of electoral districts.

9. Convention concerning Indigenous and Tribal Peoples in Independent Countries, passed by the ILO in 1989, effective in 1991, and ratified to date by twenty nations, mostly in Latin America, including the following: Mexico, Venezuela, Peru, Paraguay, Honduras, Guatemala, Ecuador, Costa Rica, Colombia, Chile, Brazil, Bolivia, and Argentina. Signatories guarantee the recognition of many rights to indigenous peoples within their national territories, given "the aspirations of these peoples to exercise control over their own institutions, ways of life and economic development and to maintain and develop their identities, languages and religions, within the framework of the States in which they live."

10. The autonomous municipalities are located in the jungle region that borders Guatemala, in the region of Los Altos, in the Lacandon Jungle in the region of Altamirano and the Morelia Communal Lands, and in the northern zone of the state of Chiapas.

11. As antecedents, in response to the commitments it incurred by signing Convention 169 of the ILO, the Mexican government sent to the ILO the agreements it signed on February 16, 1996, in San Andrés Larráinzar, with the Zapatista Army of National Liberation and other indigenous organizations, in the presence of the Commission of Concord and Pacification named by the Congress of the Union (COCOPA). Later in 1996, this commission developed a constitutional reform initiative, known as the Law of COCOPA, to comply with the signed agreements. Despite what it had formally agreed to, in 1998 the government of Ernesto Zedillo presented a counterproposal in which the rights of indigenous peoples to free determination was reduced to apply only to their "community"; it maintained that the Political Constitution of the United Mexican States "grants" rights to indigenous peoples, instead of recognizing and validating that as peoples they possess and are free to exercise their own legal rights; it maintained for the state the prerogative of validating or not the local authorities elected by traditional communal processes; it does not mention the right of indigenous peoples to use and enjoy their natural resources, lands, and territories; and it does not recognize indigenous peoples as "entities of public law," treating them instead as "entities of public interest." In 2001, during the presidency of Vicente Fox Quezada, the Mexican government countered the Law of COCOPA and the signed San Andrés Accords with the so-called Bill of Indigenous Rights. The Congress of the Union approved this counterproposal for reform, which was passed on August 10 of the same year (see Article 2 of the Political Constitution of the United Mexican States).

12. The Caracoles are defined as those spaces constructed by the Zapatistas for the purpose of organizing autonomy. There are five Caracoles: La Realidad, Oventic, La Garrucha, Morelia, and Roberto Barrios, each of which incorporates autonomous municipalities.

13. *La Jornada*, September 29, 2004: xv.

14. Secret elite society at Yale University to which both U. S. presidential candidates in 2004, George W. Bush and John Kerry, belonged during their student years.

15. In 1995 a group of Mayan teachers, commissioned by their respective communities via formal declarations of their communal assemblies, formed the Union of Teachers for a New Education for Mexico (UNEM, for the initials in Spanish), with the objective of "implementing a profound reform of the basic educational process, which will combine theory and practice under the control of the indigenous communities of Chiapas." Between 1995 and 1996, the UNEM received specialized professional training and moved ahead of the autonomous educational projects which the Zapatistas began implementing later, following the government's failure to comply with the San Andrés Accords.

The ambiguous position of the UNEM, between the state, the non-governmental organizations, and the EZLN, has allowed it to maintain a certain margin of autonomy and to constitute itself as a vanguard organization in the education field. By not being tied to a formal structure and not receiving permanent wages, the members participate in the productive and social life of the community, which has transformed them into teacher-peasants, and has contributed to the enrichment of their teaching.

To date, the importance of UNEM is not the number of its participants, which does not surpass twenty-five, but rather its ability to involve others in the construction of its alternative educational model, such as Zapatista indigenous teachers and community outreach workers, both those who are in the official education system as well as those outside of it, and also a growing number of non-indigenous academics.

Its effort has been the design of an intercultural and bilingual education from below, grounded in self-government, territorial rootedness, and the active participation of the community. Among other successful projects we can mention *Tarjetas de Autoaprendizaje* (Bertely, coord. 2004) with a run of 6,000 copies, the workbook *Los Hombres y las Mujeres del Maíz. Democracia y derecho indígena para el mundo* (Bertely, coord. 2008) with a run of 32,500 copies, as well as the collection *Sembrando nuestra propia educación intercultural como derecho* (Bertely, coord. 2009) with 1,000 copies. This collection includes, among other products, the formalization of the curricular model for primary schools.

16. One of the few Maya documents to survive the Spanish conquest, the Popol Vuh is the essential text of Mayan history and culture, equivalent to the Bible and to other sacred texts.
17. A kind of edible insect.
18. Edible vegetables.

6.

Resistance and Cultural Work in Times of War

By Elsie Rockwell, Mexico[1]

Researcher at the Center for Research and Advanced Studies, Mexico. Email: elsarockwell@gmail.com

TIME AND AGAIN, NOAM Chomsky has denounced the series of territorial invasions and direct interventions of the United States in Latin America. In the past decades, the U.S. government has deliberately attempted to impose an economic model designed to sweep away existing social and political orders, and yet refuses to abide by the very rules it imposes. Policies based on this model have all but destroyed, for example, the corn-based agriculture and culture that has sustained some 280 generations of Amerindians and twenty generations of immigrants to America from other continents. In the words of the Zapatista Army for National Liberation (EZLN for its initials in Spanish), these actions are manifestations of an undeclared Fourth World War: a war that destroys all in its path, and expels or kills thousands who attempt to survive and resist.

In the present interviews, Chomsky suggests many themes we might further explore. One concerns multiculturalism. Chomsky notes the "process of state formation that was very bloody and savage and destructive. . . . [It meant] the suppression of local cultures, local languages, regional customs, and so on." He also suggests that in this new stage, the powerful tend to "take over and distort and modify the efforts of liberation for their own purposes. So, yes, that can happen with multiculturalism and diversity."

The dialectic between the destruction of diversity through the process of state formation, and the subsequent distortion and use of multiculturalism, is at the center of current debates on popular education in Latin America.

During the past two decades, Latin American governments, including that of Mexico, often under international pressure and with international funding, have decreed laws in defense of indigenous rights and instituted programs for "intercultural education." Although these measures have to some degree been a response to strong indigenous movements, they also reveal a betrayal of grassroots demands. For example, during the San Andrés Accords[2] in 1996, leaders of various Indian groups in Mexico opposed a clause inserted by the government delegation that offered "intercultural education"; rather, they defended "self-determination of educational policies and practices by indigenous communities." Apparently, it was the government that had a clear interest in promoting "intercultural education" and in reproducing the discourse of multiculturalism. In fact, the classic discourse of a homogeneous national culture as the foundation of citizenship is now rarely expressed, and has been replaced by programs for differentiated educational services, for minority groups and students with "special needs," and most recently for "gifted students." In seeking educational alternatives that resist these policies and yet defend cultural diversity, this current situation must be analyzed with care. In what follows, I propose four themes for reflection.

FIRST THEME: WARTIME
These are times of war. Not only the undeclared wars that the U.S. is waging under the guise of the "war on terrorism," but more importantly, the long and violent war identified by the Zapatistas as the "war of neoliberalism against humanity." In the words of Subcomandante Insurgente Marcos, the Fourth World War is "the war of the large financial centers, with total scenarios and an acute and constant intensity . . . one paradox of WWIV is

that while it is waged to eliminate frontiers and 'unite nations,' it leaves in its wake a multiplication of borders and a pulverization of nations that perish in its claws. . . . It may sound contradictory, but globalization produces a fragmented world, full of pieces isolated one from another."[3] This vantage point requires new ways of thinking about cultural and linguistic diversity. The new world order prospers not so much through national or global homogeneity sought in the past, as through a process of fragmentation of humanity that hinders the construction of global resistance.

The arsenal of neoliberal policies contains weapons as terrible as nuclear and biological arms. Refined methods of economic exploitation and exclusion involve the whole world population. Famine and pandemics exile and kill millions. Transgenic species, lethal substances, and synthetic drugs threaten not only human life, but the whole biosphere, life on Earth. The battery includes strategies of "low intensity warfare," multiple forms of political persecution, and the power of rumor and misinformation. These weapons are aimed particularly towards movements of resistance and construction of a different world.

The current economic order globalizes barbarism: it fabricates poverty, destroys nature, and militarizes entire regions. It prospers with wars that generate huge fortunes. It excludes the majorities, and its policies have closed life paths for millions of young people. Its victims include cultural and linguistic diversity, but also civility, human rights, and human reason, that is, the foundations of the systems of public education in which many of us have studied and worked.

The neoliberal establishment eschews the term "neoliberal," and has fashioned a discourse in which "culture" occupies a prominent place. Cultural diversity becomes a commodity. The logic of capital leads to an appropriation of anything that can be sold for gain, such as folklore for tourists. Meanwhile it destroys public access to both local and universal cultural patrimonies and even divests those who are the true heirs of their cultural legacies. In spite of its discourse on cultural difference, the current offensive tends to destroy cultural resources produced by generations.

The prevailing view posits a purported "clash of civilizations" that justifies actions that respond to dominant economic and geopolitical interests.[4] The discourse on cultural difference, with its attributions of cultural superiority and inferiority, spreads like gunpowder and ignites racism and the perception of the "Other" as enemy. The fragmentation resulting from neoliberal policies is then again endorsed to cultural difference, camouflaging a war waged for decades. Meanwhile, new frontiers are established using criteria of "ethnic cleansing."

In Mexico, the government discourse on Chiapas presented the actions of paramilitary groups funded and trained by the army as a result of "inter-community conflicts," reducing violence to "cultural causes." This discourse figured prominently during the cover-up of the Acteal Massacre of 1997, which has continued to this day.[5] Authorities also used the discourse to distract attention from fundamental social and political demands. During the negotiations of San Andrés, for example, the indigenous leaders resisted the reduction of their demands to the recognition of "cultural autonomy," offered by the government delegation. On the contrary, they demanded effective collective territorial rights and political autonomy at the level of communities as pre-conditions of cultural self-determination.

When the government failed to respect the Accords signed at San Andrés,[6] the Zapatista communities in Chiapas in 2003 decided to construct new ways to "govern by obeying," *mandar obedeciendo*. They established their own Juntas de Buen Gobierno, drawing on their collective local histories, yet seeking to create new rules for good government. They put forth principles such as collective and rotating authority, popular referendums for all decisions, and strict accountability for all governing actions. The measures being developed will no doubt be of value beyond the communities in which they have emerged. The Zapatistas have also established an autonomous education network, though in a sense the whole construction of the autonomous municipalities (MAREZ) is in itself a unique educational process.

This Zapatista effort transforms our notions of time, upsetting the evolutionary timeline that culminates in a Eurocentric image of progress and relegates indigenous peoples to a primitive past. Having constructed their public identity in the present struggle for autonomy, the Zapatistas know they are contemporaneous with many other peoples worldwide who hope to build alternatives for good governance. They live and act fully within the present-day national and global public debate. This is the greatest challenge they pose to the state, and is one of the reasons that authorities attempt to legislate and to propagate depoliticized versions of multiculturalism or interculturalism, limited to "cultural" aspects, without conceding local autonomy and self-determination.

Rural social movements, such as the Movimento Sem Terra in Brazil, or Via Campesina, mentioned by Chomsky, place great value on the *land* as a necessary condition not only to sustain life but also to recreate culture. Though born of the agrarian world, the struggle for the land has taken on new meaning in all movements opposing neoliberal policies. Thus, the Sem Techo and many urban ecological movements also stress access to land, particularly to collective spaces, in their efforts to reorganize life in the urban settlements populated by the waves of dispossessed peasants that the capitalist mode of production has sent to the cities.

What is at risk in this war is the land, *all* of the land, Earth itself, and the biological and cultural diversity that makes life on Earth possible.[7] The defense of the land, of the local, has taken on a universal value that extends towards the defense of shelters, streets, walls, public squares, and all spaces destined to communal life and cultural creation.

SECOND THEME: EDUCATION AND CULTURE

In the effort to achieve the benefits of "education for all," we often assume that schooling is intrinsically good for all, and forget that it is always immersed in contradictory social processes. Educators tend to discuss the advances in formal education as though nothing were occurring outside of classrooms. The agendas of national and international agencies, such as the United Nations' Millennium Development Goals intended to end world poverty by 2015, project educational goals that are unattainable given the present consequences and costs of the war. Consider the conditions of millions of undernourished, displaced, expelled, and migrated children; children forced to sell their labor or their bodies; or the destruction of food and health that accompanies the present crisis. How is it possible to think of education from the vantage point of this reality, considering the war being waged on all fronts?

The present process generates structural changes in societies that radically affect the configuration and practices of schooling. One of these consequences is the fragmentation of educational spaces. In the countryside, in the face of massive displacements and forced economic migration, the response of governments has been to promote parallel segmented educational services, often called "flexible" modalities, in order to assure school enrollment. For example, one program in Mexico labels certain children as "migrants" even before they leave their hometown, and channels them through special classes as their families move from one agricultural field to another. These options are no longer financed by national budgets, but rather are dependent upon international organisms that offer recourses, in fact loans, to the developing countries and impose conditions. In cities, fragmentation follows a different path. As access to institutions of higher education has become restricted, there is a proliferation of enterprises selling spurious training and diplomas to those who are excluded.

Publicly funded quality education is again becoming an education for the elite.

The effects of the war begin to be visible in the everyday life of public schools as well. State educational services have abandoned the principle of equal schooling for all, with its guarantee of access to a common body of knowledge. Despite the implications of homogenization of this republican ideal, it did serve the claim for quality public education for all. Nowadays, the educational system, far from being homogenous, is becoming vertically and horizontally fragmented. In Mexico, schools that have always had the advantage, receive greater support. Other schools are subjected to second-class conditions, and still others, in the poorest neighborhoods, are silently integrated into the network of so-called "safe schools," whose sole innovation is a system of constant police surveillance and detention of delinquent children, with the corresponding public disqualification. This occurs not only in Mexico, but in the ghettoized schools the world over.

What does this process have to do with culture? A renewal of the discourse centered on cultural differences justifies fragmentation and exclusion in education. The discourse on cultural diversity takes on many forms: on one hand the deterioration of quality is often attributed to cultural deficits and inequality. On the other hand, the notion of multiculturalism is used to map out new borders constructed through the diversification of school services. For example, in some zones, multicultural programs have been placed under the supervision of special education services. Indigenous children in the cities are referred to sections for children with learning problems.

The discussion on culture and education today is thus not as simple as when the systems of public education attempted, with little success, to homogenize national culture, and the defense of the right to cultural identity and diversity was evident. True, economic globalization tends to homogenize consumption and restrict the autonomous control of cultural and material resources of excluded groups; it does so largely through mass media, an instrument that has substituted for public schooling in this process of forging a common consumer culture. However, at the same time, the powerful disseminate stereotyped images of religious, ethnic, and ideological difference to incite racism, and attribute to these differences the social conflicts that are resulting from the war waged on all of humanity.

THIRD THEME: RETHINKING CULTURE

Awareness of these struggles should force us to rethink the concept of *culture* as a process embedded within relationships of power. As the global dynamic creates new and stronger borders both between nations and within societies, the political use of cultural symbols confounds and reorients affiliations, often signaling false criteria of difference and identity. This process blocks possible alliances among groups suffering the same war and launches fictitious identities to mobilize support for offensives. The dynamics of culture are immersed in war.

Much scholarship on cultural dynamics and education has dealt with social structures and detected class and power relationships. Scholars have learned to value local creativity and to understand diverse meanings and interpretations of similar cultural representations. Anthropologists tend to agree that in a world of intense global movement, with transnational migrations and networks, a systemic and closed concept of "culture" as a "bounded entity" is not valid.

Yet many governments, as well as the media, use those closed concepts to construct essentialized differences among human groups; these versions become dangerous allies to a disguised racism. The U.S. government authorizes the current war through the denial of our common humanity, including biological, linguistic and cultural commonalities, and manipulates "difference" to justify exclusion and aggression. This has been evident, for example, in the discourse on the radical difference of "the enemy"

projected by the Human Terrain System, an intelligence component of the U.S. armed forces in the Middle East. For political as
well as scientific reasons, it is now necessary to build up a different
concept of culture.

For this task, we might heed two authors whose influence
in Latin America has been fundamental, Antonio Gramsci and
Michel de Certeau.[8] Various writers have noted that the *Prison
Notebooks* of Gramsci merit a new reading at this time. Chomsky
alludes to Gramsci in this final note on pessimism and optimism.
A new reading would center less on hegemony and organic intellectuals, and more on the ample descriptions of the cultural
dimensions of political process, and on the particular interpretations of common sense, worldview, and "good sense."[9]

In examining cultural processes, Gramsci focused on power
and practice and on the historical trajectories of human societies.
Some of his examples are eloquent; he carefully analyzed the effect of successive reorganization of church orders, the constitution of political parties (in a broad sense), and the rationalization
of the life of workers through "Fordism," in terms of their political and cultural logic. For Gramsci, cultural elements, whether
a Machiavelian perspective or a popular ritual, did not possess
invariable intrinsic meaning, but rather acquired new accents
and uses in each political context or conjuncture. He noted how
cultural elements were often rearticulated in each instance, from
different political positions, to give relative coherence to collective action. Since Gramsci was concerned with the constant social
struggle, he used analogies with war operations to describe cultural processes. He extended the notion of a "war of positions" to
the political dimension of the ongoing struggle, and to actions in
the cultural terrain. Analysis of the hegemonic uses of cultural elements should be understood within the logic of domination, and
likewise, counter-hegemonic actions in this terrain should take
into account the logic of resistance.

Gramsci saw cultural phenomena not as parts of a coherent

whole, but rather as a contradictory set, whose logic at any give moment could only be understood through the history of a given configuration and the political processes that exert pressure to maintain or transform cultural patterns. In order to understand cultural processes, it is necessary to identify and understand the present-day tendencies that are similar to those that Gramsci analyzed and describe the effects they have on our practices and perceptions. This holds true in all cultural spheres, those of the arts and mass media, as well as in consolidated educational systems; they constitute a huge battlefield.

The second author, Michel de Certeau, also suggests viewing culture through analogy to warfare. His concepts of *strategy* and *tactic* situate culture at the center of struggle. By making a strong distinction between these terms, and considering tactics as the weapon of the weak, de Certeau discarded coherence as a necessary trait of cultural configurations. On the contrary, he stressed the plurality, heterogeneity, and discontinuity of the cultural work taking place through networks (not fields) and noted the importance of intergenerational transformations. Subaltern groups "continually turn to their own ends forces alien to them." The basic cultural process is active appropriation, not passive internalization. For de Certeau:

> All of the essential places of a society are less marked by
> the specificities of the objects, tools or concepts that oc-
> cupy them, than by the manners of appropriating, utilizing,
> and thinking about these sets of elements. It is not certain
> that these manners of doing form coherent wholes. Their
> combinations are the result of a multitude of historical com-
> mitments which facilitate the adaptations and selections to
> come. However what is certain is that if we remove the ob-
> jects and utterances that seem to be topical from these laby-
> rinths of tactics, we will only retain a set of non-pertinent
> and inert pieces of the social body, even if their collection

induces in us the most brilliant of constructions. We must therefore return to the inassimilable practices that lay deep within a specific place.[10]

The practices of those who resist, including indigenous groups, are marked by a constant resistance in the face of direct actions from those in power, and thus become tactical movements. Culture, thus understood, is fundamentally an issue of labor; "this work, more essential than its supports or representations, is culture." De Certeau further insisted in the danger of depoliticizing the analysis of cultural processes, by transforming representations into "monuments of identification," rather than understanding them within the everyday battle to sustain a life with meaning. At the same time, de Certeau rescues the historicity of cultural processes, as "the capacity that a group has to transform itself by reutilizing for other ends and new uses the means at its disposal."[11]

A definition of culture as *labor* and *tactic* may seem strange. However, it is just this sort of consideration that renders the concept dynamic, and that places us in the ongoing struggle, with work to do, rather than within in unending chain of transmission and reproduction.

FOURTH THEME: CULTURE AND SCHOOLING IN TIMES OF WAR

The defense of public education has a strong history in the Latin American Left. The conviction is indebted to the historical link between education and citizenship, inherited from the Enlightenment. The tradition of lay, free, compulsory schooling, forged in the wake of religious conflicts in Europe, imagined a public sphere where ideal citizens might meet as individuals "without culture." Public schools therefore excluded all representations and practices linked to the private lives of individuals, including their religious, linguistic, and cultural specificity. Nevertheless, the public sphere of schooling was never really culture-free. It imposed many subtle cultural meanings and practices identified with the Western, white, masculine world. Schooling privileged practices that endangered the principles of an open public space just as the confessional models had done before. The spread of school patterns associated with a highly codified and fragmented knowledge, alien to local experience, produced the actual or mental desertion of students at all levels. This result warranted the struggle for the recognition of alternative forms of knowledge and ways of learning.

However, a new battlefront emerges today. The educational system, under the guise of recognizing diversity, imposes distinctions codified in cultural and racial terms, and channels them through institutional arrangements. In doing so, it undermines what Guillermo Bonfil[12] identified as "cultural control," the right that social groups have to determine the future of their cultural resources. In some cases, the institution does this openly, with the explicit classification of students. In others, it uses indirect means, such as the everyday discrimination that students "of color" suffer in most classrooms. In educational contexts, all sorts of measures have been designed to organize and to educate difference, ranging from systems of compensatory education to projects for intercultural education designed outside of the communities where they are implemented. The projects have in common the tendency to center attention on the culture of the "others," understood generally as bearers of a system of representations and values that are incompatible with national or dominant culture supposedly transmitted by schools. Opponents of this trend insist, to the contrary, that intercultural education should teach privileged groups about cultural and linguistic diversity, yet in Mexico as elsewhere these proposals have not prospered.

In Latin America, several voices have alerted us to the consequences of the new discourse regarding multicultural or intercultural education. Official policies that center compensatory educational action on cultural difference, though underscoring respect and tolerance, have tended to propitiate practices that are perceived as discriminatory by the students themselves. Furthermore, they individualize rights and trajectories and disregard the spaces of resistance and collective cultural construction. Distinction is institutionalized. Racism openly surfaces where it had previously been covert. Many studies have shown that it is the political use of cultural difference, and not cultural differences *per se*, that contributes to conflict and failure in schools.[13] Perhaps this explains why so many Indian students have chosen to remain "invisible" in schools and universities in order to avoid stigmatization, while others, often claiming a distant relationship, enjoy the growing number of scholarships destined to these groups.

Proposals for intercultural education take on a different meaning in contexts of deep social inequality and power asymmetry. In these situations, diversity cannot be regarded simply as an "encounter of cultures," the euphemism used to avoid speaking of the conquest and colonization of the continent. The dynamic relationship among diverse cultural practices in class societies is not a matter of juxtaposition, nor does it generate a balanced state of *mestizaje*, but rather a contested process in which some meanings and practices are valued while others are discredited. Mutual appropriation and accentuation of cultural contents follow complex paths. The centralized design of curricular components for "other" cultures has often produced cultural stereotypes, or at best, emblematic uses of cultural symbols. For example, centralized programs sometimes endorse written versions of native languages, produced by professionals, which the speakers of those languages cannot recognize as their own. Furthermore, the "intercultural dialogue" in educational spaces often implies imposition and exclusion, and generates real or symbolic violence and suffering.

Alternative projects that hope to be open to cultural diversity must build conditions for autonomous cultural production and control. Where these conditions do exist, they allow multiple processes of cultural appropriation and invention to take place, and generate internal resistance to cultural representations and practices that are considered alien by the communities (Bonfil 1991). In some communities, both in Oaxaca and in the autonomous municipalities in Chiapas, emerging conditions have allowed both a selective integration of cultural and linguistic elements that are still vital in the locality and the appropriation of other forms of knowledge, external in origin but essential to survival. An example will illustrate this approach.

One theme that has become central to alternative educational projects in Mexico is the defense of the corn-based culture common to Mesoamerican peoples. Work with a scaled timeline designed to represent history from the original settlement of America (40,000 years or more ago) to the present involves a linear calendar that may be considered foreign to the Mesoamerican concept of time as circular or recurrent.[14] However it also generates a powerful experience of valuing the magnitude of time and labor invested by the populations that first discovered the continent and domesticated the environment, and that created maize culture over the past 8,000 years. In order to connect the timeline with local identity, the centuries are translated into number of generations of forefathers. This exercise offers a different perspective on the civilizing pretentions of those people who arrived to conquer and colonize the first nations a mere 500 years ago. In this case, scientific knowledge required in the defense of corn-based culture is valued and integrated into the educational process. Yet some alternatives do not require intercultural solutions. Some alternatives prefer to separate the contexts for learning indigenous knowledge, for example, the design of language revitalization practices through intergenerational work, in communities rather than in schools.

These alternative educational practices contest programs that establish, through external criteria, strong "ethnic" distinctions between students and propose cultural contents as perceived from above. These options often confront students with alien and strange representations of their own cultural knowledge and practices. The educational materials produced for these programs generally exclude the history of social conflicts from a local perspective, and of course, leave out all reference to the present-day war against humanity. Rather than imposing external definitions of cultural contents, it is necessary to promote the conditions for autonomous educational work that might allow the selective inclusion of the communities' history and cultural resources from within. It is not an easy task, given the colonization of knowledge in all spaces. Some voices even warn against rendering local cultural knowledge—such as botanical classifications—more visible through intercultural education, as it may also become more vulnerable. The process requires constant alertness to determine the relevance of contents and the best ways of teaching certain contents to children. It presupposes an effective participation of the communities involved in the educational process, and not only their symbolic presence. This sort of project implies a considerable amount of work, in order to transform the manners of creating, representing, and sharing the sort of knowledge needed in the ongoing struggle.

Only this continuous cultural reworking from within can produce an experience of schooling that might resist the exclusion and alienation that has characterized formal education for most young people. In times of war, this sort of autonomous educational labor should be an integral part of resistance.[15] The larger challenge is to preserve the multiplicity of cultural options still available for humanity, and invent new combinations, in order to better construct that other world that is possible.

A frequent objection to these educational initiatives is that they may contribute to further cultural fragmentation. The republican ideal of equal citizens under law, sharing a common language and culture can be vindicated in defense of national state-run schooling. However, it is not clear that the existing systems of schooling are furthering that ideal; in many cases, they seem rather to be leading to new modes of privatization of knowledge. On the other hand, the most valuable efforts of local construction, those assuring the active participation of teachers, parents, youth, and teachers, tend to reconstruct or strengthen local public spheres, where social collectivities may appropriate the meaningful and relevant contents needed to face the neoliberal assault.

Social and cultural movements that take educational work seriously are essential to the survival of humankind. Many alternative cultural projects and actions, both in and out of official schools, have achieved a particular convergence of energy that far surpasses their scarce resources and the limitations imposed by authorities. Their task is to re-create and socialize cultural diversity so that it might serve in the current struggles. The inclusion of many knowledges, cultural languages, and practices in these new educational spaces is a significant contribution to the creation of *un mundo donde quepan muchos mundos*—one world in which many worlds fit.

NOTES

1. Text translated by the author. A previous version was presented at the World Forum on Education, Plenary on Education and Culture, Porto Alegre, Brazil, November 2001.

2. The San Andrés Accords were signed between the EZLN and the Mexican government in 1996, after several months of dialogue that involved the participation, along with the EZLN, of representatives of many Indian groups in the country.

3. Subcomandante Insurgente Marcos, "7 piezas sueltas del rompecabezas mundial," *Chiapas* 5: 117–43. See also: "Perfil," *La Jornada*, México, October 22, 2001.

4. On the Huntington thesis, see Edward W. Said, "El choque de las ignorancias," *La Jornada*, October 10, 2001: 12.

5. On August 13, 2009, the Mexican Supreme Court released on procedural grounds several of the material assassins of forty-five indigenous women, men and children in a chapel in Acteal, Chiapas in 1997. The complicity of government authorities

and paramilitary forces in the massacre was never investigated. The discourse of intra and inter-communal violence served this purpose.

6. The Law for Indigenous Rights, finally approved in 2003, omitted fundamental parts of the San Andrés Accords, including local autonomy.

7. A powerful statement in this direction is Armando Bartra, *El Hombre de Hierro* (Mexico: Universidad Autónoma de la Ciudad de México, 2008).

8. It is important to note that Gramsci's complete *Prison Notebooks* were translated to Spanish in Latin America since the late 1970s (*Cuadernos de la Carcel* (6 volumes), Mexico: Juan Pablos). Likewise, a number of Michel de Certeau's works were translated to Spanish, while still unpublished in English.

9. On Gramsci's concept of culture, see Kate Crehhan, *Gramsci, Culture and Anthropology* (Berkeley: University of California Press, 2002).

10. Michel de Certeau, *La toma de la palabra y otros escritos políticos* (Mexico, Universidad Iberoamericana, 1995), 220. My translation.

11. Ibid., 1995. My translation.

12. Guillermo Bonfil, *Pensar nuestra cultura* (México: Editorial Alianza, 1991).

13. For example, Frederick Erickson, *Talk and Social Theory* (Polity Press, 2004), argues that this mechanism works at the level of micro interactions in the classroom.

14. Normally, in Mexican schools the timeline begins with the Conquest, even though some mention is made of the greatness of Prehispanic civilizations, with no clear notion of their duration and transformations. The inclusion of 35,000 additional years is significant.

15. The intention is to reinforce the pockets of resistance to neoliberalism. See: Subcomandante Insurgente Marcos, "7 piezas sueltas del rompecabezas mundial," *Chiapas 5* (1997): 117–43.

7.

Political Uses of *Interculturalidad:*
Citizenship and Education

By Marcela Tovar Gómez, Mexico

Mexican professor at the National Pedagogical University-Mexico
and educational researcher focusing on education and cultural relevance; coordinator of the Internacional Network of Indigenous
Teacher Educators of the Project on Governability of Indigenous
Peoples. Email: mtovar110480@gmail.com

AFTER THE EUROPEAN INVASION, the inhabitants of Abya Yala[1]
found themselves subjugated for the first time in their history to a
single power that dominated the continent. The new social order
that emerged from the Conquest established some very precise
relationships of dominance that were based in the coexistence of
two distinct hierarchical systems: on the one hand, those of the
conquering group and the indigenous world, each with its own
norms and specific channels of mobility; and on the other, the
system that regulated the relationships of power of the first over
the second. [2]

The various wars of independence from Spain and Portugal
opened up a space for nations to emerge out of this separation, as
part of the dream of liberty and self-determination that supposedly
defined this new order, but without significantly altering the relationships of power that controlled indigenous societies. Out of this
new structure was created the abstract notion of "citizen," which
was defined on the basis of concepts of universality, equality, and in-
dividuality, and which organized the developing society on the basis of a political regimen that was representative in character.[3] This
conception was always separated from its economic dimension.[4]

From this perspective, it would seem that the citizen had already cut ties with his community identity, and that no contradiction existed between the individualization of political participation and communal behaviors, given that the vote became the mechanism whereby a citizen participated in decisions that guaranteed the well-being of the general populace.

Meanwhile, indigenous peoples had transformed their internal practices, responding to the need to survive as cultures and to conserve basic principles of their political systems, such as the existence of their own authorities and government systems. These were the very systems which made it possible for them to palliate the effects of the conditions of inequity and discrimination under which they lived. The indigenous remained trapped in a knot of contradictions, in two respects: a) they were considered citizens of a state that didn't recognize them equally with other sectors of the country; and, b) the government structures and their own exercise of citizenship weren't recognized by the state.[5]

In the case of Mexico, the presence of a large percentage of indigenous in the population allowed the liberal elite to spread the perception that the social and economic backwardness of the society was due to the ignorance of the indigenous, who had to be educated in order to exercise political democracy, which was the extent to which any sector of the population could participate.[6] Not knowing Spanish and not being strong readers or writers was considered a heavy load for the country, resulting in poor advancement in social and economic development.

This discriminatory mindset about the indigenous as a factor in the country's backwardness brought about the most consistent and sustained project of assimilation, in which the Mexican educational system played a major role. When one analyzes the educational policies of this time period, for example, it is surprising that the children of rural communities in the Tsotsil region of Chiapas had to go to the Sunday market dressed as women in order to avoid being caught and carried off involuntarily to boarding schools where they would be taught the Spanish language, as well reading and writing, in this way violently uprooting them from their communities. This happened in the decade of 1960–1970.[7] These actions show the very deep root of indigenous identity in the face of a state that, in this same time period, considered them "Mexican citizens" with all due rights and yet opposed their traditional forms of resistance based in their communal social and political organization.

The way in which the Mexican state has structured its relationship with its citizens obscures crucial issues necessary to understand the complex and inequitable relationship between the state and its indigenous peoples. First, it makes invisible "the extraordinary capacity of indigenous communities to use a liberal category like 'citizen' to defend themselves from the liberal state and its pretention to destroy community identity."[8] Resistance to domination has had as one of its main pillars the *strategic behavior* of the indigenous communities before the state, in which they adopted a differentiated usage of the liberal concept of citizenship, responding to the challenge involved in breaking their connection with the past and transforming their local communities into a source of political rights, firmly tied to their territory and their identities as original peoples.

Taking advantage of legislation having to do with municipalities, indigenous localities legitimated themselves and their forms of government before the state, although they have never been recognized as government structures or decision-making groups with a distinct notion of citizen obligations and rights. Where this unique treatment is seen most clearly is in the justice system and in the criteria for belonging to a community. These unique government systems have permitted the maintenance and also the transformation of indigenous identities, and at the same time, they have been a source of strength to resist various programs of assimilation imposed by the state.

Within this framework of contradictions derived from the existence of a dominant regime that makes use of all the means at its disposal to destroy the communities and the authentic government systems of indigenous peoples, for forty years education proposals have been put forth whose central concept is *interculturalidad*, and these have been taken up as state policies since the 1990s. However, it is difficult to accept this agenda as distinct from the persistent campaigns to teach the Spanish language (*castellanizar*) and acculturate, primarily because the new ideas are developed by the same institutions that had as their mission to eradicate the indigenous cultures.

Because of this, a central question that needs to be answered is: "what does *interculturalidad* mean for the education offered to indigenous peoples?"

Designing an intercultural proposal implies, in the first place, the recognition, on an equal level, of the plurality of cultures present in all educational spaces.

But it is of major importance to distinguish between the liberal concept of equality and equity. Equity assumes equal conditions and opportunities; it implies taking into account the social determinants in a situation and how these are distributed, in terms of their limits or responsibilities, among the distinct sectors of society. Access to education is a right of every citizen, but factors and dimensions inherent in the situation of discrimination suffered by indigenous peoples determine the share of the country's educational goods and services that indigenous schools receive.

An intercultural perspective implies taking into account the cultures that share a common space. But the way in which they should be taken into account is complex when one tries to put this into practice. More than anything, from the present framework of homogeniety derived from a neoliberal concept of education which permeates the ends and goals of the Mexican school (that is, trying to generate products by investing the least, now that the main indicator no longer is human welfare, but rather something concerning the relationship between cost and benefit), the first, human welfare, is measured as an "expense," and the second, benefit, is understood to be that which a person should know and know how to do to hold a job in the labor market. It has been a long time since the holistic development of persons was an end of education, even in the realm of public declarations. But this also has to do with students and teachers who focus their attention on technology, presuming the value and neutrality of its ends and social uses.[9]

When it comes to implementing an intercultural focus, the national education system tries to "make people aware" of the indigenous cultures, and to "rescue them," since "they are being lost." Now, one way to draw closer to knowledge of indigenous cultures has been through the oral tradition, which is "rescued" (that is, written down) in schoolwork assigned to indigenous children. However, much of the time these accounts are collected from oral narratives as homework assignments that the teacher gives to the children. Often, when these are written down in Spanish, their narrative structure is "adjusted" to that of Spanish. These stories, decontextualizeded from their cultural meaning or significance, are accepted as testimonies that reveal the thinking or worldview of indigenous peoples. At the same time, it is supposed that these stories are a faithful categorization of the "oral tradition" of indigenous peoples, and they are interpreted based on cultural schemes and structures foreign to those that authentically organize both their content and their profound significance.

In a focus in which intermingling in multicultural contexts basically presupposes the eradication of the discriminatory thinking that penetrates society, designing an intercultural educational project implies, first of all, *contextualizing* the proposal, *situating* it in the environment where it will be developed, and responding to the specific requirements of the culture where it will be implemented. In other words, designing, executing, and evaluating it in terms of local knowledge, with participation by all relevant individuals and while searching for real empowerment for all actors involved.[10] On the other hand, it is untenable to think that *interculturalidad* implies drawing close to indigenous cultures, while at the same time setting aside the possibility that the mestizo culture will find in school activities a space for reflection. It would be valuable to reflect on what the mestizo culture "is losing," as well as on the search for mechanisms to "rescue it."

The discourse about intercultural education is present in the national education system in different ways. In the programs of education for peace and education on values offered as part of teacher preparation programs, "diversity," "*interculturalidad*," and "the fight against discrimination" are terms that are constantly confused. In official government schools, the term "*interculturalidad*" is present in the rhetoric. Intercultural middle and high schools, universities, and normal schools have developed where efforts have centered on probing the "prior knowledge" or cultural knowledge of the students, since most of the professors in these institutions are not indigenous, they don't speak the languages of the students, and in the majority of cases they haven't received an education that permits them to understand what constitutes *interculturalidad*. Even if the teachers were indigenous, they must move beyond the colonized pedagogical discourse which welcomed them into the institutions of teacher preparation, and which prepares them to "bring civilization" to indigenous peoples. [11]

The perspective in programs and proposals of intercultural education has centered on valuing indigenous cultures, and specifically, on bringing students information about these cultures. Very often it is suggested that indigenous students themselves should be responsible for researching and reflecting on their culture, while the lesson plans submerge them in the traditional, "scientific" concepts of *the* pedagogy.

In this way, the possibility is lost that a sense of astonishment upon encountering the Other would permit the construction and deepening of values related to an appreciation of diversity.[12] The discourse used emphasizes the rich plurality of nations that conform the country; celebrations, costumes and dress, food, music, and, rarely, history are analyzed. The past is narrated as a sequence of specific events that display courage, beliefs, and stereotypes, in which indigenous peoples appear as societies condemned to disappear before the civilizing impulse that resulted from the invasion. The historical perspective of the winners is recreated in minute detail: it was the beliefs, prophecies, or omens that determined the attitude of the indigenous as they faced the invader. After narrating the battle that drove the invaders from Tenochtitlan, they recreated "the sad night" of Hernan Cortes, following an analytical tradition of emphasizing the psychology of historical events. [13]

If teachers had wanted to offer students some other type of information, they wouldn't find it, because what is at hand in the majority of cases consists of texts that reproduce this stereotype. The information that exists about the indigenous cultures of today is scarce, fragmented, casuistic, and written in academic language.

Society doesn't have access to trustworthy information that could reverse these much repeated stereotypes. Above all, a naïve, well-intentioned approach to valuing and rescuing cultures has resulted in prioritizing the systemization of indigenous "stories, myths and legends" as a way to get to know the indigenous cultures.

A simple review of the free government textbooks that children throughout the country receive is sufficient: hardly any images testify to the presence of indigenous peoples. The children in indigenous schools, many of them beginning speakers of Spanish, are introduced to the world of reading and producing texts with stories like "The Gnome" or "Captain Hook." Different studies of educational materials document that the indigenous are presented as people of the past: the historical Indian is the one who *had* a culture and an identity before the European invasion, but these disappeared when colonial rule began. However, the complex processes derived from the historic commingling of distinct cultures show how one cultural identity has been imposed on the other, generating inequitable and discriminatory relationships that recently are being questioned.

In Mexico, the educational processes directed toward indigenous peoples never were equitably conceived; the educational offer for indigenous peoples has been and continues to be compensatory in nature. Time and again, education reforms are worked out that propose to close the gap between what society gives to its citizens and that which is offered to members of indigenous communities, without really devising significant actions intended to achieve this goal.

There are very few social spaces in which equity and cultural relevance effectively permeate the indigenous education proposals that are elaborated by the state. In the majority of cases, the educational proposal is formulated assuming the stereotype of an injured, victimized population, from which base the educational criteria to be applied are decided. In this way, in response to the demand by indigenous communities for primary schools, "indigenous" schools were devised according to the critieria of education authorities, and were poorly equipped with the most minimum of supplies. An education strategy was designed in which cultural relevance, the use of the indigenous language, or the content to be taught, are rigidly normalized and carefully structured to support the use of the obligatory textbooks. Controlled by the school system, teachers either rebel or are coopted, and "supervisors" are held responsible to constrain classroom teaching within official limits. In the educational program offered to indigenous peoples, small concessions stand out whose possibilities to bring to fruition a culturally relevant education are infamous, such as allowing the teacher to adjust the academic content to respond to the needs and educational context of the school community. However, the teachers are prepared—if they have been prepared—in schemes in which the complex problem of the use of the maternal language as the language of instruction, or curricular design expressed through content and materials drawn from indigenous thought, are nonexistent.

In Abya Yala, increasingly systematic and consistent efforts are being made by the indigenous to define their own educational systems. This perspective currently includes high school and university education, in which professionals prepared in state universities find a place to reflect on the content and preparation needed by indigenous peoples. In this way, indigenous universities, indigenous and intercultural universities, and intercultural universitites are multiplying, displaying nuances of difference in their design that result from arduous indigenous struggles, negotiations, and the situation facing indigenous peoples. Realities such as the need to reflect on the indigenous culture itself, their insecurity and lack of experience, and the many deficiencies in their own preparation are evident in the indigenous proposals being brought forth. At the same time, these proposals are boxed in by bureaucratic requirements for which the only conceptual guideline, the national curriculum, or dominant curricular currents, or the prestige of certain educational or conceptual foci, weigh in as criteria that are used to discredit, critique, or suppress these indigenous proposals.

And underlying this complex problematic, programs of intercultural education and the preparation of intercultural teachers are multiplying.

Interculturalidad as a category accepts all the definitions and purposes that the powerful choose to assign it. It is used in official pronouncements that extol the educational successes of the government. It serves to point out deficiencies or advances in the education of indigenous peoples. What is forgotten, however, in a country whose diversity and cultural riches are a privilege, is that inequity and the imposition of cultural models that are foreign to indigenous identity can't be taken as the beginning and the end of this process.

The possibility of developing their own, authentic knowledge and thought cannot happen unless the situation of inequity that defines and controls the relations between the dominant and subordinate cultures is resolved. However, such a resolution depends upon the concrete realization of their own space, in which indigenous intellectuals decide which are the themes and perspectives that interest them, what they are interested in conserving from their own cultures and how to do that, as well as what appropriations from the foreign culture they consider to be legitimate and compatible with their own structures of thought, with their values and worldview. These things cannot be achieved until there are claims made to open up the political, social, and pedagogical space that indigenous educators require in order to raise the questions that they consider relevant and the solutions that are relevant to their lives, considering their identity and the complex demands that they face in being part of two worlds: their own and the one constructed by neoliberal policies. This moment hasn't yet arrived, although initiatives, reflections, and proposals are already emerging that express a new conception of what education should be in a country committed to *interculturalidad*.

REFERENCES

Alleyne, G. A. 2002. "La equidad y la meta de salud para todos." *Revista Panamericana de Salud Pública*11: 5-6 (May/June) http://www.scielosp.org/scielo.php?script=sci_arttext&pid=S1020-49892002000500003.

Annino, A., L. Castro Leiva and F.-X. Guerra. 1999. *De los imperios a las naciones, Iberoamérica*. Zaragoza: Iber Caja.

Araujo Grijalva, S. 2006. "Reto rural, un proyecto con pertinencia cultural." *Alli Kausay*, Folleto temático de la COSUDE en el Ecuador 8 (November 2006). http://www.cosude.org.ec.

Guerra, F.-X. 1999. "El soberano y su reino: Reflexiones sobre la génesis del ciudadano en América Latina." H. Sábato, *Ciudadanía política y formación de las naciones. Perspectivas políticas de América Latina*. México: Fondo de Cultura Económica.

Rozat Dupeyront, G. 2002. *Indios imaginarios e indios reales en los relatos de la conquista de México*. México: Universidad Veracruzana.

Political Uses of Interculturalidad

Santiz, A. 2005. "Lectoescritura en Lengua Materna." Unpublished.

Serrera, R. M. 1994. "Sociedad estamental y sistema colonial." A. Annino, L. Castro Leiva & F.-X. Guerra. *De los imperios a las naciones: Iberoamérica.* Zaragoza, España; Iber Caja.

NOTES

1. Indigenous name for the Americas.
2. Serrera, R. M. "Sociedad estamental y sistema colonial," In A. Annino, L. Castro Leiva y F.-X. Guerra, *De los imperios a las naciones, Iberoamérica.* (Zaragoza: Iber Caja, 1994), 47.
3. The concept of "neighbor" implies the existence of hierarchies, and therefore, of differences, and a corporate or communitarian concept of the social. When substituted by "citizen," which implies that "all individuals are equal," it leads the society toward homogenization. Chomsky points out: "State formation, by force mostly, has tried to impose national education standards in order to turn people into similar individuals. This happens everywhere... In the United States, for example, public education as far back as the late nineteenth century was primarily socialization of independent farmers to turn them into a workforce of interchangeable parts." (Chomsky interview 2004, this volume.) For the concept of "neighbor," see François-Xavier Guerra, "El soberano y su reino. Reflexiones sobre la génesis del ciudadano en América Latina." In Hilda Sábato, *Ciudadanía política y formación de las naciones. Perspectivas políticas de América Latina.* (México: FCE, 1999), 40–42.
4. This connection between politics and the economy has been acquiring new forms, but it continues to be one of the invisible intersections of power: "One of the effects of neoliberalism, and it's well understood, is to reduce democracy. Even just freeing financial flows. It was perfectly well understood by the economists who designed the post-WWII economic system, John Maynard Keynes, for example, that if you have free financial movement, if you have no constraints on finance, on the free flow of capital, governments are not going to be able to carry out social democratic policies." (Noam Chomsky, in the second interview by L. Meyer, 2007).
5. The new social movements to which the indigenous communities have committed their efforts in the last few years form part of the growing demand for their rights; these struggles are most visible in Bolivia. See Chomsky (2007b). Greeting to the Second National Congress of Indigenous and Intercultural Education. Oaxaca, México. October 25, 2007.
6. Guerra, op. cit.
7. Ana Santiz, A. "Lectoescritura en Lengua Materna" (unpublished manuscript, 2005).

8. Annino et al., 1999, 63–64.

9. In this way, the Alliance for Educational Quality (ACE), proposed by the Secretary of Public Education to implement education reform, proposes as one of its priority principles the access to education through computers, which suggests that they consider the ability to skillfully use technologies of information and communication to be central in the formation of children, or in evaluations that compare the achievement of students. However, "Education is not to pass exams... It is about having the ability to think, create, explore, be creative." Noam Chomsky, interviewed by L. Meyer (2007).

10. S. Araujo Grijalva, "Reto rural, un proyecto con pertinencia cultural,"*Alli Kausay*, Folleto temático de la COSUDE en el Ecuador 8 (November 2006) At http://www.cosude.org.ec.

11. Fortunately, community loyalties and values are part of the system of ethics of many indigenous teachers and of a growing number of mestizos who work in indigenous regions. However, they don't have the concepts and pedagogical knowledge that permits them to rethink their reality from their own perspective.

13. This involves, in more or less general terms, influencing the homogenizing structures of thought that are socially constructed in modern societies. It is important to highlight that a double movement operates in these processes: the "foreigner" discovers a new way of seeing the world that was always there but was hidden. The "native" looks at his or her own culture from a perspective that attempts to break the colonized thinking that accompanies homogenized thought; you can not see diversity as if it were homogeneous without hiding or devaluing the Other.

12. Rozat became interested in how the chroniclers in their writings analyze and account for these "omens" in which the invaders present themselves as gods. The victory of the Spaniards, according to this discourse, is due to the decadence of the pre-Columbian societies, that they did not know how, or simply could not, combat the Spanish invaders. Given the stories of the impact that these omens had on the attitude of the Nahuas, the question that remains unanswered is, how it is possible that peoples who had a profound knowledge of celestial phenomena, of regularities and their effects on nature, could have determined the future of their peoples based on happenings that they could have predicted with the tools and knowledge available to them? See: Guy Rozat Dupeyront, *Indios imaginarios e indios reales en los relatos de la conquista de México* (Mexico: Universidad Veracruzana, 2002).

8.

Politicization of *Comunalidad* and the Demand for Autonomy

By Gunther Dietz, Mexico

Anthropologist of German decent, professor and researcher of intercultural studies at the Universidad Veracruzana in Jalapa, Mexico, with previous research in Germany, Spain, Denmark, and Belgium, and various Mexican states. Email: guntherdietz@gmail.com

IT MAY BE PREMATURE to trumpet "the end of capitalism as we know it" as did British newspaper the *Independent* in March of 2008 (Blond, 2000), but perhaps we can begin to think of the end of globalization as we know and endure it. For decades, the keen analyses of Noam Chomsky, far from falling into the fallacies of automatism and the historic inevitability of globalization, have unceasingly pointed out those who have been pushing the deregulation of markets—those who previously clamored for the privatization of earnings from international financial transactions are the same ones who now are pushing for the state to assume the losses caused by this neoliberal dogma.

As Chomsky has stressed since the 1980s and especially throughout the 1990s, globalizing forces not only abandon society and delegitimize the state, they end up requiring arrangements that are increasingly authoritarian and not at all "liberal" to protect themselves from their own market. (Chomsky 1995) In this context, Lois Meyer's two interviews with Chomsky not only reveal the consequences that these deregulating processes have brought about in the field of education. They also illustrate the difficulties inherent in thinking, designing, and implementing educational alternatives that reconstruct what is "public" in schools. When the state finds itself in the very hands of those who are commercializing, outsourcing, and/or privatizing its functions, the ambiguity of its role as a normative, legitimate force is evident.

This makes even more attractive, if possible, the proposition of *comunalidad* developed by the indigenous and teacher movements in Oaxaca and articulated by, among others, Díaz Gómez (1992), Maldonado (2002, 2004a, 2004b), and Meyer (2004). This concept is understood as "the way of life of the original peoples of Oaxaca, shared by those peoples who came from the womb of Mesoamerica" (Maldonado 2004a:24), constituting, according to this author, not an immutable essence or cultural content, but rather a local form of organization from which education and the school must be conceived.

COMMUNITY IN INDIGENOUS STRUGGLES

Not only in Oaxaca, but in other parts of Mexico as well, indigenous movements and organizations have sought gradually to free themselves as much from the state's tradition of co-opting trade unionism as from manipulation by other non-indigenous actors. Throughout a difficult and painful process, the so-called "ethnic awakening" has enabled groups, organizations, and movements that have arisen from indigenous peoples to defy national institutions every time these have trampled on indigenous claims for rights or cultural and linguistic concessions. They have done this to recover their political and territorial autonomy. Simultaneously, as Chomsky reminds us, the progressive parceling out and privatizing of communally held indigenous lands and the rapid submersion of their subsistence economies by the cash economy threaten the very social and territorial foundations of indigenous peoples. Since the 1980s, in order to counter these trends, new movements at the local, regional, and national levels have emerged that struggle to decolonize the political sphere and recover boundaries of territorial, cultural, and political self-determination.

Politicization of Comunalidad *and the Demand for Autonomy*

In analyzing the evolution of indigenous movements in Mexico and their struggles for recognition of indigenous rights, it is worth mentioning, first of all, that the origins of this evolution can be traced in the national context of the history of relations between the state-party and rural civil society. These relations are structured out of two political traditions whose foundations date back to the Mexican Revolution: on the one hand, the "agrarianist" tradition of agrarian land reform dominated by the nation-state and its corporate, organizational networks, which are openly contradictory to the communalist, Zapatista legacy of the Ayala Plan;[1] and on the other hand, the "indigenist" tradition of development and integration policies specifically designed for indigenous regions and communities.[2]

Starting from this historic context of the Mexican nation-state, it is possible to explain the central role of the community: first, in determining the content of the claims made, and second, in the forms of organization developed by the major indigenous actors who have emerged, especially since the 1970s, in response to the consecutive failures of the state's "agrarianist" and "indigenistic" approaches to dealing with the "Indian problem" in Mexico (Esteva 1994).

By comparing semi-governmental, guild-like indigenous organizations with independent organizations and their respective struggles and "ethnic" versus "classist" claims, we are able to point out various factors that together have enabled the emancipation of rural organizations from their governmental and/or institutional dependence and the development of their own forms of organization (Dietz 2005): the crisis of the agrarian corporatism of the Institutional Revolutionary Party (PRI) as the state political party, which intensified throughout the modernization of Mexican agriculture; the failure of indigenism as a program to integrate ethnic minorities into the Mexican nation-state; the emergence of an independent peasant movement that is taking control of new areas and experimenting with new forms of organization; and the transition of these new organizations away from the struggle for land towards the struggle for control of natural resources and the production process in its entirety.

In the 1980s and with a marked increase at the start of the 1990s, both the semi-official guild organizations (ANPIBAC, CNPI, etc.) and the independent peasant organizations experienced an existential crisis. Official recognition that indigenism had failed as a means for the ethnic homogenization of the rural population, together with the withdrawal of the neoliberal state from agrarian and agricultural policy, meant the loss of the institutional counterpart for both kinds of organizations. At the same time, the organizations also lost purpose and legitimacy in the eyes of their own rank and file. In this context, both the indigenous teacher associations and the "classic" peasant movement found themselves marginalized by the appearance on the scene of a new kind of organization.

In response to the withdrawal of the state and attempts to privatize communal lands, "coalitions" made up of indigenous communities from one or more ethnic groups emerged in distinct indigenous regions of México; new regional organizations, sometimes mono-ethnic and other times pluri-ethnic, were born from within these coalitions. It is precisely these "alliances of convenience" among indigenous communities that declare themselves "sovereign" before governmental institutions and claim their traditional indigenous law *la costumbre*—which will complement their political struggle to achieve communal and regional autonomy by adding development projects they themselves have developed (Dietz 1999, Maldonado 2002).

ETHNOGENESIS[3] AND INDIGENOUS CITIZENSHIP

Since the 1990s, relations between the Mexican state and national society, as well as between the non-indigenous mestizo majority and indigenous minority-majorities, are being redefined, starting with these new ethnic-regional actors, of which the Zapatista

National Liberation Army constitutes only the most visible example. The program of autonomy subscribed to by distinct coalitions of communities is self-conceived to be the answer to the disappearance of the state as the principal protagonist of economic and social development in indigenous regions and as an example of the evident failure of the welfare and indigenistic policies of corporate control. Through the struggle for autonomy, the coalition of communities is gradually transforming itself, not only into an important entity of mediation, but also into a new level of political articulation that is inserting itself between the communities and the state.

In short, it is noteworthy that the new indigenous actors that are emerging and consolidating in Mexico in recent decades cannot be reduced to mere "victims" of neoliberalism or transitional epiphenomena of the accelerated pace of economic and technological globalization that the country has been exposed to by the governing elites over this period of time. Above all, since the unilateral cancellation by the neoliberal state of the old, post-revolutionary pact, indigenous communities are re-situating themselves and redefining their position with respect to the nation-state and the mestizo society via three profound transformations. First, in the course of the infrastructural integration championed by the policies of the indigenists and developers, a new stratum of society sprang up and took on innovative, "hinge-like" functions. Both product and producers of cultural hybridization, the most active and also deliberate members of the communities, the young generation of teachers and the former proponents of indigenist policies who now were re-communalized, began restructuring the community's internal forms of organization, thanks to their bicultural knowledge and urban-rural networks.

Second, in order to defend the traditional rights and shared interests of the indigenous communities affected by the cancellation of the "social contract," these new hybrid actors "ethnicized" their demands while simultaneously articulating them at a supra-local level. This shift towards ethnicity shared on a broader level signified a break with the localist tradition that had been imposed by the Spanish colonizers more than five hundred years earlier.

Finally, taking advantage of the simultaneous trend toward administrative decentralization, the struggle for indigenous rights is not centered on the contents of those rights, but mainly on constitutional, legal, and political reforms as prerequisites for the formulation and practice of those rights. This "right to have rights" (Hannah Arendt, cf. Benhabib 2005), symbolizing the definitive assumption of citizenship by indigenous peoples, now has materialized in the notion of "autonomy," which would imply the recognition of communities as legal and political subjects with their own identities and plans, no longer to be subsumed under the old nationalistic and homogenizing project of *mestizaje* ("de-indianizing").

The confluence of these simultaneous processes of ethnogenesis, cultural hybridization, and indigenous *comunalidad* triggers a novel dynamic of transitions: from the local to the regional or even to the transnational, from the politics of welfare to constitutional claims, from the politics of recognition to the politics of self-development and self-determination. This marks a decisive shift in the history of indigenous movements in Mexico: the innovative policies and practices initiated in the 1990s of the twentieth century have left behind the historic isolation of the indigenous community. Despite setbacks in legal reform, a local sense of belonging as well as the participation and assumption of citizenship by the communities through networks, alliances, and ethno-regional and Zapatista platforms, will end up finally forcing the Mexican state to fully recognize the individual and collective rights of its indigenous citizens and their forms of organization.

NOTES

1. A document in which Zapata denounced President Francisco I. Madero for his

perceived betrayal of the revolutionary ideals and set out his vision of land reform, devolving land back to community ownership.
2. A post-revolutionaly public policy whose intent was to support a process of integrating local indigenous cultures within the Mexican nation.
3. Emergence of a new ethnic group identity.

9.

Democracy and Changes in Latin American Education: Lessons from the Guatemalan and Bolivian Indigenous Cases

By *Luis Enrique López, Guatemala*

Peruvian sociolinguist and educator, presently working in Guatemala, with extensive professional experience with indigenous peoples in the development of programs of intercultural bilingual education. Email: lelopezh@yahoo.com

AS PROFESSOR CHOMSKY POINTS out in the interviews included in this volume, the last two decades have brought about unprecedented changes in Latin America, mostly as a result of the active political participation of indigenous organizations and leaders. Such changes are closely related to events in the field of education, and especially in the education of Latin America's indigenous peoples.

Even though by 1940, representatives of the Latin American states gathered in Pátzcuaro, México, already knew that the education of indigenous peoples could not continue to be neglected and ignored as it had been up to that time, it was only when attention to education became a demand of the indigenous movement at the end of the 1970s and beginning of the 1980s that the states truly began to work more carefully and seriously toward an alternative education for indigenous peoples.

In fact, the still young Latin American democracies today face the need to respond to the resurgence—even the insurgence—of a new and active social actor: the indigenous movement. With increasing strength since the 1980s, the national indigenous issue has become more and more evident. Indigenous claims have moved beyond the exclusive domain of ethnic interest and daily necessities experienced by Latin American indigenous peoples, to concerns about issues of *national* nature and scope, such as, for example, those related to the rational and sustainable use of natural resources, the role and operation of the state, and the current model of development and its sustainability. From this holistic perspective, the indigenous movement also questions the meaning of democracy and even the nation-state model that this part of the world adopted from post-revolutionary Europe more than two hundred years ago.

Throughout this whole process and despite the deficiencies that still characterize it, education has played a fundamental role. More often than not, traditional politicians who represent the hegemonic sectors must interact with indigenous leaders and negotiators, who usually state clearly their demands and proposals for the present and future of their societies, as well as for the countries they inhabit, due to their increasingly solid formation and intercultural vocation. This is due to the fact that, from its beginnings, the Latin American indigenous movement identified education as part of its agenda of demands.

It could not have been otherwise, since lack of access to the educational system constituted one of the most serious obstacles to the advancement of the indigenous as citizens of those same states, which practically ignored them. Through education, the indigenous tried both to achieve citizenship and to transform it. To do so, they felt it was indispensable to know the language and culture of the hegemonic sectors to socially acceptable levels of mastery. But this demand for education quickly moved beyond the initial plane to demand the right to maintain their own languages and ancestral cultures. This is how intercultural bilingual education (IBE) as we know it today was born.

In Bolivia this movement began its gestation in 1982, at a time when the country returned to its path toward democracy in a climate of greater participation by civil society in state matters, and when the indigenous movement was then led by Aymara leaders, who made their voices heard and claimed their right to be different (López 2005). In the case of Guatemala, the process emerged more through international cooperation, in a context where the country was submerged in an internal ethnic and racial war. At that time, even talking about indigenousness and suggesting the possibility of using an indigenous language in education or in daily communication in Guatemala was considered subversive, likely leading to military repression (Richards & Richards 1996). At the beginning of the 1980s, while in Bolivia the indigenous began to be recognized as valid voices and actors on political matters, in Guatemala the Mayans were persecuted, and those who could left the country to avoid the risk of physical extermination. The more substantive changes in Guatemala would arrive only in 1995 and 1996, when after thirty years of violence, through pressure by the international community, the Guatemalan army and the guerrilla movement signed a lasting peace accord. The peace agreements included various indigenous demands, and the Guatemalan state committed itself to a series of structural reforms directed toward recognition of the historical multicultural character of this country where the majority of the population is indigenous.

Only Bolivia is comparable to Guatemala on the continent, because only these two countries still maintain indigenous majorities. In Bolivia, according to official census data, more than 60 percent of the population is indigenous, and corresponding data from Guatemala report more than 40 percent. However, in both cases, although more in the Guatemalan case, it is estimated that the indigenous population is larger, perhaps by as much as 20 percent in both cases. This is because, on the one hand, the indigenous themselves feel the need to hide their real ethnic and linguistic affiliations, among other reasons to defend themselves from the racism and discrimination that has yet to be overcome, products of the entrenched colonial system still in existence. On the other hand, state officials and census takers do whatever they can to make sure the number of indigenous decreases with each count. Still motivated by the ideal of one mestizo nation and the construction of *only one* national culture, these nation-states continue to conceive of their socio-cultural and linguistic diversity as a problem, and even as a threat to their national unity and security.

Ideas such as those outlined in the previous paragraph continue to hold sway in sectors of Bolivian society that today feel themselves displaced by the indigenous insurgence and its arrival to power, and also and especially among the white-mestizo minority that wielded power in Guatemala at least since the beginning of the Republic in 1821. The paths taken by the indigenous peoples in these two apparently very similar yet still very different countries have differed, and today these two nation-states present us with very distinct contexts.

In Bolivia, the indigenous have assumed power and today they compete for hegemony and real power with the white-mestizo minority, grounding their struggle in a cultural revolution that transcends the purely political, in order to place the debate on the epistemological plane and relocate indigenous knowledge, culture, and languages on the national stage and across the country, including predominantly Spanish-speaking areas. These efforts disturb the white-mestizo minority for whom all that is Western or of Hispanic ancestry is considered "normal." In contrast, in Guatemala the control of power and cultural hegemony remains with the white-mestizo ethnic-racial minority, which has always held power. The indigenous move in the interstices of the dominant system and take advantage of the small cracks that open up in the iron walls of power in order to cautiously and timidly advance their proposals and place the indigenous cosmovision onto the national stage. However, in both countries the struggle today is epistemic, raising questions about the ontology of school knowledge, as well as of university knowledge. The indigenous peoples of Guatemala and Bolivia want their knowledge, cosmo-visions and ways of life to be recognized and accepted as systems, not as passing phenomena. As can be imagined, such a situation has serious implications for the education of all the inhabitants of these countries, not only for the indigenous populations. The pedagogical discourse that began with the reclamation of their languages and the recognition of these as valid languages for instruction later developed into the demand for the right to a curriculum that includes their own cultural elements. Today this demand encompasses the national education effort as a whole. Both countries aspire to and search for national curricula that take the matrix of native ancestral knowledge as their starting point, from there opening up to the world. For reasons mentioned previously, Bolivian indigenous are closer to achieving this goal than their counterparts in Guatemala.

In Bolivia, a new constitution recognizes the pluri- or multi-national character of the country. An effort to revise the current education law has begun by radicalizing the concept of intercultural bilingual education inherited from the original struggles and indigenous proposals of the 1980s and 1990s, projecting it from a different epistemological and political foundation, one which now calls for decolonization. Based on this new foundation, education is proposed to be both intracultural and intercultural, intracultural to reaffirm that which is inherently indigenous, and intercultural to permit dialogue with what today is seen and reconsidered as alien. Unlike two decades ago, these proposals are not intended to apply only to indigenous peoples but to the country as a whole, since their goal is to overcome the colonialist mental structures that affect everyone, and simultaneously to fight the entrenched and enduring racism and the discriminatory structure of society. Education is seen as both a crucial sphere and an efficient tool for bringing forth a new kind of citizenship—an ethnically differentiated citizenship and/or an intercultural citizenship—and for constructing the new multi-nation state required by the political constitution that was approved by the majority of the population in a referendum held early in 2009. It is clear, then, that the indigenous in Bolivia reject the alleged neutrality of education and today give it a political meaning distinct from that which it was assigned since the creation of the Republic, that is, moving away from assimilation into cultural pluralism.

It is worth noting, even briefly, that the notion of *interculturalidad* in Bolivia was adopted and adapted to the Bolivian context with active indigenous participation already early in the 1980s. However, early on, the notion of *interculturalidad* was taken beyond education, placing it in the domain of national policy, slowly extracting from the state more spaces for its application. As many indigenous Bolivian leaders reiterate, *interculturalidad* implies the transformation of social and political relations, and finally access to power (López 2005).

In Guatemala, progress on this process is slower, since the indigenous peoples have not achieved a comparable level of political advancement to that of their Bolivian counterparts. Furthermore, the power structure has adopted and assumed a neoliberal multicultural position with a politically correct discourse that succeeds in distracting and immobilizing a wide sector of the indigenous population (Hale 2007). Few indigenous leaders expose and denounce the neoliberal multiculturalism that takes priority in Guatemala or refuse to play the game, accepting instead the many positions that the Guatemalan state has opened up through what is known as "little indigenous windows" and as "permissible Indian" spaces. While in Bolivia the indigenous have advanced to the degree that they now fill positions of power as protagonists, in Guatemala indigenous people continue to fill only the positions permitted them by the white-mestizo power structure. In Guatemala, what has taken hold is the discourse of tolerance for that which is indigenous, but not yet true mutual respect and equal political participation and co-existence, beyond the slots for the "permitted Indian" (Hale 1984).

In that context, as many as three models share the education scene in Guatemala. The strongest and most supported by the state, both politically and technically, is the assimilationist model, which aims at what is euphemistically called the *integration* of the indigenous peoples into the mainstream of the dominant Castilian-speaking culture. The second is the bilingual model, based in an early transitional vision that prioritizes the use of the ancestral language only in the first three or four grades of elementary school and does not allow for a curricular transformation from below, that is, from the indigenous cultural and epistemological matrix. The third is the Mayan, or by extension indigenous, model that seeks first to strengthen indigenous wisdom, culture, and language, so that these serve as the foundation on which to approach Western knowledge. The first two receive support from the state, although to a greater degree the first one, and both share the same goal, expressed in mottos such as the "pride of being Guatemalan," pointing toward a single, homogenous Guatemala. In contrast, the third model is grounded in the contributions of local communities and international support, and is the only one that truly projects itself as an intercultural option, though at times it, too, falls into essentialist poses. Such essentialism, however, could well be strategic, given the adverse contexts in which it develops.

Although Mayan education is by nature bilingual and intercultural, strategically its spokespersons prefer to highlight the Mayan character of their education as a way to distance themselves from the state-run model of Indigenous Bilingual Intercultural Education (IBIE). While the Ministry of Education sees IBIE as a technical and pedagogical proposal, for indigenous leaders and organizations the same IBIE is primarily a political proposal that allows them, not only to give visibility to their culture, but also to construct new mental structures to overcome colonization. This is why, from the indigenous view, it is essential that parents and community leaders be actively involved in the development and implementation of education. While for the Ministry what matters is that children learn to read, write, and solve basic arithmetic operations, for the indigenous, it is also important that those children develop a critical awareness, reconstruct their history, and appropriate a set of social and life competencies that allows them to overcome the subjugated and subaltern condition to which they have been reduced. In short, we are faced with two distinct interpretations of educational quality that, still to this day, have not been reconciled.

The truth is that in both Bolivia and Guatemala the educational services available to indigenous students require urgent improvement, precisely so that education contributes to social emancipation, as indigenous leaders propose. Many indigenous students achieve only meager results, and then they confront situations that they have a very difficult time resolving with the limited competencies the official educational system develops in them.

In order to bring about an improvement in indigenous education, it is necessary to transform teachers as well as the teaching profession. On the one hand, teachers must overcome their status as technicians who apply that which technocratic elites in the Ministry of Education decide should occur in education, and instead convert themselves into true professionals who respond creatively to the specific needs of each community and each context in which they have to act. But, on the other hand, they must also overcome training they have received which has prepared them to be functionaries of the state, aligned with the assimilationist vision and mission that Latin American states have adopted. In other words, what is needed is not only professionals, but also organic intellectuals aligned with the indigenous cause and with the social emancipation of their peoples.

This becomes even more imperative when we consider indigenous teachers. In Guatemala, for example, there are more than 18,000 indigenous teachers (from a total of about 120,000), working in mainly rural schools where the majority of students are also indigenous. However, although they are indigenous and in most cases speakers of an indigenous language, they prefer an all-Castilian education. Products themselves of a conformist and homogenizing education, many indigenous teachers undoubtedly feel trapped between their own training and the politically correct discourse of the Guatemalan state that promotes bilingual education, even when it is only transitional.

As was said above, an improvement is urgently needed in the quality of what occurs in classrooms and schools attended by indigenous students. Equally necessary is an effort to transform initial teacher education and the continuing professional education of all in-service teachers. But in order to make professional teacher education transformational, it must locate technical and pedagogical aspects within the larger political context of the civil, political, cultural, and linguistic rights of indigenous peoples.

Needs like the ones briefly delineated here not only describe the educational realities in Guatemala and Bolivia—they are characteristic of all Latin America. The gap in educational achievement between indigenous and non-indigenous students grows ever larger. This same inequality characterizes the services available to indigenous students, especially those living in rural areas, as compared to students living in urban areas.

Latin America's historical debt to its native peoples includes a quality education, meaning not only equality of access to state-provided services, but also and most importantly social relevance and cultural and linguistic appropriateness. A quality intercultural bilingual education (IBE) could contribute to this end, but as of today bilingual education programs are still limited and do not reach the majority of indigenous students. Furthermore, their quality is limited and, as mentioned previously, the required number and quality of bilingual teachers is not yet available.

But today, IBE is carried out in seventeen different Latin American countries and is an integral part of the majority of educational systems throughout the region. In some cases, it involves a large part of the indigenous student population through state programs, such as in Bolivia and Guatemala; but it is also present in Brazil, Chile, and Costa Rica, in specific sectors of remote indigenous communities. There also are cases where IBE is implemented jointly with indigenous organizations and communities, as in Colombia and Ecuador. Mexico and Peru constitute the two countries with the longest tradition of searching for an alternative indigenous education, but in these two cases most of the efforts have come from the state and the academy, histories which have compromised the development of truly alternative programs. In other countries, such as Bolivia and Ecuador, IBE emerged mainly from the bottom-up, not from the top-down. This fact definitively marks their histories and makes the educational project in these countries an integral component of a much more comprehensive effort to reinforce and redefine democracy and, simultaneously, to critically review the current model of liberal democracy, in order to construct viable and useful alternative models in multi-ethnic, pluricultural, and multilingual societies, as most Latin American countries are today (López 2009).

A common denominator of this educational alternative is the proposal of *interculturalidad*, today a reclaimed demand of indigenous peoples in their questioning of the nation-state model and in their struggle for a distinct and differentiated citizenship that recognizes their socio-cultural and linguistic characteristics. Nevertheless, today the indigenous do not reclaim *interculturalidad* only as an indigenous right, but as a necessity and also a right for everyone, even those who belong to hegemonic sectors. They hold the view that only through a self-confrontation of Latin American societies with themselves, and through positive acceptance of the diversity that defines them, can a more valid and lasting democracy be built.

In this way, through education, Latin American indigenous peoples seek to achieve equality, but with dignity. To this end, the demand for a different education constitutes only one part of a larger agenda that includes the rights to territory and natural resources, particularly water, defense of the environment, and in sum, the right to life. This is the context in which they situate the right to the use and enjoyment of their language and culture, and also the right to education. Unlike those of us who are not indigenous, for indigenous peoples, education is not an isolated and discreet issue, but rather, from their integrated or holistic vision, it is one important component, but not separate from their more comprehensive future and life project.

As can easily be understood, despite the changes Latin American states have inserted into their constitutions during the last two decades, precisely to recognize the multiethnicity, pluriculturalism, and multilingualism that characterize their countries, these states are not yet ready to embrace the changes desired by the indigenous and their organizations. While for the states IBE is only a pedagogical response to a problem that they have finally managed to understand, lack of communication in the classroom and in the school, for the continent's indigenous peoples, intercultural bilingual education is above all a tool to accomplish their social liberation, as many of them repeatedly point out (López 2009).

In all countries, intercultural bilingual education is seen today as a state proposal, and in some cases, strictly official or governmental. Even when it includes the teaching and using of indigenous languages, together with Castilian, as well as the possibility of diversifying the school curriculum to incorporate indigenous values and knowledge and everyday practices, in many places throughout the continent indigenous peoples are pressing for a more radical focus which they consider to be more endogenous, more their own. What is interesting is that, regardless of its name or orientation, this educational focus neither seeks nor contemplates isolation from the rest of the country or from the other socio-cultural groups that compose it, but instead participation in decision-making and the capability to decide the type of education their communities and peoples require today. In sum, what they seek is an education that begins with their needs and expectations, and one whose development they control, if not exclusively, then at least in interaction with state authorities. They consider it their own to the extent that they have control over it, but it is also bilingual and intercultural, because history and current conditions require that it be so.

If this is an adequate analysis, state-controlled IBE, as well as efforts of international cooperation, must necessarily modify their focus in respect to indigenous education. First, it is necessary to restore the political face of IBE, which was present since its beginnings but largely neutralized in recent years, at least so far as to assure that there is joint development of education together with indigenous organizations and communities, toward the construction of the real and participatory democracy the indigenous movement demands. Secondly, international cooperation agencies should work not only with states, but also and most importantly with indigenous organizations and with those authorities who are legitimately recognized by indigenous peoples and communities. If what we are confronted with is a question of rights, the approach to indigenous education should above all be political, as it arises from the larger question indigenous people have about their subaltern condition and social emancipation.

In Guatemala, issues such as these will unavoidably require a reform of the current political constitution of the state. Bolivia has just accomplished this and has incorporated fundamental aspects of the indigenous cosmovision into its legal framework, such as the recognition of communal justice and the application to all persons of indigenous notions such as the "good life" or "living well"—*sumaq kawsay*, in Quechua, *suma qamaña*, in Aymara. By means of these concepts, the indigenous seek to contribute to a reconciliation of human beings with nature, as well as to a reconstruction of current lifestyles. Mental structures such as this allow for a repositioning of IBE, in order to build with and from it a different history of relationships between the indigenous and non-indigenous populations, in response to the pressures and demands that come from below.

Those in Guatemala with a hegemonic view observe indigenous advancement with profound caution and concern, often defending their position with the indisputable fact that not all indigenous parents understand what IBE is about and what it implies. By deliberately and strategically doing this, they avoid a historical analysis of the situation and the deeper understanding that such actions and behaviors are only vestiges of still current colonialism and the condition of suppression in which indigenous existence is still enmeshed.

However, when Guatemalan indigenous who today reject IBE become aware, as others have already done, that IBE constitutes a tool for creating new mental structures rooted in a position opposed to the old racist and discriminative ideas, they will declare, as indigenous leaders of other Latin American countries are already doing, that intercultural bilingual education is not only a response to their needs but also a possibility and an attempt toward constructing a different future.

Noam Chomsky views with hope that which is occurring among indigenous peoples in our Indo-Latin America. He also sees that education can be a promising space when it takes on the cause of the dispossessed, and in our case, he aligns himself with the indigenous and proposes that they be empowered. I fully share these views, and I believe that the brief review of indigenous education I have attempted here allows us to look to the future with some hope, though, too, with the critical lens that is still necessary.

The changes that have occurred in the education of indigenous peoples since the 1940s, when educational outreach was thought to be a compensatory and largely paternalistic measure, and when it only sought to dilute the indigenous population by submerging it within the mestizo masses out of which the nation-state was to be built, witness to a unique evolution in the

Latin American states regarding the acknowledgement of the socio-cultural and linguistic diversity that characterizes the societies of this part of the world. These changes are products of the greater visibility and active presence of more than 40 million indigenous who inhabit Latin America and, at the same time, the increased democratization of this region. Education constitutes the social laboratory par excellence where new ways of coexisting and perhaps more creative forms of state formation and organization could be gestating in all Latin American countries, forms that might overcome the limitations of the historic nation-state model as it has been experienced in the Americas since its importation more than 200 years ago. It appears that the indigenous peoples of the Americas are helping us to accomplish, or create, these discoveries.

REFERENCES

Hale, C.A. 1984. Rethinking indigenous politics in the era of the indio permitido. *NACLA. Report of the Americas.* September–October:16–21.

———— 2007. '*Más que un indio*': *Ambivalencia racial y multiculturalismo neoliberal en Guatemala.* Guatemala: AVANCSO.

López, L. E. 2005. *De resquicios a boquerones. La EIB en Bolivia.* La Paz: Plural Editores.

————. 2009. *Reaching the unreached. Indigenous intercultural bilingual education in Latin America.* Background Study for Education For All Global Monitoring Report 2009. Paris: UNESCO.

Richards, J. B., & M. Richards. 1996. Maya Education: A historical and contemporary analysis of Mayan language education policy. In *Maya Cultural Activism in Guatemala,* ed. E. Fischer & F. Brown, 208–221. Austin: University of Texas Press.

10.

Indigenous Education and "Living Well": An Alternative in the Midst of Crisis

Ruth Moya Torres, Guatemala

Ecuadorian sociolinguist, bilingual intercultural educator, and curriculum designer presently working in Guatemala, with extensive work history at all school levels among diverse indigenous peoples in Ecuador, Nicaragua, Honduras, Bolivia, and Guatemala. Email: ruthmoyatorres@yahoo.com

IT IS A PRIVILEGE for me to comment on some aspects of Lois Meyer's interviews with Noam Chomsky. I am interested in analyzing Chomsky's ideas regarding the following topics: the capitalist context and its repercussions on education; the issue of standardization in general and, in particular, standardization in education; and, the possibilities that education could reconstruct elements of *"comunalidad."* I will illustrate my ideas with a few examples. Chomsky's reflections applied to indigenous education in Latin America constitute, without doubt, an important contribution.

THE MACRO-ECONOMIC AND MACRO-POLITICAL CONTEXT IN WHICH LATIN AMERICAN EDUCATION DEVELOPS

Chomsky alludes to world capitalism and the multilateral bank—the International Monetary Fund, for example—to show the complex and unequal relations between the powerful countries and the "emergent" countries that find themselves severely pressured to define their own projects and concepts of social development. Chomsky illustrates the situation with examples from Venezuela and the Southern Cone, but it is well known that these examples could be multiplied many times over.

In effect, since the nineteenth century, the governing classes of Latin America have committed a large part of the financial resources of their countries to paying the external debt. The very independence movements in these countries, which occurred about two hundred years ago, developed under conditions of indebtedness to foreign capital. In Ecuador, for example, this debt, known as the "English debt," was only cancelled in the mid-1970s with resources from petroleum sales. It is well known that the most aggressive levels of Latin American indebtedness occurred in the second half of the twentieth century, to support a foreign model of "modernization" that didn't correspond to the hopes and needs of the national majority populations. Many Latin American countries invested more than 40 percent of their income to pay the external debt. These payments were directed almost exclusively to debt "management." Finally it became apparent that the debt was unpayable and the lenders had to concede to cancel the debt. Under these conditions, it is not difficult to imagine the subordination of poor countries to the strategies of the rich countries in the framework of the so-called free market. This forced "alignment" has to do not only with the economy, but with all spheres of political and social life, including education. Latin American indebtedness is a reoccurring phenomenon, a consequence of having to finance actions that devolve from the implementation of education policies and reforms which, in general, pay off in the development of competencies intended to help students compete in the global market.

In this first decade of the twenty-first century, some Latin American states have accelerated and even canceled segments of their external debt. Paradoxically, these payments have been viewed by the multi- or bilateral banks and their political spokespersons as "dangerous" messages for other countries, resulting in the cancellation of any possibility that these countries might access "fresh capital" to pay for their "development," meaning, to indebt themselves even further. Payment of debts to the International Monetary Fund by Venezuela, Argentina, or Ecuador has meant that these countries are added to the list of countries deemed unreliable from the perspective of the market economy. A country's ranking of reliability for the global market, as is well known, is determined by the same countries who lend out capital and who sell worldwide the technology bought with that capital. As Chomsky suggests, in the end corporations are totalitarian economies that do not assume responsibility for the general population, that is, average people. A reflection such as this leads us to a simple assertion: "the people" are not part of the political class and, inside a country, the political class hides itself behind big corporations. Usually, this Latin American political class ardently defends corporations, the free flow of capital, etc., and it does so in the name of economic freedom and development. Strictly speaking, it is actually defending its own interests.

What is the relationship of the logic of globalization with education? Does the "comparative advantage" of poor countries in the market economy include biological and cultural diversity? If so, this same diversity becomes a commodity and, as such, it is exposed not only to pillaging, but also to an extractive logic, displayed in Latin America by world powers since earliest colonialism. In this political and economic climate, the principle victims are indigenous peoples and African-descent communities.

First, according to capitalist logic, the function of states is to avoid protectionism, but it is well known that, both in Europe and in the United States, protectionist practices have held sway. Social frictions that have arisen out of the negotiations or signing of free trade agreements between the United States and Latin America evidence that the question of protectionism is not banal. The fact is that for centralized economies, protectionist measures are nothing new. Think, for example, about the policies of the

Bourbons that were implemented by Spain in the late colonial period in the Americas.

Today, the crisis in the financial system that has been unleashed in the United States since 2008 shows, without doubt, a new style of protectionism, oriented toward financial capital more than toward the recuperation of the real economy. Such distortions already are having grave effects on the U.S. economy, with worldwide repercussions. If protectionist measures are declared by capitalist countries to be anticompetitive, considering that competitiveness is the ethical paradigm of the transnationals, how are we to understand "competitiveness" in our countries? For what reason or purpose are we to be competitive? How are we to orient public education so that it contributes to the common good?

STANDARDIZING EDUCATION

Chomsky suggests that people live and resolve in diverse ways the balance between national standardization of education and the attention to their own educational characteristics and necessities. For Chomsky, the education system has as its objective the "leveling out" or homogenizing of people and, as a consequence, the destruction of what is called "individual culture", which is taken up in complex ways and is based on traditional practices. The result of this leveling out, says Chomsky, is obedience, passivity, and the adoption of behaviors and values that do not question or challenge. The education system, highly stratified, places people in socially specific roles, which requires the elimination of individual, cultural, group, or linguistic identities and differences. Chomsky's example is the "blocking" of bilingual education in various parts of the world.

I agree with several of these views, for example, that the school plays an homogenizing role, and the stratification of the school system operates to assure that individuals fulfill functions that are equally stratified, resulting in social inequities and polarizations. In this sense, the stratification of the education system is an effect and not a cause. I do not agree that individuals carry within themselves an "individual culture," even if what is referred to is the existence of complex cultural and social relationships that generate an individual culture. The notion of individual culture is unacceptable for indigenous peoples who claim the collective production, throughout history, of all systemic expressions of their particular cultures. This is precisely the foundation of indigenous educational projects.

From another perspective, standardization in Latin American educational systems is similar to, as well as different from, the standardization evident in educational systems in other countries of the world. This is because other standardization efforts have sought to serve purposes other than those that respond to the educational necessities emerging from an education for socially relevant, viable, and sustainable development. For this reason, I find it interesting to think about the relationship between standardization of education and education's utility for life, which has to do not only with the *quality of education*, but also with the *quality of life*. Here Latin America finds itself embroiled in a debate, still inconclusive, and one to which indigenous peoples have contributed.

Since the year 2000, Latin American countries through their ministries of education have committed themselves to complying with the Millennium Development Goals (MDG).[1] In educational terms, this commitment means guaranteeing that by 2015 there will be student access to, retention in, and completion of studies, at least for basic education (eleven or twelve years if schooling). To achieve these goals, Latin American countries have made important budgetary commitments and have indebted themselves even more, despite the fact that they cannot, in general, fulfill these goals. An even more delicate situation concerns the achievement of the MDGs for the indigenous peoples and African-descent communities of Latin America.

It is not always clear, nor is it always easy, to achieve consensus on the budgets which support notions of quality. There exists a reductionist understanding of educational quality. In essence, educational quality is confined to students' abilities in reading and writing skills in the language of the nation's elite class, and also operational skills in basic mathematics calculations. No substantial gains have been achieved in the acquisition of language skills, and very little is happening in the learning of arithmetic and science. Instead, a set of "values" is clearly present (such as obedience, passivity, etc.) which serves to homogenize the behavior of individuals and social collectives, as Chomsky notes.

And again, there is no significant relationship between what is learned and the usefulness of this learning, especially for indigenous and African-descent students. In part, this is because the indigenous students speak one or more of the 500 ancestral Latin American languages, and because some, though not all, of the African-descent students speak a Creole language which developed as a result of slavery and colonization. But this is not the only problem: there is the content to be learned, the same content that impedes the process of endoculturation which enables the affirmation of one's own identity and provides the foundation for developing intercultural relations based on social, economic, political, cultural, or linguistic equity.

Going a bit deeper into notions about the creation of individual culture, it seems to me that these are inspired by liberal philosophy, even though it is recognized that individuals have social contexts that make them carriers of culture. It is not always evident that culture is molded by the hegemonic classes, and the apparatuses of the state serve this purpose, among these the education apparatus. Any education project that diverts from these purposes is considered to promote the decomposition of the national state. For its part, the state promises symmetries, following the concept of equality before the law. We know these symmetries do not exist, and that there are enormous difficulties in escaping institutionalized violence, impunity, racism, sexism, the lack of conditions for reproducing one's own culture, among others. As a consequence, for indigenous peoples education has lead to acculturation and ethnic shame. However, this panorama should not dishearten us too greatly, if we count on indigenous peoples' capacities to resist and to propose alternatives.

There is no doubt that the same scheme of liberal thinking (in a philosophical sense) has favored the exercise of individual rights, and that in this ideological scenario it has been a complex matter to move toward the recognition of collective rights. It is almost paradoxical that both individual and collective rights are currently guided by standards devised by the same political and elite classes in power. The relevant question, then, is: how much can social collectives influence the definitions of ethical norms and social, cultural, and economic ways of life in their nation-states?

Conceiving of indigenous education as a question relating to peoples as bearers of collective rights is perhaps one of the major conceptual advances that has been made.

It seems to me that indigenous peoples and African-descent communities of Latin America attempt to resolve through differentiated mechanisms the balance between official standards and attention to social, cultural, and linguistic peculiarities, as well as attention to their own educational needs and aspirations. This is because indigenous peoples and African-descent communities experience very diverse social, political, economic, and cultural realities, which are then inscribed into national and international relations of power.

In countries like Guatemala, especially since 1996 when the Peace Accords were signed which put an end to the so-called "internal war," the Mayan people have concentrated their struggle in two areas: a) achieving a legal standard that protects their educational and cultural rights, as well as transforming the educational bureaucracy to make room for a bilingual and intercultural education (BIE) that would include Mayan demands for a broader and better education; and, b) accomplishing a general sense of well-being, fundamentally centered on the question of legalization and adjudication of lands. Themes such as expanded coverage of educational services and health care, as well as access to a judicial system that counters impunity and facilitates internal reconciliation, were some of the themes of the Mayan movement. In the area of education, this movement was expected to make political and theoretical concessions to promote reconciliation, for example, by accepting that the Ladino segments of the national society be designated a "people," despite the fact that the elite Ladinos, throughout the history of the republic, have assumed as legitimate the foregrounding of their interests as if they were the interests of all, ignoring the ethnic and social inequities experienced by the Mayan people. The reality is that more than ten years after the signing of the Peace Accords and the initiation of education reform, and though there has been a proliferation of legal standards addressing bilingual intercultural education, a report in 2007 by the National Permanent Commission of Education Reform reported that these laws have not been carried out. Neither has the exercise of language rights as described in the Law of Languages been protected.

In countries like Mexico, with a long institutional history of public indigenous education, and with changes in the normative standards regarding linguistic rights (for example, the existence of the General Law of Linguistic Rights of Indigenous Peoples) and new priorities and policies for the development of intercultural, bilingual education, the development of a relevant, quality education for indigenous peoples has still not been achieved. This is seen clearly in the case of Oaxaca, which is alluded to in the interviews that are the object of this commentary.

In all of Central America, despite significant differences by country, laws and institutional changes have been developed regarding educational, linguistic, and cultural rights of indigenous peoples. In all of these Central American and Caribbean nations

(Guatemala, Nicaragua, El Salvador, Honduras, Costa Rica, Panama, Belize, Jamaica, Curacao, Aruba, Bon Aire, Guadalupe, Haiti, etc.), there are peoples who speak languages of Mesoamerican, Caribbean, and Arawak origin, or Creole languages developed by those of African descent, such as Creoles of English, French, or Hispano-Portuguese origin. However, in very few of these countries have public policies been developed that support the linguistic rights of original peoples. Perhaps it is useful to note the case of Nicaragua where, since the first Sandinista government, proposals were developed about regional autonomy, which in the area of education were concretized in the Regional Autonomy Education System (SEAR, for its initials in Spanish). However, even here little has been accomplished in terms of institutionalizing bilingual intercultural education.

In South America, the situation is quite diverse, particularly given the mobilizing capacity of indigenous organizations. The case of Colombia is worth highlighting. Despite the fact that indigenous peoples constitute less than 2 percent of the total population of the country, they have managed to generate a national discussion around "ethnoeducation." Ecuador and Bolivia are also unique in that the indigenous peoples who form part of the ethnic and social diversity of these states are composed not only of the majority Andean peoples, but also the minority indigenous peoples from the tropical jungles, and both countries increasingly have recognized the territorial rights of these peoples, especially of the minorities. Regarding education in both of these countries, BIE is recognized and intercultural education is promoted for all students, not merely those who are indigenous. It should be mentioned, however, that there is more progress in the development of BIE in Andean languages (Quichua/Quechua in Ecuador and Bolivia, and Aymara in Bolivia) than there is in BIE efforts among minority peoples of the tropical jungles.

"COMUNALIDAD"

The question of whether state education systems might be able to promote and protect communal ways of life deserves special attention, as does the question of whether the sense of *comunalidad* emerges from indigenous peoples, or if eventually it also could emerge from democratic segments of civil society. Chomsky suggests that these two themes eventually can converge.

A more adequate approach to this topic would take inspiration from the political practices of Latin America's indigenous peoples and African-descent communities. A community-based society, when viewed as the insertion of individuals into the structures of power, does not always result in the common good. Also, "community-based" is defined differently in different contexts, responding to specific cultural patterns. For tropical jungle cultures in general, and for Amazonian cultures in particular, what creates the sense of social cohesion is kinship relationships and alliances. This is because, de facto, there does not exist social development in the form of established communities, as in the highland cultures. *Comunalidad* should not be understood as equivalent to sedentariness, a distinction which is especially important in the case of indigenous peoples from tropical contexts.

We must recognize, however, that the peoples from the tropical jungles are linked to world capitalism. A good example is provided by the Waorani, an Amazonian people in Ecuador, who are hunters, gatherers, and itinerant horticulturalists. Not many years ago, through co-optation of their leadership, the Waorani sold part of their territory to a Ukrainian business for twenty thousand dollars. This process was finally stopped, but it illustrates the importance of making territorial decisions based on the rights of historic social collectives to prior knowledge and informed consent. Another example is the indigenous community of Sarayaku, also in Amazonian Ecuador. Sarayaku was able to successfully sue a North American company for environmental contamination and damages to the environment and to human life, due to exploitation of petroleum resources. This case was appealed in international courts of justice, with the support of solidarity sectors both within and outside the country. The examples can be multiplied. The fact is that indigenous peoples have lived diverse forms of resistance to preserve themselves as social collectives above and beyond their status as individual subjects of a society. If it is true that the forms of indigenous struggle have had diverse priorities and emphases, it is no less true that, during the modern period, resistance efforts have passed through two great moments: agrarian struggles, and land and territorial struggles. The latter are associated with the plundering and dispossession of ancestral lands, natural resources, and territorial boundaries. This does not mean that either agrarian problems or territorial questions have been resolved. Instead, these two sets of indigenous demands cohabit in the same national space, and they result from the political praxis of distinct organizational forms and different but contemporaneous historical contexts. On the other hand, all expressions of indigenous resistance are threatened by co-optation through mechanisms of power and corruption.

Internal cohesion among indigenous peoples depends on endogenous and exogenous factors and on the kinds of external pressures experienced by a given people, as Chomsky states so well. For indigenous peoples and African-descent communities, the primary pressure is economic and takes many forms: colonization, the expansion of agricultural acreage, the presence of the livestock, forestry, or tourism industry, and in general, the presence of extractive mega-companies. Right now, the communities are involved in the sale of CO_2, which seems a slight compensation for the political practices of oligarchies and the destruction of the natural resources of the planet. Nevertheless, failure to recognize the material and spiritual links of indigenous peoples with their environment continues. The so-called "voluntary isolation" of indigenous peoples in reality covers up the ethnocide carried out at the hands of the governing classes. The rebellions of Peruvian Amazonian natives which occurred in 2009, brought about by violations of their territories and ways of life, are a variation on this same problem.

The concentration of these phenomena not only motivates society's intuition and social imagination; given that these actions arise from the basic need for survival, their intensity forewarns of abuses and extermination practices closely linked to state terrorism and ethnocide. World crises such as climate change can contribute to new reflections that are more congruent with the concept of "living well" fostered by indigenous peoples, as well as the alignment of democratic forces to favor the development of new forms and meanings of governability and democracy. This would be the work of a new education.

NOTES

1. In September 2000, world leaders adopted the United Nations Millennium Declaration, committing their nations to work together to reduce extreme poverty, and setting eight Millenium Development Goals (MDGs) to be achieved by 2015, including ending hunger and poverty, universal education, child and maternal health, and environmental protection, among others.

11.

Repress Ideas to Consolidate Nation-States
. . . or Re-create Ways of Thinking to Strengthen Balance

By Guillermo Chen Morales, Guatemala

Maya Achi popular educator, human rights activist, journalist, and director general of the New Hope Foundation in Rabinal, Baja Verapaz, Guatemala. Email: guillermochen@yahoo.com

I BEGIN BY EXPRESSING my deepest thanks for the opportunity to comment on the theme of communitarian thinking, and, of course, to Noam Chomsky for his interest in knowing the work of the original nations.

Reflecting on what is occurring with indigenous languages is one of the actions that the New Hope Foundation, Rio Negro, has engaged in since 1997. After the signing of the Peace Accords in 1996, we, the original peoples, began a process of social restructuring, given that the Guatemalan government, with the weight of genocide on its shoulders, managed to disarticulate and destroy entire indigenous communities, among them Rio Negro[1] and Plan de Sanchez in Rabinal, Baja Verapaz. In the same way, they carried out ethnocide, and with it, we lost many speakers of Maya Achi.[2]

Now they continue with other kinds of extermination, like homogenous state education and the use of the media. During the present government of Álvaro Colom (2008–2012) one hears talk of a free education, a constitutional right written into article 74 of the political constitution of the Republic of Guatemala. But Article 76 also indicates that instruction should be carried out

225

bilingually in zones with a predominantly indigenous population. What is not said is that the free education that is promised assumes the process of "castilianization," that is, the expected, forced use and teaching of the Spanish language, and excludes the right to be educated in a bilingual way, regardless of the language of the local linguistic community. In Guatemala, when one speaks of bilingual education, there exists the stereotype that everyone immediately thinks about the "poor Indians" who should learn Spanish, not about the *mestizos* who should learn an indigenous language. The others, the non-indigenous people, could be bilingual in Spanish-English, Spanish-Japanese, and even become multilingual or hyperpolyglots, but they would never speak an indigenous language, as that would be degrading.

Another erroneous idea is to believe that bilingual education means directly translating academic content from Spanish into indigenous languages. This homogenizing action in Guatemala is implemented through the New National Base Curriculum—CNB—put forth by the Guatemalan Ministry of Education or MINEDUC. There is much theoretical talk about the "new model"; however, to what degree can the teachers apply it in their classrooms?

I would like to emphasize Chomsky's comments about Kenneth Hale's actions to create a program of cultural and linguistic defense, reconstruction and revitalization in indigenous communities, and the experience with the Hopi reservation.

Since 2002, we have focused our attention on the recreation of an educational methodology that comes from the communities and is constructed together with them. For us, it is not sufficient that certain cultural elements of indigenous communities are "included" or "added on" to the official curriculum of the basic cycle of education (grades 7 through 9), and that this is proclaimed to be an intercultural education system. In Guatemala, there are multidisciplinary teams that work on developing an Intercultural Bilingual Education, or EBI. The problem is not in the technical teams but rather in the lack of a long-range educational policy. Every four years national elections are held to elect a new president, and whoever comes to power improvises in the area of education, changing everything that has been done in past administrations. We do not have a national vision, let alone a vision for intercultural bilingual education. We could write hundreds of books criticizing the Guatemalan education system but it would be a waste of time if we do not propose modalities of community education.

For this reason, our hope centers on the Methodological Re-Creation of Intercultural Bilingual Education Achi/Spanish (RE-MEBI). What does this process consist of? We have shared with our indigenous brothers and sisters from other countries and we have witnessed progress in this theme of intercultural bilingual education. We have also worked with methodologies that are effective for rural areas. We try not to reinvent the wheel, but rather to take the elements of innovative methodologies and adapt them to our contexts. That is why we are calling it "re-creation," as this means "take all the best" and insert it and adapt it to indigenous ways of thinking. We are not trying to be purists; rather, we look for the most pedagogical and communitarian forms which are still true to our indigenousness. We propose an alternative to ameliorate poverty and to strengthen and value the Achi culture through our young people, so that they come to be the vehicle of change through education. This concept is not isolated from an equal strengthening of other cultures, as we seek to establish a fluid and equal relationship with and among the distinct cultures in our country and across the continent. This will not be possible if coming generations do not acknowledge the value of indigenous thought, and respect it.

We will implement part of the Tutorial Learning System (SAT), a methodology created by the Foundation for the Application and Teaching of Science (FUNDEC) in Cali, Colombia. This system allows us to provide a complement to the Western and rural perspective, taking into account Latin America's socio-economic reality. We recognize the SAT and its objectives as a starting point for developing the REMEBI Achi/Spanish.

If the REMEBI is to reflect the culture and language, we believe it is indispensable to work from and with the communities so that they are the protagonists of this new educational model. Western knowledge often is incompatible with indigenous thought, especially regarding language, which preserves in every word the essence of the community, as well as the idea of unity in diversity. The communities, especially the elders, possess and protect all the wisdom of the ancestors. We have found people of advanced age who still remember their parents' and grandparents' wisdom, representing approximately two hundred years of continuous, undisrupted wisdom, in that it reflects thinking from three generations.

The REMEBI research began with short monographs about the home communities of youth and others who are registered in the New Hope Education Center.[3] The most pertinent themes are those of health care and the community. This initial process helped the young people know the members of their community better and select the individuals who are knowledgeable about very specific topics. They began a cycle of interviews with traditional healers, *comadronas*,[4] bone-setters,[5] spiritual guides, and other experts. A group of scholarship recipients from our organization worked assiduously in the transcription of these interviews, translating from the Maya Achi language to Spanish. From the beginning, we have sought out professionals to process the information and develop its pedagogical applications. The multidisciplinary team is comprised of an anthropologist, a spiritual guide, a social worker, a curriculum and instruction expert, and a graphic designer. Two advisory councils have been formed, one of which is local, comprised of spiritual guides, linguists, *comadronas*, parents, and elders. The international council is comprised of experts in anthropology and archeology, as well as sociologists and researchers. We want all of the research that is undertaken to be shared with these two councils in order to have a broader vision of the work of REMEBI.

The parents of youth at the educational center maintain constant communication with the multidisciplinary team to confirm the information that is gathered. Once the information is corroborated and confirmed, it is recast into a specially designed format for pedagogical use, and then made available to the tutors for field-testing. This process is extremely important because the success of this new methodology in terms of strengthening our culture and language depends on it. Our products will be *educational codices*, with themes of health care, traditional medicine, nature and the environment, community, rights and values, spirituality, wisdom, astronomy, Mayan mathematics, Mayan calendar, art, and ancestors, and genealogy. We will represent the life of the Maya Achi community in these documents.

The methodology applied in the classrooms consists of using round tables representing the community way of working. At each table are seated four students—two males and two females—to promote duality of the elements, more than equality of gender. Sharing life experiences is much richer if one locates the students at different cardinal points. Here is where we break with the traditional form of educating. With these practices guiding the experiences of the youth, we convert them away from theoretical thinking toward balance. We also eliminate the individualistic form of educating, given that we do not line students up in rows. In stark contrast to this new communitarian modality, individualistic consciousness is deeply rooted in educational centers, allowing young people to be formed exclusively and solely as cheap hand labor. In stark contrast, the community form of educating seeks to draw its power from indigenous knowledge and to generate new thinking in order to motivate development and seek a balance between the human being and Mother Nature.

In recent internal evaluations, we have seen how teachers have valued this methodology. But there is a very surprising discovery—explanations that are given in class in Spanish are discussed and analyzed by the young students in their mother tongue, Maya Achi. The level of progress is much better than in other state education centers. Despite the fact that there are funds designated in the budget for bilingual teachers, the contracted teachers do not teach one word in the Maya language because they feel ashamed. Their excuse is that parents prefer that their children be taught Spanish, rather than strengthening their mother tongue

During three consecutive years, the New Hope Foundation has formed young people with critical and community-based thinking. Our problem stems from the absence of this effort in the following educational levels.[6] We offer the basic cycle at the middle level and a preparation program for community nursing assistants. In the foundation's Strategic Plan, we have proposed the creation of a diversified cycle, and then the creation of a university extension with courses of study that reflect the indigenous cosmovision. This would mean that youth would not have to break with their community education.

Starting at eleven or twelve years old, they would begin an education in accord with and relevant to their cultural values. We do not attempt to repress ideas to consolidate the state; rather, we wish to recreate ways of thinking in order to strengthen the balance between human beings and Mother Nature. Strengthening and promoting the Maya Achi language will help transmit our philosophical and cosmic knowledge, as well as serving as the basic communication vehicle for carrying out work in the communities. Spanish will be the common language of communication to rethink historic events and translate them into the maternal language in order to improve life in all its splendor.

NOTES

1. A community located 27 kilometers from the urban center of Rabinal that suffered

four massacres during the war, the most notable being the massacre of Pak'oxom, Río Negro, on March 13, 1982, when 107 children and 70 women were killed on a hillside three kilometers from the center of the town.

2. Maya Achi: Linguistic community of about 100,000 speakers, located in the state of Baja Verapaz, Guatemala. (Census 2002/ Richards, M.)

3. A community educational center created in 2003 by the New Hope Foundation for Achi indigenous youth from Baja Verapaz.

4. Women who specialize in caring for pregnant women before, during, and after they give birth.

5. Community health workers who treat dislocated or fractured bones.

6. In Guatemala, schooling begins with preschool (ages 3–6), then primary (grades 1 through 6, or ages 7–12), followed by the middle level, which is divided into two education cycles: basic (grades 7 through 9) and diversified (grades 10 through 12). The final level is higher education. The New Hope Foundation primarily attends to the needs of students in the basic cycle, which refers to grades 7-9. However, its concerns lie with continuing education, in every way and at every educational level that this might be possible.

12.

Reading Noam Chomsky from an Educational Experience of the Kuna People in Panama

By Reuter Orán Bodin and Kikadir Yadira Orán, Panama

Reuter Orán and daughter Kikadir, both bilingual teachers from San Ignacio de Tupile, Kuna Yala, Panama, are part of the Technical Team of the Implementation Project for Intercultural Bilingual Education (EBI) throughout the Kuna territories of Panama. Reuter, now retired, helped draft the curricular proposal for an authentic Kuna EBI and still advises its development. Kikadir, a technical teacher with the Panama Ministry of Education, teaches Kuna reading and writing and provides professional development for EBI teachers. Email: kikadiroran@ymail.com

THE KUNA PEOPLE OCCUPY and govern principally the Atlantic islands on the Panama coast. Like other indigenous and non-indigenous peoples around the world, we Kuna have always fed the flames of our past. Our last armed struggle took place in 1925, when the national government tried to strip us of our culture. Our people rose up in arms, evicting the colonial police from our territory, because the police did not respect us and actually violated our most fundamental rights.

Today we live with relative autonomy, recognized by the Panamanian government. From the depths of our culture, we are attentive to world affairs. This is why we feel very content participating in this international dialogue with Dr. Noam Chomsky and many important colleagues and academics throughout the Americas. The opinions of this illustrious professor seem interesting and instructive to us from our perspective as persons involved in an educational process of our people. We will comment on the first two interviews.

Regarding one of Dr. Chomsky's opinions, it is clear that world history has been and continues to be a chain of bloody and interminable struggles. The most powerful impose their laws and customs, confiscating the property, culture, government, and history of those they dominate. All continents have lived this tragic situation that, unfortunately to this moment, humanity has been unable to overcome.

The situation of anguish and uncertainty that the original peoples of America have endured and continue to endure is the fruit of these abuses that Europeans have perpetrated ever since they invaded this continent. Once they decimated the indigenous peoples, they imposed their cultures and languages. Since that time, the autochthones' cultures have been devalued; they are considered obstacles to development and a danger to national unity in countries throughout this continent. With these criteria, the Latin American countries developed their educational systems and converted education into an instrument of domination. In this way, they continue to subjugate and vilify the original peoples of this continent. Therefore, we consider that the opinions of Dr. Chomsky are sound.

Indigenous peoples should become conscious of this reality and unite, so that together we advance on the road to liberation. The Kuna people still keep our customs alive because we practice them. Our authorities are named by the people themselves, in accordance with our norms. The communities administer justice, and only if a crime is grave is it turned over to the national authorities. The official language in the region is the Kuna language, and it is used in all situations of daily life. Our women wear their traditional clothing, and our past history, referred to as "myths" by anthropologists, is transmitted daily to our children and young people.

Our people are conscious of the damage done to them by the traditional education system. This is why we demand a new education focus and we participate in all movements that advocate for respect of human rights, especially those of indigenous peoples.

Now, the great majority of the elite rulers of this and other continents use their powerful media and employ euphemistic names and labels to try to cover up their attitudes and justify our misery. The contempt toward indigenous cultures that began during the conquest is part of a colonial vision against which we must continue to struggle.

This is why we consider the opinions of Dr. Noam Chomsky to be instructive. His clear, global vision of what has occurred with humanity, and what is occurring in modern times, helps us to orient ourselves on the path we so anxiously want to travel: that is, to be subjects of our own destiny.

Thank you, Dr. Chomsky, for being at our side, for helping us to see through the eyes of a wise person that there is hope in this world, that human beings are becoming conscious of their own reality, a reality that deserves to be analyzed carefully in order to make firm and adequate decisions. We cannot continue to allow human beings to self-destruct and terminate the planet on which we live, to continue abusing nature until they kill Mother Earth, the name we give her, following the tradition of our ancestors. Now that diversity is considered a valuable resource for development, both indigenous and non-indigenous peoples are called upon to demonstrate that life on this planet is truly diverse and that it is possible to cohabitate here, respecting our differences.

Intercultural bilingual education exists in different contexts. Its progress is greatly influenced by the attitude of the state and the situation in which indigenous communities find themselves, as Dr. Chomsky discusses. The Republic of Panama is one of the youngest countries in this region. Barely 108 years have passed since its formation out of the Independence Movement. Since its birth, this nation has applied the traditional vertical education model that converts our peoples into objects of education. Our peoples have become accustomed to this method, to the point where they are capable of defending it. This is why it is important that, over time, they come to know the principles, foundations, and advances in our new educational focus.[1]

In 1972, the Panamanian constitution was reformed. One of its articles manifests the following: "The state recognizes and respects the ethnic identity of the national indigenous communities." Furthermore, it mandates that "the aboriginal languages will be the object of special study and dissemination, and the state will promote bilingual literacy programs in the indigenous communities." These articles would not have been more than words on the page of this document if we had remained with our arms crossed, waiting for the state to comply with the constitution.

In the 1980s and part of the 1990s, one school took the initiative and clandestinely put bilingual instruction into practice. Later, the Panamanian Organic Education Law was modified and eight articles were introduced that comprise concrete steps toward the development of intercultural bilingual education (EBI) in the indigenous communities of Panama.

As a fundamental task of our Implementation Project for EBI in all Kuna territories across Panama, the Kuna people developed and presented our new education proposal to the national government, which approved it in December 2008.

Faced with the imminent scarcity of bilingual teachers, the Specialized University of the Americas opened its doors to offer a bachelor's degree in education with an emphasis in intercultural bilingual education. This demonstrates the advances of EBI in Panama, though not at the rate we would have liked. But it shows that the state reacts only when we demand it to, and this we must continue to do.

What is needed is for the state to assume its full responsibility to provide continuity to this project, providing the necessary resources to ensure its development and expansion to cover all levels of basic general education, as the Panamanian constitution and the laws of the republic establish.

Returning to the interviews with Professor Noam Chomsky, we recognize in his comments three distinct fronts on which indigenous peoples must act head-on to be able to reach our goals. One front is that of the huge international corporations that watch out for their own interests; a second is that of the governing elite in our countries who manipulate resources and public policies from their government positions, at the cost of supposed freedom and democracy; and a third front is that of our communities, who have lost faith in their past, which is why we must revitalize and strengthen them.

Fortunately, we no longer are alone in this struggle. The world is clamoring for a new economic, social, and political order. And we must direct ourselves toward that path if we do not want to destroy ourselves, due to our lack of vision.

The idea of compiling these interviews and complementing them with our commentaries is a powerful demonstration of what we can do, counting, of course, on the insights of the great teacher, Noam Chomsky. Such an action is important, especially at this time when diversity is recognized more and more to be a valuable resource and not an obstacle to development, as it was claimed before.

These actions will allow us to develop our own liberation strategies. This means that we will have the opportunity and the responsibility to create and oversee the implementation of educational models that truly respond to our interests, based in our own pedagogy and cosmovision. Of course, we must not prevent changes that bring dynamism to our cultures. In other words, we seek to advance from what is uniquely ours, toward the creation of *interculturalidad.*

NOTES

1. The Implementation Project for Intercultural Bilingual Education (EBI) is a project of the Kuna people. It began in 2006 with efforts to sensitize the communities that comprise the Kuna Yala region. The development of this program began in 2007 with children in early education (ages 4–5). The following year it continued with children in the first grade (ages 6–7), and this year it continues with children in second grade (ages 8–9). The project is sponsored by the Spanish Agency of International Cooperation for Development, and it terminates at the end of this year. But our traditional authorities, convinced of the importance of this new educational model, are negotiating to continue this much-desired program.

13.

Abya Yala and the Decolonization of Democracy, Knowledge, Education, and the State

By Luis Macas Ambuludí, Ecuador

Kichwa anthropologist from Ecuador, linguist and J.D., member of the Political Council of the Confederation of Indigenous Nationalities of Ecuador (CONAIE), and executive director of the Scientific Institute of Indigenous Cultures (ICCI). Email: info@icci.org.ec

EDUCATIONAL STANDARDS ARE NOT only totally foreign in most cultural, social, and political contexts, but are especially alienating from the perspective of an ancestral, millenary culture that responds to its own processes of historical construction. The state education system provides for and is implemented out of a completely Eurocentric conception of reality. It violates the principles, values, and knowledge base of the indigenous or native peoples of this continent, who remain distant from Western culture and knowledge.

For this reason, we believe that there are several aspects of this topic that must be analyzed and reflected upon. First, we take for granted that a differentiation between the two cultures or civilizations is fundamental; though they share a common ancestry, they are distinct in their respective cosmovisions. Plain and simple, we are different in our conceptions, principles, sciences, knowledge, and our processes for constructing knowledge and identity. Second, educational standards, as we understand them, are not simply a way to move in with mandatory instruments, information, or the delivery and reception of knowledge (which is called education), nor is it the state's responsibility to deliver or "deposit" knowledge. Fundamentally, the delicate process of education, particularly in our region of the world, is controlled by the consolidation of an ideologically determined process, and obviously originates in the dominant sectors of society, where it has been specifically designed to impose and sustain dominant interests, disregarding and excluding other sectors. Third, the education systems of the Latin American nation-states, under the control of the dominant sector and converted into a vehicle for political and ideological manipulation, have not evolved in this way by chance. Historically they have been a tool, not only to preserve and maintain the current economic, political, and social systems, but unquestionably to perfect the capitalist system, which has permitted the accumulation of wealth by very few and the poverty of many. It is these educational standards, serving the purposes of the capitalist system, that now are caving in due to the most profound crisis of their existence.

The goals of a state in the global economic and political system seek the regeneration of the global system by imposing an education system that is compatible with generic standards of education. At the same time, the education system has the mission to transform the individual into an interchangeable human tool, serving the established order, or to convert the individual into an efficient, competitive, and disciplined laborer, willing to fulfill a designated role in a society that conforms to the current way of life.

From this perspective, the homogenization of educational standards not only plays a prevalent role in cultural transformation and in the destruction of identities. Educational standards have much more drastic consequences. They have outcomes that promote the disintegration of the social fabric, the dismantling of indigenous *comunalidad*, and the disarticulation of concepts from the very thinking patterns of communal ways of knowing.

We agree with Professor Chomsky that the homogenization of cultures, identities, the diversity of peoples and systems and diverse forms of life, by means of educational standards, is not a casual or isolated act. It is a perfectly planned response to the interests of the global economic system, in response to a particular perspective that humanity is now enduring. Perhaps it derives from a more perverse intentionality by those who flout power in society, that of wiping out the diversity of identities, cultures, and systems of life.

Facing these realities, our leaders, both men and women, with more than sufficient reason counsel us in our communities in ways that turn out to be paradoxical:

> The official and conventional education system, the communication media, schooling—these are all enemies of indigenous communities because, in the end, the individual whose being is intrinsically communal, whose behavior and life style are collective, is culturally alienated, individualized, confused, and adopts strange behaviors and even behaviors antagonistic to the community. Therefore, education should be communitarian, a responsibility of the community, within the community, and for the community.

Chomsky affirms this same way of thinking in the following excerpt from the interview of 2004:

> I can even remember some of this from childhood. My family happened to be first generation immigrant working class, most of them. Many of them never went to school, perhaps no further than fourth grade. But they lived in a world of high culture, the Budapest String Quartet, debates about the latest performance of a Shakespeare play, Freud, Stekel, every possible form of political radicalism—in my life, it's the most lively intellectual culture I've ever been in, including the Harvard Faculty Club. But mostly these were barely

educated, unemployed working-class people, seamstresses, shop boys, that sort of thing. And this was a large part of the culture of the people—I don't want to say "popular culture" because that makes us think of television sitcoms—but the culture really of the people, which was complex and rooted in their own traditions. The culture of the people absorbed a lot of world culture but also had its own independent roots and character. Well, all this gets leveled in educational homogenization. Now it's a very different popular culture.

In this context, native cultures have endured for millennia and have diverse identities; they are different ways of life. Contact with the dominant society and culture, schooling, foreign educational models and standards, negation of the community and instead the acceptance of a very different and pervasive reality, aggression by the mass media that tends to distort and degenerate, that is distorting the very essence of the original, millenary cultures. By these means and others, these cultures are changed into something superficial, simple *folklore*, a tourist attraction, until they end up as what is referred to as "popular culture." Finally, they disappear into the homogenized world.

So, the strategy of instituting official education standards is designed to be the firm foundation that will bring about a global economic system, resting on the current political and social order. This is a good way to finance the system and the global economic model—an economic model based on accumulation that generates much poverty and inequality in the world. Obviously, we are talking about a violent process, deadly, that annihilates cultures and identities. We are talking about an excellent tool for ideological domination, serving to reproduce the global system and current economic model. But this model is going through an imminent and perhaps irreversible crisis; perhaps this will be the moment when good times draw near and coalesce to bring about the resurgence of our peoples.

THE FORMATION OF THE NATION-STATE

Addressing the subject of the formation of nation-states, Chomsky lays out many reasons why this process, which was developing for hundreds of years in Europe and other regions of the world that later were conquered, represented destructive processes and bloody, murderous scenes that went on for generations, with the goal of delimiting national borders according to the particular interests of royalty and kingdoms. Ultimately, the formation of the nation-state became an unprecedented historic crusade, the consequences of which are marked with blood and fire and much human cruelty. It signified the destruction of cultures, customs, identities, even the physical disappearance of millenary peoples and nations. That is to say, the horrible carrying out of this crime exceeds our concepts of "genocide" and "ethnocide." The nations and peoples of this region of the world, known as Abya Yala in the indigenous language of the Kuna, a term which now all of our peoples have adopted as our own, draw attention to the fact that quantities of debris and ashes remain, and also an incalculable historic debt.

Prior to the formation of the Latin America nation-states, or Abya Yala, there was the European invasion and brutal subjugation of millions of human beings, thousands of cultures, languages and identities that already were formed as nations and peoples. This regime of genocide and bloody colonization resulted in the raid of our territories, the armed robbery of our natural resources, the irreparable destruction of Mother Nature, and the creation of functional colonial structures, which then justified the institutionalization of our extermination and humiliation.

In this way, the nation-states of Abya Yala were born out of the bloodstained ruins of civilizations, out of the burning cross and gunfire of a heinous regime. This is why the political system and the state structures implanted in our region are colonial, as is the imported democratic system. The fundamental characteristics that make up this type of state, from our point of view, are hierarchical, one-nation, one-culture, one-language, exclusive, and capitalist, characterized by enormous social inequalities.

The formation processes of those states meant the wrongful seizure and distribution of whole regions and continents of Indian lands, auctioning off their wealth, and exploiting indigenous labor and black slaves. These conditions have been the important foundations and pillars of the institutionalization of the nation-state in this region. Latin American states are poor copies of the European state, evidenced in many ways: they still maintain colonial characteristics, ways of thinking and a Eurocentric institutional vision that are recognizable in present state institutions.

Therefore, state construction in our regions, aside from being questionable, is unfinished and in a condition of stagnation, or even in an embryonic stage. This means that the conditions exist for modifying or even reconstructing these states.

In this context, we, the indigenous peoples of the region, have put forth the need to reconstruct the present states, creating a new state that includes everyone equally. One state, democratic, free, just, equal, unified, and plurinational. For us as indigenous peoples, the construction of a plurinational state is an urgent priority.

This proposal reflects our questioning of the structures of the traditional, exclusive, homogenizing, and racist state. Construction of the plurinational state consists in recognizing the cultural, social, and political diversity of our peoples. That is to say, recognizing the presence of multiple nations inside the nation-state, millenary cultures and civilizations that have existed for thousands of years, incorporated into a state that was born only 179 years ago, in the case of Ecuador.

Furthermore, state institutionalism finds itself in a process of decay and irreparable failure precisely because it is inherently colonial and lacks historical legitimacy. For this reason, this proposal from the indigenous movement has lodged itself in the debates taking place within both national and international communities.

Due to the force of the mobilization efforts on its behalf, this proposal has been incorporated into the political constitutions of Bolivia and Ecuador during their recent Constitutional Assemblies, convened out of the necessity to decolonize democracy, the state, and education, and to articulate the thought, science, knowledge, and paradigms of Abya Yala. In these two Andean countries, the construction of the plurinational state, now incorporated into the new constitutions, has already begun.

RESISTANCE

The perverse reality which confronts *comunalidad*, indigenous nations, and all humankind poses a risk, not only to the preservation of multiple and diverse cultures and identities, but above all, the danger that the universal sciences will stagnate. Nowadays, the sciences are fed by local processes of knowing, knowledge generation, and regional identities which receive no formal recognition. But the danger goes far beyond science or the academy; confrontation among indigenous peoples is imminent in the form of fighting and ethnic, religious, and cultural wars. For this reason, it is absolutely necessary and urgent to search for mechanisms to establish tolerance and effective recognition and acceptance of the Other.

From our modest life experiences, we are able to suggest some policies and strategies, not only to fortify an identity-based cultural resistance movement of indigenous peoples, but also to bring about social consensus regarding topics that we absolutely share. These policies and strategies would be directed both from within our communities, as well as from without.

In this regard, academic institutions, society, and the state must generate opportunities to debate these topics which have not yet been addressed deeply or with great rigor. We say this because resistance to this aggressive and violent world cannot simply be the concern of a single indigenous person, or indigenous peoples collectively, or the community, *la comunalidad*. If the entire world is at high risk, if the global catastrophe is going to destroy the planet, then resistance, or the search for mechanisms to resist, is an obligation of everyone. Additionally, the "Indian problem," if it is a problem, is not a problem of indigenous peoples. The topic or question of indigenous peoples should be taken up globally, addressing all its implications, such as the topic of natural resources, territorial rights of indigenous peoples, the topic of *interculturalidad*, plurinationalism, etc.

We should ask ourselves: what have academic institutions contributed to this debate? How have they handled indigenous topics? At the very least, we know, tangentially, that the universities, the institutions of higher learning, are called to debate, to reflect on real social, economic, and political relations in the world, and to contribute to fundamental change. Furthermore, institutions of higher learning have the conditions, opportunities, and means to create these dialogic spaces. However, there seems to be total apathy toward indigenous issues, or a lack of vision; meanwhile, it is evident that there is abysmal ignorance concerning indigenous topics. From this perspective, as articulated by our peoples, the education system at all its levels facilitates and reinforces and extends the established order.

On another matter, what have been the role and behavior of the nation-state in relation to the decisive issues of indigenous peoples? From our perspective, we contend that the state should represent everyone equally; it is the organism whose functions are general, intended for all citizens. Therefore, it is the appropriate entity to generate public policies and programs that attend to the needs of society and, in particular, indigenous peoples, given their historical demand for justice or, perhaps, for the historic debt the state owes them. The establishment of equitable relationships, mutual respect, and the knowledge and strengthening of cultures and identities are supreme duty of the state through its education system and other state media. In this vein, opening the debate, the discussion of the indigenous question, establishment of internal recognition, achieving harmony among peoples and cultures, are obviously all responsibilities of the state. But instead, the state prefers to generate problems for indigenous peoples, creating obstacles that increase their struggles and hamper their process of development and their possibilities for change. That which historically has opposed indigenous struggles has been the state.

It is within our prerogative as indigenous peoples, communities, and organizational structures to bring about consensus through internal debates and through dialogue with the national society about the indigenous agenda, which includes topics that are claimed internally by the indigenous movement, as well as national and global issues. Also, an action agenda has been designed, growing out of our social mobilizations. Our struggles to bring social pressure to bear are peaceful, important, and necessary mechanisms in the process of consolidation and development of our peoples.

These agendas and actions of the indigenous movement in some South American countries were established out of our necessity to devise mechanisms of resistance and to search for answers to the painful problems of our peoples and the general crisis that is afflicting all of humanity. The indigenous agenda responds to a historic and collective process of construction; it is not an arbitrary and unilateral creation. It is the product of our experiences of struggle and of its own historic process of organic, political and ideological construction. From this perspective, both the agenda and the political project it represents anticipate actions that are immediate and intermediate, situational and strategic.

This agenda identifies priorities, one being to forge unity among peoples, to consolidate our organizations, and to work on constructing proposals, such as the following: the right to bilingual education, property (territorial) rights, and our political projects, such as plurinationalism and *interculturalidad*, among others.

At all moments, in all spaces, and in any of our struggles, the indigenous movement considers that determining its own path is fundamental. And that path is the organizing and unifying of indigenous peoples. This is the indispensable requirement in this process of struggle for resistance and the construction of proposals. Without the slightest fear that we are mistaken, we believe that change comes from and is generated by the base, the rank and file, of a people. Structural changes work from the bottom up, not from the top down. For this reason, special attention is given, and the time necessary is committed, to the action of organizing and unifying peoples—this is the strength and cornerstone of the contemporary indigenous struggle.

From this social base and political consistency, struggles are begun, proposals are constructed, claims are defended, changes are initiated.

We will try to illustrate this, using some applied experiences in our country, programs like the Bilingual Intercultural Education Program, which is designed in response to doubts about the national education system after the many documented failures of the official system in indigenous communities. The official education system has been hierarchical, homogenous, and monolingual (Spanish-only), a system that does not reflect the social and cultural reality of our society, much less the communities and the indigenous peoples.

Our experience has created a system of intercultural bilingual education that, first of all, is the result of collective action and was developed through indigenous organization at all levels. Second, the programs, content, and methodologies are generated by our own wisdom, principles, and knowledge. Third, the teachers are from the community and their social commitments and professional guidance are responsibilities of the community. The task of preparing teachers is based in community knowledge, facilitated by indigenous persons who are responsible for educational administration.

The educational administration is relatively autonomous in relation to the state. Naturally, though, the state is financially responsible for the process of bilingual education in such things as the salary of bilingual teachers, professional development, development of educational materials in indigenous languages, and equipping educational centers.

In this regard, the Intercultural University of Indigenous Nations and Peoples (Amawtay Wasi) in Ecuador, the Indigenous University of Colombia, and three universities in Bolivia, have joined this process, forming a sequential and complimentary stage in bilingual education. These are all projects that attempt to rearticulate the science, knowledge, and paradigms of Abya Yala. That is to say, we feel it is necessary that our reality be recognized within academic, political, and ideological contexts. In the same way, we feel urgency to decolonize our thinking and our philosophies, in the search for an alternative system of higher education, rejecting some principles of the classic system such as educational norms. Our proposals are in a stage of development and refinement.

Another proposal for a real, liberating alternative, one that has been considered important for indigenous peoples and for other sectors of society, is plurinationalism and *interculturalidad*. Plurinationalism acknowledges the real, undeniable diversity of life in nations and among peoples, as historically defined and differentiated economic, political, cultural, spiritual, and linguistic entities. Plurinationalism defends fairness, justice, and both individual and collective freedom. Through this project we promote our principles of life: reciprocity, solidarity, mutual respect, redistribution, the complementarity and unity of all peoples, respect for Mother Earth, and harmonious cohabitation with her.

Toward this end, plurinationalities are a model of political organization: the organization of the state, society, forms of government or authority, systems for administering justice, and a system of government that applies justice, liberty, and well-being equally to all, and the dismantling of colonialism, racism, and discrimination. Also, the self-governing of our peoples inside the nation-state, allowing for affirmation of diverse identities and cultures, in order to generate spaces for debate and dialogue about *interculturalidad*, which has been an aspiration and historic proposal made by our peoples.

We, the original nations and peoples, are working toward harmonic cohabitation among all humanity, our equilibrium and cohabitation with Mother Nature, justice, and human equality; in other words, a sense of complementarity with the planet. Therefore, the aspirations, dreams, and proposals of indigenous peoples are not only for indigenous peoples. In our minds, they are alternatives to solve the problems of humanity as a whole. Resistance, then, must become a real convergence of efforts among all sectors that are conscious and committed to humanity, Mother Earth, and life.

14.

Kichwa Resistance in Ecuador

By *María Yolanda Terán, Ecuador*

Kichwa educator and researcher from Ecuador, presently a doctoral student in Education and Indigenous Languages at the University of New Mexico, EEUU, and coordinator of education for the Andes Chinchasuyo Indigenous Organization of Ecuador and the Network of Indigenous Women in Biodiversity. Email: yolanda_teran2003@yahoo.com

"OUR INDIGENOUS LANGUAGES ARE the heart of our peoples, of our cultures . . . in the face of globalization, we have to reinforce our cultures, spirituality, languages and local powers."—JRM, indigenous leader of Ecuador, 2008

As an indigenous Kichwa woman from Ecuador, I am aware of the series of problems we—as a family, as students, and as part of a mestizo society—had to confront in order to survive. After my parents were married in the community of Peguche, Ecuador, they traveled to the Sanctuary of the Virgin of Las Lajas in Colombia. On the return to their community, the bus in which they were traveling broke down, so they stayed several days in San Gabriel, a city located in northern Ecuador. Repairing the bus took longer than expected, so my parents accepted the invitation of close relatives to stay on and live in the city.

The change of residence meant both advantages and disadvantages for our family. On one hand, leaving the community of Peguche meant distancing ourselves from close family; on the other, it opened up the possibility of enrolling in the formal education system, something that would have been denied to us, especially the girls, if we had continued to live in our community.

In the city of San Gabriel, my parents quickly felt the effects of racism and exclusion. In order to attend public schools, my brothers had to cut their long hair and shed their traditional clothes, all this so that we would be accepted without problem at school and in mestizo society. In our case, as girls, we always kept our traditional dress and way of being. Because of that, we suffered even more than the men, both in school and out.

My father understood that one of the ways to get ahead in mestizo society was to learn and use the dominant language, Spanish. He made us learn to speak the best Spanish in all of Ecuador. Meanwhile, my mother continued speaking our language, Kichwa, in and out of our home. Thanks to this brave and rebellious act on her part, we learned to understand Kichwa but we lost our oral fluency due to school pressures and our fear of being rejected. Furthermore, the negative concept of Kichwa was engraved in our hearts by our own indigenous classmates, who referred to our language as "Yanga Shimi," a language with no value, a concept inherited from colonial times and still prominent today, despite many widespread efforts to change this perception of our mother tongue.

Throughout my life, I have clearly seen the negative effects of the state policies implemented during each era, how these policies were able to subordinate and dominate our people, through deception, ransacking, violation of our rights in the most cruel and unimaginable ways, dispossession of our lands, our cultures, languages, life styles, and cosmovisions. They turned us into a people without land, a people with low self-esteem, weighed down by suffering, poverty, extreme poverty, desolation, and anguish.

For example, the "whitening" of Ecuador was intended to negate the rich cultural diversity of the country and the great potential of the indigenous peoples. Many years had to pass before the ruling leaders of the time were able to accept and understand that we also have the capacity to contribute to the country's development, and that together we will achieve sustained development and an identity characterized by mutual respect and understanding.

Throughout our history, indigenous men and women worked together to guide us and give us the necessary direction to end these abuses. As for education, our peoples were forced to receive an education foreign to their cultural context. Kichwa-speaking students had mestizo teachers who were unfamiliar with the mother tongue of their students. In this unequal context, there were various violations and mistreatments of our children because the teachers taught in an unknown language and used methods that conveyed an image of the teacher's superiority and arrogance. The teacher was never a friend to the indigenous child. These teachers used the excuse that "they were doing Indians a favor by teaching them, and that Indians didn't understand what they were taught because they were inferior." Then they proceeded to punish our children. Here the saying "beat them until they learn" was rigorously applied.

Faced with these abuses, the dispossession of our ancestral lands, the excesses of the Catholic Church, the robbery and rape of our indigenous women on the plains as they collected wood for cooking, and a series of other abuses, indigenous peoples began various educational initiatives, initiatives that valued and applied the indigenous cosmovision, science, art, customs, languages, etc. This type of social venture was viewed negatively by the landowners who persecuted, murdered, and imprisoned various indigenous men and women, with the intent of terminating the rebirth of indigenous education.

Finally after years of tension, in the 1980s the National Direction of Bilingual and Intercultural Education (Dirección Nacional de Educación Intercultural Bilingüe, DINEIB) was created, an institution that once again would take responsibility for the system of indigenous bilingual education. It was the first educational department of its kind in Latin America, and since that time DINEIB has tried to fill the existing void in indigenous education. It is currently working on the quality of our education, which basically seeks an integral and holistic education through and for a sustainable way of life. We have this department, which does not receive sufficient government funding but which carries out its tasks because of the commitment of its employees and sustained international support.

The new constitution of Ecuador recognizes the collective rights of indigenous peoples, and among these the existence of indigenous languages, acknowledging Kichwa and Shuar as official languages. Nevertheless, we are aware that appropriate laws to exercise our language rights to their full extent are lacking. We are also lacking the necessary financial resources to create educational programs in our languages, developed from within our cultures and by our indigenous professionals, whether or not they have Western academic degrees.

We know that there are numerous Kichwa speakers in Ecuador and the Andean region, but if we don't use our language, if we don't *speak* it, we run the risk that its *vitality will diminish*. In this regard, it is essential that we work with parents and schools to create a link, a bridging of our work that creates an educational extension, so that what is learned through the indigenous language at school continues in the students' homes. Then it will be crucial to develop cultural and linguistic policies to define our short-term, intermediate and long term goals. These policies should be defined through full and effective involvement of all community members, so that all have an understanding and ownership of the policies and work plans, which are to be designed according to their own concrete needs. In this new approach to work, we urgently need "community collaboration (*minga*) for the life and existence of the indigenous peoples, community collaboration (*minga*) for the indigenous languages and cultures," in order to avoid their loss due to rapid sociocultural and political changes and the effects of out-migration and globalization.

In the face of globalization, inadequate state policies, unsatisfied basic needs, the impossibility of having a dignified life or reaching collective and individual well-being, we as indigenous people must work to strengthen our local power and our cultural identities, reclaiming our ancestral values, principles, and rules of holistic coexistence, recovering the lost harmony among humans and also between humans and Mother Nature.

We have to grow together, men with women; our self-esteem has to improve. Through our knowledge and our intercultural relations based on equality and respect, we will achieve our long awaited "*Sumak Kawsay*," our good life, that will be framed within our rights to self determination, free prior and informed consent, the right to our ancestral lands, among others.

We must keep our hearts and minds open so we can understand societal changes, but our love for and conviction toward our roots should be strong and firm in order to continue our fight for survival. Therefore, it is important to educate ourselves both formally and informally, and to count on the support of our elders, women, and youth. All of us have to know and understand the significance and extent of our constitutional rights, as well as the Declaration of the United Nations on the Rights of Indigenous Peoples, and several world-wide international documents, and we must know how to use these in our favor. How long will we live in a world of inequality and injustice? Why don't we remember that "when we die we are all the color of the earth" and try to see ourselves as brothers and sisters, taking care of and protecting each other as such?

Considering the national and international negotiations that were held around the world on topics related to indigenous peoples, I began to follow the work of United Nations agencies in Quito to understand their work dynamic for our peoples. As part of the National Council of Indigenous Women of Ecuador (CON-

MIE), I worked with other Ecuadorian indigenous colleagues to bring about changes in the United Nations system, through the inclusion of our ways of thinking and our experiences regarding several topics. As CONMIE, we have invited the United Nations "to work from the field, not from a desk in the city."

In 2002, during a workshop organized by the United Nations in Quito, Ecuador, indigenous representatives felt obligated to use our indigenous languages. This happened because of the difficulties we had discussing certain topics in Spanish, or when we saw and felt that many important decisions concerning indigenous peoples were going to be delayed or ignored, or when we realized that a work agenda not reflective of our reality and needs was being imposed on us. It was a critical moment when we began to speak Kichwa in front of the delegates at the United Nations. The last session was very intense; no resolution seemed possible, and things became tense and heavy. Then an indigenous leader spoke in Kichwa with great energy, saying: "We need to take this issue into our own hands, now, not tomorrow." Then she assigned responsibilities to each of us. Some were to write a document, others were to reach an agreement of understanding with the U.N. delegates, and others were to make a final decision about the conformation of the Indigenous Advisory Council for the United Nations in Quito, Ecuador. Our "indigenous response" to the work agenda imposed by the United Nations brought this system to a halt and caused it to pay more attention to our demands.

U.N. representatives from the United States, Europe and Ecuador were surprised by our collective stance and asked for translation. Our leader called on me to speak, to remind the system that the moment had arrived for its employees to learn our languages, in order to have better communication with us, just as indigenous peoples in the past and even today have been forced to learn the official languages of the United Nations. After this cordial invitation, I translated into Spanish only a portion of our previous discussion in Kichwa.

To speak different languages in the United Nations, we have to have the courage to speak in languages that are not our own. Still, as women we should accept the challenge of doing so, so that our voices are heard directly, not through intermediaries or poor translations.

In 2003, I began my international work on some of the United Nations issues: education, health, indigenous languages, traditional knowledge, genetic resources, cultural indicators, etc. I have participated in the Permanent Forum on Indigenous Affairs for eight consecutive years. In 2006, as regional coordinator for Latin America and the Caribbean for the Group on Indicators of the Convention on Biological Diversity (CBD), I organized in Quito a regional workshop on Indicators of Traditional Knowledge.

For several years I have been the education coordinator of the Andes Chinchasuyo Indigenous Organization of Ecuador and also of the Network of Indigenous Women on Biodiversity of Latin America. Furthermore, I am part of the Subgroup on the Rights of Indigenous Children, among others. At all the international meetings, I have had to take a great leap to reach full, effective participation, both personally and as part of the group of indigenous women and colleagues from Latin America. The use of other languages to present our ideas is critically important. I have to use English, Spanish, Kichwa, or Portuguese, depending on the situation. On several occasions, I have had to translate for my friends when no translator was available or due to a poor translation. Of course, this has caused conflict within some agencies because "speaking so many languages has given me power," which is true in a sense, because we are no longer acting blindly or failing to understand in international gatherings.

15.

Indigenous Peoples Contesting State Nationalism and Corporate Globalism

By Stefano Varese, Peru

Peruvian of Italian descent, professor in the Department of Native American Studies and Director of the Indigenous Research Center of the Americas, University of California, Davis. Email: svarese@ucdavis.edu

THE LAST FIVE DECADES of Pax Americana in the Americas have witnessed a process of social and spatial restructuring, expressing itself in the transformation of old cultural and national loyalties into new trans-ethnic, transnational, and multidimensional identities. The growing phenomenon of an Indian diaspora in Latin America and beyond that transcends national borders is questioning conventional ideas and practices of nationalism, citizenship, and territoriality. The various cultural patrimonies of each expatriate indigenous group seem to be redefined within the new social context through a process of negotiation with the dominant "other," in which culture and identity enter into a contested domain, a field of negotiation, adaptation, and limited compromise. What is being outlined as the central theme of negotiation between the increasingly trans-nationalized states and the indigenous peoples in transit toward a multiethnic diaspora, is the issue of new notions of citizenship: expanded, flexible, multidimensional, multiethnic, de-nationalized. These new forms of citizenship should guarantee the political, economic, social, cultural, and linguistic rights of a new hemispheric—and world—resident who is no longer the subject in exclusivity of a particular nation-state to which unconditional loyalty is due, but rather a citizen of multiple social, political, and territorial spaces cohabited and shared in different moments of life. In this manner, issues of indigenous sovereignty, autonomy, and self-determination that are recurrent obsessions of Latin American governments and the U.S. federal government could become less threatening and more manageable were a multiple and non-exclusively-state-oriented conception of citizenship to be adopted.

It is obvious, however, that re-conceptualizing and repositioning the concept and practice of citizenship within contemporary nation-states implies bringing into the debate what Etienne Balibar (1991: 96–100) has called the "fictive ethnicity" of the community instituted by the nation-state. This is a fabricated entity and personhood reproduced torturously and intentionally through the process of nationalization of different peoples into the social formation that constitutes the nation-state. Ethnicized (and culturally homogenized) peoples within the nation-state are "represented in the past or in the future as if they formed a natural community, possessing of itself an identity of origins, culture and interests which transcends individual and social conditions" (ibid. 96). The nation-state's need to establish its hegemony through the construction of "fictive ethnicity" has had two types of non-mutually exclusive consequences in the Americas: 1) on the one hand, nation-states have privileged policies of assimilation which claim equal rights of citizenship only to those individuals and groups that participate in identical manner in the national fictive ethnicity. Cultural/ethnic diversity is presented as cause of political and economic inequality; 2) on the other hand, the same nation-states institutionalize concealed segregationist policies in which ethnicized/racialized groups and individuals are differentiated (stratified) and delivered different levels of citizenship and political power. Implicitly or explicitly, the promise of the nation-state is that each citizen on her/his merit may share the advantages of democracy, freedom, and equality if she/he is willing to socially behave in adherence to the rules or "values" of the new globalized nationalism: "the Global West," "the Global North," or simply "neoliberal globalized nationalism." The unfinished relation between the indigenous peoples of Latin America and Euro-American humanism (and social science) has traced a delicate and ambiguous dialectic that began with the contradictory letters of Columbus to the Spanish Crown and continued during five centuries with the unequivocal defense of the indigenous by Bartolomé de las Casas, the repeated attacks on native institutions, ideas, and civilizations by missionaries and colonial administrators, and the constantly nebulous alternation between some sympathetic accounts and an overwhelming amount of superficial views, racist prejudices, and expressions of absolute contempt for the Indians. Both modern anthropology and the contemporary indigenous political movement carry the colonial burden of this long process of mutual misinterpretation. I think, however, that in this complex and long-lasting relationship, the last quarter of the twentieth century and the beginning of the twenty-first century can be identified as founding moments of approximation and mutual cooperation between the ethno-political indigenous movement of Latin America and a limited sector of the fields of anthropology, social sciences, and the humanities. Within this frame of analysis I intend to render tribute to both the indigenous intellectuals/activists and the anthropologists/humanists who have surmounted the colonial barriers and prejudices of separation, thereby contributing to the establishment of an environment of collaboration and cultural creativity. I find, therefore, a certain pleasure in celebrating this newly achieved alliance because its origin coincided, years ago, with some sort of collective birth of conscience among a group of us anthropologists and indigenous intellectuals in Latin America who were willing to choose academic and tribal heterodoxy in order to protect freedom of cultures against a massive imposition, from both sides of the political spectrum, of a homogenizing social project.

THE POLITIZATION OF INDIGENOUS PEOPLES

Although the indigenous peoples of the Americas have been struggling against colonial powers for five hundred years, it was mainly after World War II that they initiated political mobilization at the national and international scale in order to resist oppression. There were hundreds of indigenous insurrections, messianic movements, and ethno-nationalist independence rebellions that took place during the Iberian colonial administration and the following Republican period, as well as many other examples of early Indian political activism expressed in "modern" terms in the various national territories of Latin America; however, it is only during the last five decades that evidence of a substantial national and international indigenous movement can be found in the massive proliferation of native organizations and supporting institutions of civil society (NGOs).

The structural reasons for the rise of an international indigenous movement can be traced to what has been called post-World War II Pax Americana, characterized by the massive expansion of the industrial base in the "core" countries, the dependent development efforts in Latin America connected to the expansion of the internal national frontier in search of energy resources, and the readjustment of the nation-state structures in order to facilitate national integration and ethnic assimilation. Explorations and resource exploitation of peripheral regions by multinational corporations and their local national representatives became suddenly the single most threatening event for indigenous peoples and territories that had enjoyed relative isolation and autonomy. In the course of a few decades, indigenous peoples of the relatively marginal areas of the lowlands of Central and South America became "internal refugees of underdevelopment." The traditional strategy of retreating to isolated areas, the "zones of refuge," became less and less viable, forcing the indigenous communities to go on the offensive, while recognizing the changing characteristics of the antagonistic forces now increasingly transnational and relatively out of the control of the regional elites.

STATE NATIONALISM AND TRANSNATIONALIZATION

A basic paradox appears, however, in this process of transnationalization of the political economy of Latin American nation-states. On the one hand, the programs operated by transnational corporations in Latin America mitigate the need for Latin American states to play the entrepreneurial role in substitution for the national oligarchies and bourgeoisie that traditionally have been passive. On the other hand, the multinational corporate project creates for the state a problem of national security by challenging precisely a weakly integrated and vulnerable national entity. Two antagonistic forces thus came into play in the Latin American scenario during the last few decades: 1) a strong trend toward national consolidation, in which the state continues to act as the founding and generating principle of the nation, reshaping and attempting to give a sense of unity to heterogeneous territorial and ethnic spaces for the benefit of the ruling class; and 2) the need of the same state, under pressure by the transnationalization of the political economy, to transform itself ideologically and objectively from a liberal nineteenth century institution (centralized, authoritarian, homogeneous) into a more permeable, flexible, less "nationalistic" entity, open to corporate penetration and transnational forces.

The expected result of these contradictory trends has been increasingly the movement of transnational capital to less controlled areas, to open regions: to indigenous territories, not yet totally exploited, where environmental regulations, labor unions, and political organizations do not exist or are weak and controllable. Concurrent to this process of internationalization of capital, labor, and environment, the privatization of the state becomes a key requirement. Even basic state functions such as police control are increasingly relegated to private concessions, resulting in the

1980s in the proliferation of paramilitary forces in charge of repression and control. The ideology and actual process of national integration and ethnic assimilation of indigenous peoples comes, therefore, under the ambiguous jurisdictions of a neo-dependent state formally in charge of defining the terms of citizenship for each member of the national community, and the informal, hidden, and powerful authority of transnational capital.

MANY INDIGENOUS PEOPLES AND FEW ANTHROPOLOGISTS
It is in this context that, in the 1970s, a new encounter between a handful of Latin American anthropologists and indigenous leaders and intellectuals took place and generated some unexpected and creative alliances. The 1970s and the 1980s, "the lost decades of Latin America," had been characterized by paranoid and violent military dictatorships, obsessive attempts, never fully successful, to bind illusory nations together by force, compulsive ventures of capitalist expansion on barely integrated national markets, and systematic assaults on indigenous peoples, territories, resources, and human and cultural rights. The 1970s, however, had also inherited years of colonial critique and anti-imperialist struggle. The writings and actions of Frantz Fanon, Albert Memmi, Jean Paul Sartre, Amilcar Cabral, Aimée Césaire, Ho Chi Minh, Che Guevara, and those of the rediscovered indigenous critics and leaders, such as Huamán Puma de Ayala, Túpac Amaru, Túpac Katari, Juan Santos Atahualpa, and Quintín Lame, had been nourishing the thoughts and political experiences of new generations of anthropologists and indigenous. Some of the latter, especially in the Andean countries and Mesoamerica, were already urban and proletarian, politicized in principles of class analysis and labor unionism, internationalized in their perception of the world system and the politics of blocks. The massive process of indigenous rural-urban migration caused by the expropriation of communal lands by landlords in the Andean countries and various other indigenous regions of Latin America in the 1950s and

1960s had exacerbated the long-standing historical process of cyclical deterritorialization of indigenous peasants. The novelty in this phenomenon that began in the late sixteenth century with the uprooting of indigenous community members through the obligatory "mita" service in the Andean mines was that now the indigenous workers, miners and seasonal farm-workers, thrown into the middle of a dependent capitalist market, were exposed to new political ideas, other workers, new forms of organization, new strategies of resistance and opposition, and a new array of social, cultural, and ethnic information.

Starting in the second half of the 1960s, vast regions of the Peruvian Amazon were also laid open to guerrilla movements of Marxist inspiration. Ashaninka, Nomatsiguenga, Machiguenga, Shipibo, and Quechua colonists were forced to choose between an armed and urban political project not particularly sensitive to ethnic rights and autonomy, and a repressive army that had traditionally equated indigenous people with subversion. Indigenous peoples of Chile, Bolivia, Colombia, El Salvador, Nicaragua, Guatemala, and finally Mexico, were also going to be increasingly involved in armed political movements and genocidal wars (cynically called "low-intensity wars" by the U.S. State Department) that would re-create the reality of the Conquest in indigenous territories.

In June 1971, a dozen Latin American anthropologists, accompanied by a U.S. ethnologist expatriate to Mexico and an Austrian social scientist, met on the island of Barbados under the sponsorship of the World Council of Churches to discuss the situation of the indigenous peoples of Latin America. The Barbados I meeting, as it became known afterwards, produced an impressive book of denunciations of human and ethnic rights abuses carried out by governments, missionaries, the private sector, and even social scientists, and a short declaration which soon became a banner for some of the emerging indigenous organizations of Central and South America. The Spanish edition of the book, published in Montevideo, never reached the shelves of bookstores: it was burned by the Uruguayan military dictatorship, a curious act of racist zeal and political conservatism since Uruguay is one of the few countries of Latin America that does not have a substantial indigenous population. No indigenous people were present at the Barbados I meeting. It would take another six years for the Barbados group to convene a larger second meeting of thirty-five participants, this time including eighteen who were active militants of the indigenous Latin American movement. Some of the indigenous members who attended Barbados II traveled to the island clandestinely; the Guatemalan Maya and Colombian Páez participants were actually risking their lives by being at the conference. Finally, in 1993, twenty-three years after the first meeting, the Barbados III group met in Río de Janeiro, to mourn the death of one of its most enlightened members, Guillermo Bonfil Batalla, and to address again old indigenous issues of neocolonialism, wars, land eviction, genocide, human rights abuses, and cultural destruction. The new twist on these long-standing abuses was that they were now presented by the transnational community of capital as the inevitable price to be paid by the weak to allow for the globalization of the economy and the establishment of a "new world order."

The three Barbados meetings can be seen as a synopsis of twenty-five years of accompaniment of the indigenous movement of liberation by a minority of Latin American anthropologists. The Declaration of Barbados I, "For the Liberation of the Indigenous People" (1971), was a strong denunciation and demand to the state, the church, the private sector, and the social scientists to satisfy the basic human and ethnic rights of the indigenous peoples. Barbados II (1977) reflected both the Indians' and anthropologists' activism and direct involvement in the social movement of liberation, assuming all the risks of such a decision. Some of the indigenous participants and some of the anthropologists already were living either clandestinely in their own countries or in exile. The Declaration of Barbados III, "The Articulation of Diversity" (1993), evaluated the previous twenty-five years of Latin American anthropology and its contributions to the indigenous struggle of decolonization. There was little optimism in this assessment that recognized the ethical distortions of contemporary theoretical meandering and self-gratifying solipsism that disguised the lack of commitment by academic anthropology to Indians' liberation struggles and, for that matter, to the struggles of the oppressed. Finally, Barbados III recognized that at the end of the century the indigenous movement of the Americas was a fundamental factor in the international scenario that would have to be taken into consideration in any major decision regarding world peace and development.

THE INDIAN REVOLUTIONARY FIRE IN NORTH AMERICA

In 1994, the Mexican government claimed that by signing NAFTA, Mexico showed that it was part of North America, at the same time that the struggle of the rebel Mayan communities in Chiapas displayed a very different truth that penetrated to the heart of global humanity. Just a few weeks after the meeting of Barbados III, on January 1, 1994, Tzeltal, Tzotzil, Chol, Tojolabal, and Zoque Maya communities of Chiapas who had clandestinely organized ten years to form the Zapatista National Liberation Army (Ejército Zapatista de Liberación Nacional, or EZLN) declared war on the Mexican government, quickly establishing the military occupation of four major municipalities in Chiapas, Mexico. An indigenous army of 800 combatants occupied the city of San Cristóbal de las Casas, seized the municipal palace, proclaimed their opposition to the "undeclared genocidal war against our people by the dictators," and described their "struggle for work, land, shelter, food, health, education, independence, freedom, democracy, justice, and peace."

This Mayan armed movement of an estimated 2,000 combatants and thousands of supporters, has as fundamental objectives the defense of indigenous land, natural resources and the achievement of regional ethnic autonomy. The EZLN has also expressed its firm opposition to the North American Free Trade Agreement, which is considered a "death certificate" for the indigenous peasants, and to the modification of Article 27 of the Mexican Constitution, which permits the privatization of indigenous and peasant collective and communal lands. "This Article 27 of the Constitution, they changed it without asking us, without requesting our input. Now it is time for them to listen to us, because to take our land is to take our life." After an initial violent repression by the Mexican army that included air raids and indiscriminate bombing, disappearances, and summary executions that caused an international scandal, the Mexican government agreed to initiate a peace negotiation process. Today, after more than two years of tense negotiations between the Mayan insurgents and the Mexican government, and despite a massive mobilization of the indigenous peoples and organizations of Mexico as well as the civil society, the demands of the Zapatistas have not been met.

The demands of the Mayan rebels in Chiapas summarize two crucial concerns of today's Latin American indigenous movement. The first is the right of self-governance and autonomy. These rights are becoming an increasingly prominent part of the democratization process in various Latin American countries. The Mayan insurgents demand communal and regional autonomy, free elections, self-rule, and guarantees of nonintervention on the part of the government in their internal affairs. The second concern is their right to territorial and resource sovereignty. Their demands for ethnic self-determination and autonomy include full control over the lands, water, and resources that fall within their defined ethnic boundaries.

The recuperation of indigenous land and political autonomy is based on three principles, the first of which is the historical depth of the claim. The current territorial fragmentation and reduction in Latin America is the result of centuries of colonial and post-colonial expropriation; therefore, restitution of land and/or reparation are major issues. The second principle is based on the ethno-biological integrity of territories traditionally occupied by specific indigenous groups. In other words, bioregions and ethno-regions were largely coincident before the territorial disturbances of Europeans. There is no such thing in contemporary times as natural, untouched landscape; rational intervention by indigenous civilizations over millennia shaped and molded the environment and its biotic resources. The third principle is the repudiation of any solution to territorial and environmental claims that would involve the commoditization of nature. As one indigenous leader from the Amazon is reported to have stated in objection to the celebrated debt-for-nature swaps[1] promoted by some Northern environmentalists: "It is our nature—and it's not our debt." Recognition and respect for these principles must constitute the ethical framework for any political and economic negotiations between indigenous peoples and national and international entities regarding political, territorial, and resource sovereignty.

INDIAN SOVEREIGNTY AND GLOBALIZATION

Until the Mayan rebellion of Chiapas, the issue of indigenous sovereignty was unspeakable in Latin America. The terms "sovereignty," "autonomy," and "self-determination" referring to indigenous peoples could barely be whispered by anthropologists and indigenous intellectuals and easily could be denounced as subversive proclamations. Following a strict Napoleonic tradition, the notion of sovereignty pertains exclusively to the nation-state. After more than two years of public debate in Mexico and in the world through the Internet, the concepts and possibilities of indigenous sovereignty and ethnic rights to self-determination and autonomy have become part of the accepted political discourse of indigenous peoples. The specifics of what may constitute ethno-sovereignty rights are still in the making and need to be addressed in each specific regional and national case. First and foremost,

there is the important question of the social and spatial definition of indigenous peoples, communities, and groups. According
to the "indigenistic" legislation of various national governments,
the indigenous ethnic groups are legally defined by their respective constituent communities (e.g., the *resguardo* in Colombia, the
comunidad nativa and *comunidad campesina* in Peru, the *comunidad
indígena* and *ejido* in Mexico, etc.). The communities have legal
standing as subjects in the law, but the ethnic groups do not.[2]
Nevertheless, the indigenous organizations of Ecuador, for instance, have succeeded in obtaining the state's recognition of the
term "nationalities" for various indigenous ethnic communities,
but this seems to be an exception in Latin America.

In view of the disagreements and confusions throughout
Latin America regarding ethno-social definitions and boundaries,
indigenous leaders are addressing two levels of sovereignty that
are rather complementary: one is "communal sovereignty," which
is implicitly recognized by the state although seldom honored. At
this level there are local indigenous institutions and authorities
and clear social-ethnic boundaries. The rather murky and more
complicated biotic boundaries pose a more complex problem of
resource and genetic control and sovereignty, which is becoming
increasingly important in these times of bio-piracy and renewed
environmental exploitation.

In contrast, the concept of "ethnic sovereignty" is legally rare
or nonexistent from the state's point of view but is increasingly
becoming the goal of indigenous organizations. Total ethnic sovereignty is represented by the numerous indigenous ethnic organizations that have a legal and fully institutional existence. The
ethno-political boundaries of these larger and multi-communal
ethnic sovereignties may imply legitimization of the historically
traceable ethnic frontiers, even if these are not presently under
ethnic control and the return of their control is a political objective of the organization.

Finally, indigenous peoples are facing the challenge to further develop organizational and legal forms that recognize and meet the needs of the ever-growing populations of de-territorialized communities who reside in cities and in nations far removed from their traditional homelands and modes of existence. This is the case of thousands of refugees and migrant workers from Central America and Mexico who have moved to the U.S. and Canada. Since the outbreak of war in Guatemala during the 1970s, some tens of thousands of indigenous have been killed and many thousands more have fled the country to seek sanctuary in Mexico and in the United States. On the basis of shared cultural heritage, the need to defend themselves as aliens in a strange and often hostile land has motivated them to form several interethnic associations.

Comparable to the presence of Guatemalan Mayan refugees in the United States is the presence in California and other U.S. states of tens of thousands of indigenous peoples from southern Mexico. At any given time there are some 25,000 to 50,000 Mixtec migrant farm workers in California alone. The Mixtecs, Zapotecs, Chinantecs, and Triques are mainly economic refugees from extremely impoverished and ecologically deteriorated regions where subsistence farming is almost impossible. Since the 1980s, people from these indigenous communities have organized transnational and multiethnic organizations for the defense of their labor, human, and cultural rights. The history of the mobilization and organization of Guatemalan and Mexican indigenous groups in California is perhaps one of the clearest examples of the transnationalization of Latin American indigenous politics, in that the primary locus of these international groups has been outside both their home territories and Latin America.

NA IN THE GLOBAL NORTH, IP IN THE GLOBAL SOUTH

One cannot easily forget that the first and most accomplished victims of U.S. imperialism were and are the Native Americans of the United States, followed by the native Hawaiians, other Pacific Islanders, Filipinos, Puerto Ricans, and all other peoples who were occupied and "assimilated" by U.S. expansionism. The success of U.S. imperialist cultural and political annexation is visible in what Gramsci called the establishment of hegemony—more than naked power and brute force—on subaltern and subjugated peoples. The central notions and values of the expansionist imperial state would require a much longer and deeper analysis.[3]

The most important of all these values, the one that articulates all of them in a coherent system, is the "capitalist ideology, its cosmology and its practice," and the political economy of the capitalist market that permeates the life of every individual living in the core of the capitalist empire, be they native or non-native. All these may sound like grand rhetorical words of the old Left, but old intellectual emotions and analyses carry the wisdom of experience, and the experience of many concrete struggles.

The lukewarm and distant relations that most Latin American indigenous peoples have maintained with the nation-states, their lack of true incorporation/assimilation into these largely fictive political entities, their lack of "patriotism," their marginal and weak position within the capitalist market, the survival and resistance of their subsistence economies, have put them in a relationship of ideological and practical autonomy to the system of values and political practices of the modern nation-state. We could argue that colonialism and imperialism failed to achieve their ideological goals in terms of the indigenous communities of Latin America. In Gramscian terms, they could not establish their hegemony. On the contrary, in the North, in the United States, in the core of the empire, the colonial-imperial power was much more successful with the Native Americans after they were defeated militarily. Native Americans became good imperial subjects, and as such they hesitantly adopted the imperial and capitalist language, the whole package of values including a degree of ethnic/racial contempt for anything originating south of the border, a kind of xenophobia, a patriotic and proud sense of being a U.S. citizens, joining willingly the U.S. Army in its imperial

wars and its invasions of foreign countries and peoples, and finally, projecting dangerously their own fully assimilated imperial
values onto other indigenous peoples, at times thinking that their
best option is to become like themselves: citizens of the United
States, U.S. Native Americans.

FINAL NOTE ON THE POWER OF IDEAS

Many of the founding members of the Group of Barbados have
since died. Two of them have special significance. Guillermo Bonfil Batalla, who brought to the forefront of the Mexican and Latin
American collective consciousness the profound injustice and racism of the social order in which indigenous peoples are forced
to live, was killed in 1992 in a car crash. Guillermo Bonfil had
predicted for years the re-emergence and consolidation of that
"Deep Mexico" of Indian civilizations that could finally change
and energize the frozen Mexican Revolution and establish a democracy of cultures, a realm of creative diversity, and the conditions for a truly autonomous multiethnic development. Bonfil's
prophecy came alive and was actualized in 1994 by the Zapatista
insurgency which continues to this day. At the other end of the
hemisphere, in Brazil, Darcy Ribeiro finally gave in after fighting
a disease that was supposed to have killed him more than twenty
years before. Actually, it was this disease that convinced the military dictatorship of Brazil in 1973 to allow Ribeiro's return from
a long exile in Uruguay, Chile, Venezuela, and Peru. The military dictators of Brazil thought that advanced lung cancer would
be enough to guarantee the silencing of this insubordinate mind.
Darcy Ribeiro—the anthropologist, the minister of education,
the novelist, the senator of the new Brazilian democracy—survived the generals and brought back to his beloved Brazil a vision
of the future that included the indigenous. In addition, Darcy's
vision of the future of the Americas was permeated by the cultural
beauty of Amazonian indigenous communities. For Darcy Ribeiro, the "dilemma of Latin America," existing as it does between

modernization and tradition, loss of identity to neo-imperial power and obsolescence, could find its solution in the respectful rediscovery of the indigenous civilizations that compose our tortured continent. More than any other Latin American anthropologists and intellectuals, Guillermo Bonfil Batalla and Darcy Ribeiro believed in the power of ideas, in the mobilizing strength of cultural imagination, and in the contributions of every single indigenous people of the Americas to the construction of a new type of Latin American social citizenship: multiethnic, democratic, local and cosmopolitan, communal and universalistic.

REFERENCES

Balibar, E, and Wallerstein, I. 1991. *Race, Nation, Class*. London: Verso.

Grunberg, G. (coordinador). 1995. *Articulación de la Diversidad: Pluralidad Etnica, Autonomías y Democratización en América Latina*. Quito, Ecuador: Grupo de Barbados, Ediciones de Abya Yala, N. 27.

Kearney, M., and S. Varese. 1995. Latin America's indigenous peoples: changing identities and forms of resistance. In S. Halebsky & R. L. Harris, *Capital, Power, and Inequality in Latin America*. Boulder: Westview Press.

Maiguashca Bice, M. 1994. The transnational indigenous movement in a changing world order. In S. Yoshkazu, *Global transformation: Challenges to the state system*. Tokyo, New York, Paris: United Nations University Press.

NOTES

1. In this financial arrangement, one nation or nongovernmental organization cancels out a portion of another debtor nation's foreign debt in exchange for local investments in conservation measures. This obligates a debtor nation's continued investment in conservation measures despite substantial foreign indebtedness.

2. See Bertely, this volume, for a more complete explanation of the complexity of indigenous peoples' legal status in Latin American nation-states, specifically Mexico.

3. Some of these notions are: citizenship (imperial, central, privileged, similar to the Roman Latin idea of "civis romanus sum"); freedom (selectively allowed after struggles and negotiations and revocable, mostly concerned with the market); electoral democracy (linked to the arithmetic of the voting process and its scandalous funding so that at the end of the day the winner is the wealthiest or

the one supported by the capitalist elite); individualism (in its extremist expression that opposes the collective, communal good as anti-modern, anti-progress, anti-capitalist); human rights (conceived and practiced only as individual rights if they are fitting the Western Eurocentric and modern conception derived from E. Kant and the Enlightenment); Governance-Government (structured and strictly organized along the paradigm of Euro-American style of government).

16.

Education from Inside Deep America

By Grimaldo Rengifo Vásquez, Peru

Peruvian agrarian engineer, founder and coordinator of the Andean Project of Campesino Technologies, and director of the "Childhood and Biodiversity" Project. Email: pratec@pratec.org.pe

COMMENTS ON THE FIRST INTERVIEW

Dr. Chomsky is aware of the fact that no solution exists outside the world of corporate life.[1] Each time he is pushed to give a response, he considers it almost irresponsible to offer an alternative and he opens up an array of diverse possibilities for an "other" life.

One of the questions posed to Dr. Chomsky throughout the interview is the meaning and achievements of *comunalidad*, and its relationship with the global project of neoliberal capitalism. Everyone has their own ways of understanding what the concept of community means, and Dr. Chomsky is no exception. He believes that the statement by Dewey, which to my way of thinking centers on the individual and his/her relationships, does not conflict with his way of understanding community. From the Andean point of view, community is understood as *ayllu*, a collective of human beings that also includes the world beyond humans, that is, nature and deities. Given this, human decisions are not only human, but also they are based on a consensus achieved with the world that is beyond human. The entire project of modernity, and especially that which is guided by the school, has been destined to destroy this relationship and mold it according to the interests of human beings living in society, that is, according to the interests of each individual who makes up the totality of society.

The survival of these communities—*ayllus*—in the Andes and their relationship with institutions and with the entire global conglomerate has been marked by the notion of nurture (*crianza*). Nurture is a relationship of affective caring among the beings that make up the *ayllu*. It involves bringing up and being brought up in a relationship of equality that includes all entities that inhabit the cosmos. It so happens that the school, the church, and also the hacienda,[2] are not now and never were in colonial times, nurturing institutions. Instead, they are oppressors. They were constructed for this purpose, as Dr. Chomsky clearly describes in the case of the school. What happens is that the *ayllus* don't differentiate between that which nurtures and that which does not. Instead, it is possible to nurture all entities, no matter what their origin, but each one in its own way and space, and each according to its circumstance. This is well known by the Andean *ayllus*, which had to endure the hacienda for five centuries until they could make it over, to mark it as community. Dr. Chomsky is right when he warns that no single solution exists to break out of coloniality. The *ayllus* have theirs, which is a way of seeing and living life that has permitted that the Andes still today, despite nation-states and industrial conglomerates, is an enormous center of biodiversity on the planet.

COMMENTS ON THE SECOND INTERVIEW

Dr. Chomsky offers us the possibility of a global understanding of why there are new and positive ways of drawing close to what is generically called "tradition." This process keeps in its sights a phenomenon which has come to be called the "re-turn" of indigenous peoples, which gives us all an "optimistic spirit" as we face ecological disaster and social exclusion, the intellectual analysis of which is rationally "pessimistic."

I would like to add to Dr. Chomsky's comments two elements that arise from dialogues with Andean indigenous peoples concerning the topic of education, and which have placed the institutions and persons that participate in educational dynamics, whether these be from the classroom or the community, contemplating new horizons.

The first is related to the request by peasants and indigenous peoples for an education that integrates that which is their own with that which is modern. In Quechua this is called *iskay yachay*—two knowledges, in Aymara, *paya yatiwi*. Fifty years ago, it was common that Aymara families determined that their children "would not be peasants like us," and they asked the school to incorporate their children into the system of education it offered. Now this situation has shifted; they want institutions that support them in nurturing a diverse world, and they place as the central principle of their demands the "recuperation of respect," among human beings, with nature, and toward the sacred. This demand is understandable if we analyze the role that institutions played in the more than half a century of compulsory modernization through which the indigenous were dragged, with disastrous results for the convivial relationships among community members and with nature. The indigenous usually say, "We have to die three times in order to learn." It's like someone saying, "You have to taste poison to know what it is." In local indigenous thinking, living is what gives knowledge, not gathering up a lot of *a priori* facts about the nature of things. As they say, "To know, you have to live." There is no such thing as a definitive, *a priori* judgment of a person, proposal or entity; it is in the course of relating to them that one comes to know or recognize what a person is like. To know what the school is like, they have had to live it. However, even despite their awareness of the role of the school in the present ecological, social, and spiritual crisis, they don't want it to disappear, nor do they want to abandon it. They need the school, but on the condition that now it helps them with a new agenda: the recuperation of respect. This seems to be the Andean communal project of this new era that we have now entered.

The second element relates to the dialogue between systems

of knowledge. The question is how to establish dialogue between two understandings of the world that appear to be, or that really are, "incommensurable": the "living world" of the indigenous in which everything is experienced as alive and imbued with personhood; and a "mechanical world," a world of objects which is the one lived and projected by modernity. Here we are not merely taking about children and their families recuperating a diversity of seeds and knowledge, growing a garden at the school where they familiarize themselves with variations of seeds, or motivating solidarity between young people from the North and indigenous movements in Deep America. Neither will the problem be solved if, instead of the mechanical conception of the world, only the experience of an animate world is taught and reinforced in indigenous schools. If we truly are talking about diversity and respect, it is imperative that there be conversation and dialogue between both cosmovisions, a situation which is still not resolved in school curricula or within institutions in general. So far, *interculturalidad* has gone the route of translating indigenous languages into the mechanical world, or using local experience as "prior knowledge" in order to lead the indigenous girl or boy toward the kind of objective knowledge promoted by science. The indigenous families and groups of teachers involved in this debate have a focus oriented toward diversity that so far appears to guide their actions; however, due to its very limited development, it is not able to overcome a certain mixture of understandings of the world.

The crucial point to which one must aspire is that each fact or domain of knowledge would be displayed and discussed within its own cosmovision, so that the indigenous boy or girl knows when they are in one universe or the other. This requires that teachers, among other things, "return to the school of life" to relearn modernity, or unlearn it, should such be the case, and to make of their experience with indigenous communities a discourse equivalent to that of modernity, to the end that the knowledge of each tradition encounters and dialogues with the other on an equal plane. But even within a horizon of optimism, this path still requires an equally optimistic intellect, something, it seems to me, that Gramsci did not live out.

NOTES

1. Here "corporate" refers to collective, the life within organizations and especially communities, reinforced by *comunalidad*, as the source of resistance and alterative life ways.

2. The hacienda system of Argentina, parts of Brazil, Chile, Mexico and New Granada, was a system of large land-holdings that functioned as plantations, ranches, mines, business factories, or often a combination of these. The *hacendado*, the person to whom the expanse of land was granted by the crown, enjoyed complete control over the estate and all its resources, including human inhabitants.

17.

The Path of Decolonization

By Carlos Mamani Condori, Bolivia

Professor of history at the Universidad Mayor de San Andrés in La Paz, Bolivia, and Aymara member of the Permanent Forum for Indigenous Issues of the United Nations. Email: pakamamani@gmail.com

INDIAN NATIONS, AS THEIR histories confirm, have had few and scarce allies who, in addition to showing sympathy, also invested time to learn about the misfortunes they have endured. Travelers who searched for the "good savage," as well as anthropologists like those who subscribed to the Barbados Declaration, became convinced that the Indian must not only be seen as an object of study, but also as the subject of political struggles, and most importantly, the subject of their own liberation. In the interview that we are commenting on, Professor Noam Chomsky shows a very positive sensitivity and closeness to indigenous peoples in general and to the challenges they face in regaining control of their educational processes whenever the nation-state has had homogenization as its objective. This interview allows us as Indians to locate where we and our peoples are situated in world opinion and global analysis, to assure the visibility of our processes, the leadership of Evo Morales, and above all, to verify the traumas caused by colonization, the genocide that marks the relationships between our peoples and the corporate, state, and imperial powers. Within this frame of reference, we intend here to formulate our ideas, more than commentaries, which I believe focus on the hard road toward decolonization, more than on the pure and simple defense of our traditions, labeled by some as an archaic utopia.

In the responses that Professor Chomsky has formulated to the questions asked by Professor Meyer about topics as important as language, education, and rights, we can appreciate his profound libertarian convictions, all of which are contemplated in relation to democracy in a neoliberal context. My personal question is this: what is it that indigenous peoples project onto the global stage, considering that the words of an eminence such as Chomsky have the virtue of establishing such an agenda, or of calling attention to the many problems that deserve the attention of global powers, and at the same time of public opinion?

Bagua,[1] the blood spilt in the Peruvian jungle, has shown us that we Indians, when unified, can establish our own worldwide networks and platforms to pressure for the defense of one of our component parts. But with the aforementioned as a preoccupation, the first and not-at-all-gratifying assertion is that we Indians are of little interest to the world, we are the periphery of the periphery. How much can we impact the balance of power and movements on a global scale? This depends on our efforts, on our capacity to make a global impact, to clearly and convincingly point out the problems we face, as well as the solutions we can envision from our countries and our realities.

Though it may seem repetitive, it is important to state that the formation process of the European nation-state was based on the expansion capacity of each one of its political entities, while during that same time period our nations and our state formations were devastated and destroyed, precisely by that same European expansion. Strictly speaking, the structure of the indigenous community represents the importation to the so-called New World during colonial times of a Spanish peasant organizational model, which was then superimposed onto the fragments that remained after the colonial devastation of indigenous life. One of the ironies of colonization is that we Indians find ourselves obligated to defend an institution, a name, "community," as though it were an inherent part of our identity and our possibility for survival.

The indigenous community is the concrete datum of the colonial situation that indigenous peoples continue to live. Fragmentation leads us to see only communities and not nations; this excessive localness works against our possibilities for political realization. In the Americas, as Chomsky rightly states, genocide and extermination constituted the origin of the modern nation-state; it was the colonizers who constituted their republics and led the processes of separation from colonial powers, celebrating independence days that covered up and denied the existence of Indian nations. The colonies, now converted into republics, developed processes of ethnic cleansing through "Indian wars," which were no more than raids that cleared out certain territories for the settlement of colonists brought in from Europe. This was the crude, cruel, and bloody history up until the first decades of the 1900s.

However, it is important to recognize that this means of appropriating land and resources has not ended; Israel's theft of Palestinian land displays this same objective on the part of a colonial power. The same occurred just a few days ago in Bagua, where transnational corporations imposed on the Peruvian state a predatory colonial vision that collided with the expressed will of the native peoples to undertake the defense of their territory in accord with the terms of resolution typical for these types of conflicts.

State terrorism is, then, ever-present; colonialism has been established through the deployment of the most incredible resources for violence. Most of the colonies—today republics—are violent in their very essence against their native inhabitants, against whom they apply antiterrorist laws, as in Chile, which is why one of the main topics on the agenda of the organizations of the region is the struggle to decriminalize protest. In Bagua, the Awajun people have been described by the government and the media as "genocidal," while the state shields itself in a supposed international conspiracy. Colonial society is violent by nature in that its political base is war and devastation in order to plunder land and other resources.

The means used to legitimate and coverup crimes has primarily been through the monopoly of writing; whoever has the ability to write, print reports, newspapers, and books has the capacity to impose their own truth. There was a time in the Andes when the Indians invested their greatest efforts in learning the language of the colonizer, speaking it and writing it. Then in 1931, the government took control of indigenous education. Warisata (Bolivia) was the co-optation of a totally indigenous self-generated educational initiative. Knowing the Spanish language, the *ayllus* (communities) were successful in defending their territories from creole and mestizo usurpation.

Colonial states require policies of cover-up and forgetting, *not talking about their own crimes*, genocide, just as the atrocities of the unjust Indian wars are conveniently hidden behind celebrations such as the bicentenaries of national independence. Will the groups in power ever acknowledge the crimes committed by the state against indigenous peoples, the construction of nation-states on top of the destruction and plundering of indigenous peoples?

Indigenous peoples in a colonial situation, such as the one in which they still live in this part of the world, are not necessarily "beneficiaries" of state policies that tend towards homogenization. For this to be the case, there would have to be an acknowledgement of equality, and if that has ever occurred it was recently, since the 1950s. Indians continue to be the "others," those who are permanently ignored, because, for the purposes of colonial degradation, it is important that there exist no "subjects." In South America, there are distinct forms of making the Indians invisible, because their very presence makes them the subjects or legitimate recipients of rights. The words "integration" and "recognition" witness to the ideological and political games played by the groups in power that control the state. To integrate the Indian is to assimilate him, to acculturate him, to convert him into a peasant who will wander through the streets of the capital cities or other cities around the globe. Now he is to be recognized, but only on paper, which has been the fate of the International Labor Organization's Convention 169, and perhaps also will be for the U.N. Declaration on the Rights of Indigenous Peoples. Meanwhile, the colonialist idea of *terra nullius*, vacant lands, is applied currently in the contracts that states celebrate with transnational corporations. There was a time in the Andes, up until 1950, when, if an Indian learned how to read—in Spanish, of course—they would remove his eyes and cut off his fingers; there was no written law, only the force of colonial practices and customs.

Indigenist policies and the adoption by some states of racial intermarriage as an important part of their ideology have led only recently, during the last half century, to universal schooling. Of course, it was assumed that the Spanish language would be learned to the detriment of the autochthonous languages; still, it has been important that Indians succeeded at using the language of colonization. In Indian struggles, the strategies used have not always been the same; there have been very important changes. During the first half of the twentieth century in Bolivia, the struggle was carried out under the banner of equality, which included access to the Spanish language. Then, during the second half of the century, appreciation of the native languages and cultures was the goal, and struggles for language preservation were important. With this, the indigenist policies of assimilation were denounced as another form of genocide. Education has become a battlefield between those groups that seek to preserve the privileges of the colonizer language and indigenous peoples who push toward policies of *interculturalidad* and dialogues between civilizations, between systems of knowledge, etc. Bolivia's adoption of pluralism as a crucial, inherent part of the state is one of our major achievements, viewed by indigenous peoples as the beginning of a process of decolonization. In Latin America, indigenous efforts and struggles are, above all, directed toward the restitution of rights and the reestablishment of cultural and political institutions. This process has been significantly reinforced by the U.N.

General Assembly's adoption in 2007 of the Declaration on the Rights of Indigenous Peoples.

What is the real and effective possibility that the project promoted by indigenous peoples will meet with success? Chomsky contrasts it with the projects and needs of corporations, that is, development, as it is called and imposed in each of our countries. But Chomsky discounts this claim:

> Corporations, after all, are just tyrannies, basically totalitarian command economies largely unaccountable to the public and with a huge link to one another, a link to powerful states. They are trying to impose an international system which will work in their interests—it has nothing to do with development.

Indigenous peoples have survived a permanent holocaust for five hundred years; in countries like Mexico, Guatemala, and the Andean region, they still number in the millions and remain majorities. This is an initial achievement, greatly valued and esteemed by the members of Indian nations. It is indigenous peoples who have protected the most important and exquisite values which sustain humanity, such as respect for life; the Aymara phrase *suma qamaña*—to live well—has been adopted by *indianidad* worldwide and by the *altermundistas* (e.g., the World Social Forum gathered in Belem). The concept of Mother Earth, *Pachamama*, is written into the text of the Constitution of Ecuador, and President Evo Morales has managed to get the U.N. Assembly to declare April 22 to be the Day of Mother Earth. Efforts are being made by indigenous peoples, civil society, and governments to reestablish the rights of Mother Earth. There is a growing acknowledgement of the moral authority of indigenous peoples for preserving human values, biodiversity, and the defense of Mother Earth from voracity and devastation.

With globalization and access to communication, it is more possible to successfully confront colonialism and the tyranny of transnational corporations. The efforts invested by indigenous peoples in the education of their children and youth, as well as in the recovery of cultural values, have no other end than this: the free determination by indigenous peoples, in opposition to the old processes of nation-state formation, to pursue the path toward reestablishment of universal human values and the recognition of the earth as the big home for us all.

NOTES

1. Peruvian massacre carried out by Peruvian Special Forces against indigenous protesters on June 5, 2009, resulting in at least thirty two deaths. Protesters were demanding the repeal of legislative degrees issued last year to bring Peru into compliance with the U.S.-Peru Free Trade Agreement, which took effect earlier that year. The Peruvian Rainforest Inter-Ethnic Development Association (AIDESEP), an umbrella organization representing most of the country's approximately fifty Amazonian indigenous ethnicities, claims the government decrees will allow deforestation and privatization of their traditional lands and natural resources.

18.
Aymara Resistance

By Felipe Quispe Huanca (Mallku), Bolivia

Aymara historian, belonging to the Pachakuti indigenous movement, who founded the Tupak Katari Indian Movement in 1979 and the Tupak Katari Guerrilla Army in 1990. His honorific name, Mallku, refers to the spirit of the mountains that surround and protect the People, and therefore is the source of life. "Mallku" means "peak," both in geography and in hierarchy, and is the name the Aymaras give to their highest authorities, as they did to Tupak Katari, a heroic leader of indigenous rebellions in Bolivia in the 1780s. Email: wayllas@gmail.com

I AM AN AYMARA Indian, so I prefer to "write with a different ink" about the interviews Lois Meyer conducted with Noam Chomsky on very important topics for native nations. I am sure that the kind reader will perceive the smell of Indian and of Pachamama[1] in my words.

I must state that the great problems concerning the education provided to Indians are not pedagogical but structural. The cause of many of our problems are erroneous education policies, generated and regenerated by neoliberal and pro-imperialist education reforms, which are foreign, and colonial impositions whose content and racist spirit are entirely anti-Indian, and thus they are intended to destroy our millenary and ancestral culture.

From this perspective, I agree with Dr. Chomsky when he states that the languages are dying out from one generation to the next. In his words:

> [I]f you go back a little bit, a generation or two . . . these were local dialects. People spoke their own languages.

Right now, if you are an Italian, let us say, you may not be able to talk to your grandmother because she talks a different language.

The community where I live, and many other Indian communities, are experiencing exactly what Dr. Chomsky describes. The Aymaras who emigrated to other countries for work, to Spain, Argentina, the United States, even to the Bolivian lowlands, suddenly return with children born in those faraway lands who are quite "whitened" by Western culture, and they speak Spanish. They don't speak Aymara anymore and they cannot communicate with their grandmothers and aunts. They only make themselves understood by means of hand signs as if they were deaf-mutes.

All these behaviors are characteristic of today's Indians, "modernized" because they were born in foreign lands, and who furthermore have lost the Aymara style of walking, dancing, eating, and getting drunk. A pathetic case of this is prominent on the political stage: the outlandish Evo Morales Ayma, who does not speak either Aymara or Quechua, only Spanish, hence just like the whites he only communicates through hand signs with the Aymara people. You know and recognize that language is ideology, and ideology is thought. So if Evo thinks in Spanish, he is a colonized president; he does not have the essence or the Indian presence of the *ayllu*.

What has brought about this colonial fandango? Education, because the school is a factory, like a brick or adobe factory; there they educate us according to a rigid mold, and thanks to that mold we are where we are. This is why Chomsky ponders this idea: "The process of education destroyed individual culture." In prefabricated Bolivia, the colonial culture has destroyed almost the entire communitarian and millenary Aymara nation, which was polished and refined since the times of the Tiwanaku[2] and the Inca Empire.

The ill-fated invasion, colonization, and conquest brought

private initiative, exploitation, racial discrimination against the indigenous, evangelization, diseases, and other ethnocidal consequences.

There is a very important passage about the consequences of schooling in which Dr. Chomsky comments: "State formation, by force mostly, has tried to impose national education standards in order to turn people into similar individuals." In reality, not only has this been tried, but a foreign education has been imposed on us with extreme cruelty. And because of this rigged education policy, today I feel deformed or transformed in my way of feeling and thinking. But, who is to blame for my transformation? It is precisely the schooling inculcated in me by the colonial government to make me obedient and disciplined.

When I was twelve years old, I entered the school run by the hacienda of the gringo Arnold Friedrich, a native German. This house was converted into a classroom of knowledge and perhaps also into a physical, psychic, moral, material, and spiritual torture chamber. There the white-mestizo teachers expounded at great length and pressed us into a tremendous colonial mold. We even felt as though they punctured our cranium to poison our Indian brain. So since that time, the literate Indian has two brains; one is poisoned by Spanish and the other continues to be Aymara. We have two cultures, the colonial and the original Aymara culture. There is no fusion of brains, nor fusion of cultures. One dominates the other.

This is not all. Chomsky continues to talk with us, this time about educational homogenization. To be clear, I should state that I am neither a pedagogue nor a demagogue. I only want to express my views opposing the old educational paradigms of the prevailing system. In reality, since 1952, the Bolivian colonial system has formed us as if on a shoe or hat mold, melted and molded by the heat of punishments in schools and rural educational institutions, so that we may serve as living tools for the capitalist system.

The military barracks are our second school, where they

have emptied us into a more brutal mold. There we learned to kill, to steal, and to rape women, and in this way to make ourselves into evil men. It is a military institution that de-Indianizes us, de-ideologizes and de-Aymarizes us even more than the classroom. The white/mestizo military re-Bolivianizes us and re-colonizes us in a violent and cruel manner, and they make us sing lies in the hymn of Bolivians: "It's already free, this land is free, its subservient condition has ended." The cruel reality is that this land is not free; it is sold to the transnationals and the multinationals who exploit the natural wealth that Pachamama has given us. Nor has the "subservient condition" of the Aymaras ended: we were servants of the Spaniards, and now we are servants of the Bolivians. There is another passage in the National Hymn that repeats this refrain: "to die rather than live as slaves," but as Indians, we continue to be slaves of the capitalist and imperialist system. Really, it is a ridiculous stupidity for a Qullasuyan[3] Indian to swear with such a false oath.

In this sense, the whites homogenize us, they transform us into a species of mass eunuchs who bear the whippings of both the oppressors and the oppressed.

There is another passage of Chomsky's which deserves our close attention: "if children do exhibit [independence] anyway, they often become what are called behavior problems."

In so-called Bolivia, from a very early age they have imposed on us forms of control already devised and implemented by our executioners in the Colonial Age and during the Republic, up to contemporary times. Who carries out that task of keeping the Indian blindfolded with such an impenetrable cloth? There are the Catholic and Evangelical churches, the nongovernmental organizations, the political parties of both Left and Right, and also the radio, television, the press, magazines, textbooks, the official history of Bolivia and other novels, etcetera.

The following concepts are taught in rural schools:

About white people	About indigenous people
The white man is intelligent and scientific.	The Indian is lazy and useless.
The white man is courageous and creative.	The Indian is cowardly and weak, always a loser in every respect.
The white man is educated and elegant.	The Indian is dumb, slow, barbaric, and opposed to science. The Indian is ignorant and rude.
The white man is fair, honorable, and a good Christian.	The Indian is a criminal, a thief, and an atheist who doesn't believe in God and dies without fearing God.
White women are lovely and sexy.	Indian women are ugly, with dark splotches on their faces, smelly and undesirable.
Whites are saints, they worship only one great God, who is bearded like them.	Indians are sinners, wicked and satanic, who adore thousands of gods because they are ignorant.
Whites are to be imitated. They deeply respect gringos and hate the native Indian.	Indians are admirers of the *Q'aras* (whites, Europeans and gringos).

From this is born the superiority and inferiority complexes, which they have imposed on us by bloodshed and violence since the Spanish invasion, colonization, and conquest. Will we ever be able to discover what is behind this type of teaching? Here in the misnamed Bolivia, there is no danger so long as the Indian giant, sleeping his profound sleep for more than 500 years, does not awaken. For this reason, the exploiters want the Indian to remain asleep for another 500 years, if possible. This explains why the Indian is not allowed to think with his or her own brain, and from childhood they teach us that we will and must always remain dependant on someone who is superior.

Noam Chomsky raises an interesting topic regarding the best administrators of the capitalist interests of the empire. Where is the factory that produces them? Let's listen to the author:

> [If you graduate from] Yale, Harvard and Princeton, you are prepared to be a manager—economic, political, doctrinal; if it is a community college, you are prepared to be a nurse, policeman, factory worker, or something like that.

It is clear that the dominant elite has always had men created in this type of university. For example, in the United States all the presidents from James Madison to the current president, Barack Obama, have been educated in elite institutions.

This does not seem strange to an Aymara. We know very well that life engenders more life; likewise, the group in power reproduces itself and generation after generation maintains the capitalist and imperialist political and ideological apparatuses.

The University of San Andrés also inculcated in me and convinced me that the graduates from universities like Yale, Harvard, Princeton, and other imperialist universities, are good rulers and respectful of laws, treaties and agreements. Is this true? No! Noam Chomsky touches a sore spot when he states the imperialist view of a university education, a view held just as much or even more by our whites when they hold out the grand falsehood that men and women educated in those halls of higher learning supposedly are privileged minds, honest politicians, capable servants of the fatherland who govern with brilliant ideas and never make mistakes.

If truth be told, those men and women have never been and never will be good "managers," nor honest politicians, nor ideological leaders, because they defend the capitalist, imperialist system. They are no more than assassins and butchers who bathe in the blood of the poor and of the peoples who long for their total and definitive national liberation. Am I right, Professor Chomsky? Here we have to be realists and not say that it is God who has put us where we are and therefore we have to live in these miserable conditions forever.

In the favorite daughter of Simón Bolivar, Bolivia, we peasant Indians have gone outside the box with our armed mobilizations from 2000 to 2005; we have broken the stigma that only university graduates can govern a country. No! We are experimenting with a semi-literate Indian, who doesn't even have a high school degree: Evo Morales Ayma. Chomsky sees Evo Morales as an example, and yes, he can be an example for countries with indigenous majorities. For the Aymaras he is not news, not even an example. Already since the Republic and the post-Republic, Indians here have achieved positions in the government: we have had Andrés de Santa Cruz Calahumana, president of the nation in the first half of the nineteenth century; Victor Hugo Cárdenas Condori, vice-president under Gonzalo Sanchéz de Lozada, and now Evo Morales Ayma, with the ultra-indigenist front man, Álvaro García Linera. All changed their last names and bathed themselves in mutual admiration along with the whites, though they could not change their Indian faces. The bizarre Evo Morales Ayma is a mannequin who is managed by the smuggler Juan Ramón Quintana, Álvaro García Linera, Walker San Miguel, and the other white-mestizos who believe themselves to be first-class people or a privileged, palace caste. They are seeding all the discouragement, all the shams and lies, and like a malignant cancer, this has paralyzed the Indian movement in its totality.

Where are our *ama suwa, ama qhilla, ama llulla* (do not steal, do not lie, do not be lazy)? During the Inca Empire, there was a cosmic law that today is trampled upon and prostituted by that criminal colonial lineage, which has corrupted and narcotized it worse than the ultra neoliberals, and they make us look bad to the new generation of Indians.

Chomsky asks himself: "What happened in Bolivia?" We, from the trenches of combat, respond to you: since 1988, Evo Morales has been the elected leader of the Coca-mama[4], which is why he has been involved in many anti-Indian measures by the various governments during these years. He never knew how to stand up against a neoliberal government; he was a timid leader, a sell-out, who did not defend his supporters in the Indian cause.

We, the Indianist-Tupakarists, have been following through with our ideological political work since 1970, preaching Indian revolution, self-government, our own Aymara state, the reestablishment of the ancient Qullasuyo-Tawantinsuyo.[5] For this sacred cause we have been persecuted, exiled, confined, and imprisoned for our armed uprising.

As a consequence of these historical facts, in 2000 we broke our silence. The millenary Indian went public with first and last names, with armed roadblocks, with blockades of agricultural produce, and by encircling cities in the style of our great Tupac Katari. With this type of organized communitarian struggle, through the Single Union Confederation of Farm Workers of Bolivia, we have managed to bring down three governments: that of General Hugo Bánzer Suarez, that of Gonzalo Sánchez de Lozada, and that of Carlos Mesa Guisbert. We even politically and ideologically destroyed the political parties of the Left and Right.

Thanks to these resounding mobilizations, Evo won the 2005 elections. But he never participated in the mobilizations; he was always a natural ally of the neoliberal governments. For this reason, in 2003, Evo never went to the mobilizations. He had to flee the country so he went to Libya, then Geneva, and finally to Venezuela.

We who have risked and lost our lives have been the authors and actors of these struggles. Now, we are not part of the present Movement Towards Socialism government, nor are we its opposition; we are in the field watching out for a hybrid government.

About the Aymara nation, I know that Chilean or Peruvian Aymaras worry, as do we, about the situation of our people, and on this topic Chomsky says that the Aymaras of Northern Chile and the Bolivian Aymaras do not have contact, but this is the author's hypothesis. We Aymaras have no borders, we have nothing to do with the Pacific War of 1879, led by the group in power that served the interests of the imperialist capitalists. Nowadays, the Indians of misnamed Bolivia are passionately interested in creating one united great nation (as Bolívar would say). The banner of our struggle is to re-establish the ancient Qullasuyo.

The earliest colonial creoles have Republicanized us, Bolivianized us, Peruvianized, and Chilenized us. Nevertheless, the Aymara Nation vibrates and pulsates underneath each autochthonous native dress. From this trench of combat, we convoke and invoke all Aymaras who suffered Republicanization by the colonial white-mestizos: we cannot continue to be manipulated and governed by the usurpers, oppressors and exploiters.

Perhaps I do not deserve to be part of the discussion about the interviews of Noam Chomsky that were conducted by Lois Meyer. So many elements are talked about, and it is difficult for me to say anything more concerning the political, economic, social, and cultural issues expressed in the author's long exposition.

This text was conceived in Aymara and written with difficulty in Spanish because I don't handle Western categories or terms like traditional intellectuals. This is because I belong to another political and ideological culture. For this reason, my forms of expression are not exactly like the ones used by the descendants/ascendants of the emissaries of the abominable evil of the centuries.

I hope that Dr. Chomsky does not think of me as demonic. For more than five centuries, we have lived under the tutelage of the cross and the sword, and under an educational policy of the Inquisition.

NOTES

1. A goddess revered by the indigenous peoples of the Andes. Often translated as "Mother Earth," a more accurate modern translation of "Pachamama" would be "Mother cosmos or universe."

2. Inhabitants of the prehistoric city of the same name which at its apex influenced religiosity in the southern Andes between A.D. 500 and 950, at which time it was mysteriously abandoned. According to the Incas, Tiwanaku was the birthplace of mankind. It remains an important religious site of Andean peoples in Bolivia today.

3. Indians inhabiting the southeastern provincial region of the Inca Empire. Qulla Suyu referred specifically to the Aymara territories, now largely incorporated into the modern South American states of northern Chile and Argentina, Peru, and Bolivia.

4. The complex coca drug economy in Colombia and Bolivia.

5. Historically, Qullasuyo was the southern part of Tawantinsuyo (the Inca Empire), incorporating those who are traditionally Aymara. Today the term is used to encompass much of the former Inca Empire, including the modern states of Bolivia, Peru, Ecuador, Chile, and Argentina, as indicated by the hyphenated reference.

19.

Changing Mirrors: Looking at Ourselves in Latin America

By Norma Giarracca, Argentina

Argentine sociologist, professor, and researcher at the University of Buenos Aires and coordinator of the Study Group of Social Movements in Latin America. Web site: www.ger-gemsal.org.ar

THESE SUGGESTIVE INTERVIEWS CONDUCTED with the North American intellectual Noam Chomsky lead us to reflect on the problems of constructing nation-states in Latin America, and the communal forms of life of many of the peoples who inhabited or inhabit these territories, forms which reemerge as political options in the last half of the twentieth century. I would like to focus on the presence of these processes in Argentina, since its strong public image identifies it as the most "Europeanized" country in Latin America, a nation where "coloniality" (Quijano 2000) took such deep root in the cultural soil that the "thoughtful" or "progressive" sectors traditionally have acknowledged only a part of these problems (the emergence of the state), seldom addressing the hidden face of capitalist modernity: the operation of cultural subordination upon the various peoples involved. The indigenous question was confined to a colonial anthropology with obvious racist influences;[1] when this question arises today, it is because intellectuals like Osvaldo Bayer[2] and the social actors themselves—indigenous communities and peasant populations—insist on raising it on the dramatic stage of the agrarian soybean expansion.

In postcolonial studies, the notion of community appears as a strong mechanism against the state and its capitalist organization;

this concept of community—*comunalidad* as the Oaxacans call it[3]—offers a political arena for the subordinated, the excluded, and the dominated, and a clear "de-colonial option" (Mignolo 2008). In this regard, the question appropriate to a country like Argentina is, to what extent during this neoliberal period of unemployment do the popular majority sectors remain at the margins of the de-colonial options made possible by the *comunalidad* that is so present in Bolivia, Ecuador, and Mexico? While in these countries also worker movements appear in "medium-term memory" (Raúl Prada: 2005), in Argentina they were at the center of the social, cultural, and national resistance for much of the twentieth century, while peasants and the indigenous occupied a less prominent position. This is an issue worth pondering in the country's current political phase, especially after the brief life of the unemployed workers' organizations and the co-optation of some of them by the post-crisis governments of 2001–2002. The other aspect is the resurgence of the voices of indigenous, peasants, and Andean peoples (in the foothills of the Andes), as one of the most significant phenomena of this century. Those previously marginalized in the construction of the nation-state and Argentine capitalism today are significant actors who radically question these outcomes. Despite their importance, in terms of population they represent a clear minority in comparison to the large masses of the unemployed or precariously employed in the great metropolises of the country who ultimately determine electoral contests.

The formation of modern Argentina began to consolidate with the so-called "generation of the '80s" (1880s), more precisely with the military invasion of the last free indigenous territories, after centuries of entrapments and massacres. Before that time, some indigenous populations coexisted with the *criollos*, the Spaniards and their descendents from the colonial era, with the population of African descent,[4] and with the new Spanish and Italian migrants who came as wage earners or agricultural colonists. It is calculated that between the middle of the nineteenth and the beginning of the twentieth centuries, more than five million Europeans entered the country, almost three-fourths of whom were Spaniards and Italians. These ethnic mixes represented a great obstacle for the governing elites, who since the time of Domingo F. Sarmiento and Juan Bautista Alberdi aspired for a modernizing "civilization" through migrations from Northern Europe and the whitening and academic schooling of the population. White Northern European populations were zealously encouraged to enter the country; at the same time, the Mediterranean Europeans who actually arrived in these lands became part of the problem, not the solution.

EDUCATION

In Argentina, just as Chomsky describes for the United States, the transition toward homogenization was occurring through processes of control in all aspects of life, and the education system here, as there, fulfilled a key role in this process. Pedagogy served as the skilled craftsman of a modern subjectivity, while at the same time producing "the invention of the other," the sense of otherness that is required in the molding process of a particular subject (one who is modern/white/educated). Castro Gómez attempts to identify founding moments of the Latin American nations, their "constitutions" (the moments in which they "invented citizenship," that is, a collection of homogenous subjects who make the modern/capitalist project possible) and to relate these to education. School, says Castro Gómez, sets itself to interject a discipline over the mind and body; children's behavior must be controlled, carefully supervised, and subjected to the acquisition of knowledge, abilities, habits, cultural models, and lifestyles that equip them for conversion into "productive" entities for the imagined society.

In Argentina, "the father of the classroom," the physical and symbolic site of school learning, is Sarmiento, who not only produced the basic educational legislation that accompanied the 1853 Constitution (to which Alberdi contributed with his "enlightened" ideas), but also the symbols, practices, and discourses of public education that have lasted to this day. Sarmiento was fully conscious that, just as the format of the National Constitution was inspired by the great thinkers of the North, so education should do the same. In a pedagogical conference in 1881, the question was asked: "Do we educate in an Argentine manner? No, he contended; we should educate as the North American Mann, the German Froëbel, and the Italian Pestalozzi have taught us to educate our children. We make them learn in a rational manner everything that is taught today in the well organized schools of the world" (Cited by Ocampo, 2004, 47).

Sarmiento represented not only the political intellectual of Latin America who attempted by blood and fire to impose "civilization," that is, modern colonial capitalism, but also the purifier who persecuted and prohibited any cultural trace of indigenous peoples, or the least indication of the resistance leaders of the Andean peoples I mentioned earlier, in the very region where, paradoxically, he had been born[5].

The "sarmientine" education proposal was based in the strictest cultural control, homogenization even in forms of dress, imposing for this purpose a white apron to cover the child's clothes, prohibiting the languages of the indigenous communities (Guaraní, Quechua, Mapuche, etc.), and very closely supervising the attempts of the European communities to maintain their languages or dialects. Children with diverse accents were disregarded, mocked, and became targets of the epithets that even today circulate throughout the discriminatory Argentine culture: "tanitos" (Italians), "gallegos" (Spaniards), "rusito" (Jews), "turco" (Arabs). The migrations from neighboring countries have added: "bolitas" (Bolivians) and "paraguas" (Paraguayans).

Those who created these hierarchies and minoritized or subalternized "the others" in this way were the white elites, who also fomented discrimination among the minoritized groups themselves. One of the dramatic consequences of this cultural operation was the racialization, inferiorization, and social hierarchization signified by the phrase "little black heads" (*cabecitas negras*), used to refer to the emerging working class in the middle of the twentieth century. In sum, "little black heads," "indios," "tanitos and galleguitos," "rusitos and turcos," all helped produce the otherness that the nation-state requires to create the identity of white, educated, civilized citizens that would become part of the imagined "republic" after the operations of repressing and hiding ethnic, cultural, and social differences. This is a republic that looked at itself in a Europeanizing mirror, one that reflected back a false and distorted image of that which, in general, gives us good literature and good art:[6] the image of a diversity of skin colors, languages and accents, eye colors, ways of being children, women, elders. This identity distortion hindered the governing elites from producing an agenda of the problems that the project of the nation-state, even within its own logic, had to consider and resolve.[7]

In synthesis, for those generations that constructed the Argentine nation in the nineteenth century, the most important goals were populating the feared deserts (in the territorial images that Sarmiento disseminated) with Europeans, and also education, in order to achieve what was required so that the state could bring about the development and progress to which they aspired. In the fifty years that passed between 1880 and 1930, the stunning development of export agriculture actually put the country among those with the greatest economic growth, leading to the belief that "populating and educating" were the mechanisms capable of creating a white nation (in the first century after independence from Spain in 1910). For that nation after its first century (as for the one that now prepares to experience the Bicentenary in 2010), there existed neither ethnocide, nor savage land appropriation, nor subordination of peoples in the name of a capitalism that reserved a promised place for very few countries. The 1930 crisis ended that illusion, and what awaited Argentina was a cyclic history of democracies and dictatorships that only concluded twenty-five years ago when the bloody dictatorship of 1976–83 was brought to an end.

EDUCATION, TERRITORIES AND RESISTANCES

Argentina is part of that Latin America that Perry Anderson describes as the territory where the world's greatest number of national, social, and cultural resistances takes place. The twentieth century is not only remembered here in the South for the countless large worker strikes and uprisings of European agricultural colonists demanding land, but also for the long marches to Buenos Aires by indigenous communities in the north, the "*Malón de la Paz*" (Indian peace raid) who insistently demand return of their ancestral lands seized by the owners of the "prosperous" sugarcane industry. The anarchist and socialist ideas brought by those European migrants who disappointed Sarmiento and Alberdi, together with the ideas of nationalists like the "FORJA" group[8] (Arturo Jauretche, Raúl Scalabrini Ortiz, Juan José Henández Arregui, etc.), the persistence of an indigenous way of thinking reinvigorated by Latin American intellectuals like José Carlos Mariátegui or the authentic indigenous voice of Bolivian-Aymaran Fausto Reinaga, and the so-called "dependentist" ideas, above all of Don Pablo González Casanova, were the intellectual influences that accompanied these resistances.

The "workers' world" of the large cities generated heroic struggles against the cyclic dictatorships and the processes of transnationalized economic concentration. This world also received the most concentrated state attention: education and control of their territories (the "worker neighborhood" encircling each factory) were foci of repressive attention by the military governments. For example, in the populous industrial region known as La Matanza (The Killing), special repressive police battalions were created and used during the factory strikes, and they gathered "intelligence" in the neighborhoods. More could be said about educational matters, where rigid bureaucratic structures included the figure of the "inspector," a type of "pedagogical police" who went to a school and observed a class without receiving permission, or the "guard," who oversaw especially the conduct of children and youth.

Faced with this degree of undeniably ominous domination, the multiple expressions of youthful resistance of the era centered their efforts at the level of territory and education. And this is because in Argentina, as Chomsky also makes explicit for his country, "the 1960s were a period of emergent activism." In the political climate of the 1960s and '70s, neighborhood-territorial forms of organization were valued and promoted in order to achieve autonomy from the bureaucratic political apparatus of the dictatorships and to demand and to wrest by force social and citizen rights. This territorial activity presupposed a strong, Gramscian-like belief in a "popular culture" (a nucleus of "good sense") that included solidarity and daily resistance, which gave support to the plebeian politics represented primarily by combative forms of Peronism and which was hated by the dominant classes. In some sense, the "neighborhood" of those times was equivalent to the peasant and indigenous communities, above all in that strong sense of solidarity that came from men knowing each other within nearby factories, and the sociability of women and children in a space that was set apart—"practiced" in de Certeau's terms—and cared for by them.

To change the orienting principles of "sarmientine" liberal education was another principle of activism in those years. In 1968, an education commission was formed in the "CGT of the Argentines" (General Confederation of Labor), made up of honest union members detached from the official CGT and committed to struggle. According to an official press release, the commission's goal was to:

press for the formation of a guild and political consciousness among Argentine educational sectors; achieve the
nationalization of the aforementioned sectors, which are
mostly middle class—separating them from every trace of
influence of liberal currents; disseminate the postulates of
the CGT of the Argentines...; initiate contact with all entities that bring together Argentine teachers, with the goal of
coordinating their struggles with those that are liberating
workers throughout the country.

Likewise, it is not by chance that the Arancibia brothers,
Tucuman rural teachers and founders of the union in their prov-
ince, were murdered at the very beginning of the military dictatorship of 1976–83.

In the brief "democratic spring" of 1973–74[9] when activists
took on some public responsibilities, Paulo Freire made frequent
visits to the country and his followers visited not only every cor-
ner where alternative public policies were being designed, but also
schools throughout the country. Indeed, when the Ministry of
Education was recovered in 1973, freed from the mix of sarmientine liberalism and Catholic conservatism that controlled it during the dictatorships, a very interesting experience developed. It
was the National Directorate for Adult Education (DINEA) that
embraced the postulates of Paulo Freire and attempted to decen-
tralize educational programs, taking into account the diversity of
the provincial populations. Even with the scarce information that
is available about this experience, there is no indication that there
was ever any discussion of the possibility of "bilingual education"
for the indigenous regions.[10]

POST-DICTATORSHIP AND DEMOCRATIC CONSTRUCTIONS

The worker neighborhoods were the center of terror and repression during the "damned dictatorship" (1976–83), when civil
governments returned, industrial jobs dwindled by 25 percent,

delegates of the combative unions had disappeared and salaries were the lowest since the postwar era; work in the informal economy and fear were rampant. Education once again was characterized by centralized control from Buenos Aires and the ever-present ambition—present as much in dictatorships as in civil governments—to homogenize diverse populations through schooling. The "neoliberals" and the sordid authoritarian Right had done their job at the cost of 30,000 disappeared, as well as thousands imprisoned and exiled. As for economic policies, little or nothing came back from the state during twenty-five years of democratic governments; the "worker world" drifted into the "world of the unemployed" or the economically precarious, who were the object of focused social policies by multilateral credit organisms (like the World Bank and the InterAmerican Development Bank) that aligned with the client policies of the "conservative Peronism" apparatus (emptied of its foundational content); likewise, processes of impoverishment and violence emerged, as occurs in all major cities of Latin America. Nevertheless, a new kind of activism is spreading within those urban worlds and education is again a central concern. The so-called "Popular High Schools" for young people and adults[11] are flourishing in neighborhoods where college students affiliated with territorial organizations proposed other teaching programs and they themselves teach youth and adults marginalized by the neoliberal order. Many of these high schools are officially recognized and are considering expanding the experience to primary education, the first stage of schooling. But they are still far from being those worker neighborhoods that we dared to compare to peasant and indigenous communities.

Then, at the margins of these scenes of still very incipient urban experiences, the new century draws Argentina close to the popular resistance movements that are occurring throughout Latin America. Their center no longer emanates solely from the "worker world," but also from the social worlds of those other actors marginalized by the industrial and agricultural export capitalism of the vast Argentine plains known as the pampas. The centrality of financial capitalism and a new international geopolitics based on the violent appropriation of natural resources lead to the displacement of resistance efforts from big cities to small towns, to intermediate-sized cities (less than 50,000 inhabitants), and to indigenous communities and communities of peasants. The struggle for land and territory, the defense of the Andean mountains threatened by open-pit mining, the spread of soy and other transgenic crops, forest activity tied to the large paper mills that pollute the rivers, threats to the aquatic reserves, to biodiversity, to the hills, to the rainforests, to the glaciers—these are the new faces of a savage capitalism that recalls the age of colonial looting and pillaging. And this new reality draws us closer to the problems of the rest of Latin America and enables a dialogue among indigenous sisters and brothers of other nations about new ways of thinking, what we call "decolonial options," that are emancipatory and libertarian. For the first time in our history, for example, bilingual education is being discussed in indigenous communities; for the first time, recognition of indigenous identity is part of the demands of the peasant groups; for the first time, the state must acknowledge the existence of peoples with rights to their culture, their language, their autonomy, and their territory as it is established by international legislation.

The proximity to Bolivia and its intense transformational process, the circulation of Latin American intellectuals committed to social movements and institutional changes, but above all, the emergence of the public voice of specific indigenous and peasants from these territories bring this profound America near to my country. The voice of the state and the dominant Argentine sectors (and the well-off in general) continues to insist on the image of the Europeanizing mirror, no matter how much the past resists being hidden. A Mapuche person reminded us at a seminar in the middle of the city of Buenos Aires in 2006:

A little while ago, while I was waiting for the break to end
and I was trying to concentrate on what I was going to say,
I had a sense of enormous responsibility. Why? Because
I remembered that almost a hundred years ago on this
same street (First Corrientes Ave.) our *cacique* passed by;
they were taking him to La Plata were he ended up dying. I thought, too, about what Cacique Pincén must have
thought when they were taking him in chains to Martín
García Island. Our tradition is entrenched in the tradition
of these same struggles. They, like us today, tried to defend
the vital space that would allow them to continue living as
they had until then. (Chacho Liempe, Mapuche of the Indigenous Advisory Council; see Liempe, 2008:124)

We are also drawn closer to Latin American struggles by
the Mapuches, hemmed in as they are by the power of Benetton
and Soros[12] (who snatched up their territories), and who join together in a single demand with their Chilean sisters and brothers
and the *qullamarka* Kolla.[13] Also, the assemblies of the Andean
peoples (Esquel, Famatina, Chilecito, Andalgalá) who, like the
Peruvian, Ecuadoran, and Guatemalan communities, denounce
the ransacking of the transnational mining activity. All these Argentine peoples are minorities at the moment of casting their
votes to elect authorities, and the majority of the urban population is trapped in a clientelistic network[14] of the old, worn-out
Peronism. Even so, the winds of change from countries that demand intercultural dialogue in the style of Bolivia and Ecuador,
and that contemplate other possible types of states (plurinational
or pluriethnic), or the ones that blow in from farther north, like
the neo-Zapatista cry "one world in which many worlds fit," arrive and refresh the stodgy colonial thought that endure in the
central spaces of Argentina.

When I read Dr. Noam Chomsky, I realized that the resistance efforts and proposals that emanate from the profound soul

of America, resound in all of Indo-Afro-America, from Canada to Argentina, despite the fact that their historical paths have differed, along with their specific manifestations.

REFERENCES

Castro Gómez, S. 2000. Ciencias Sociales, violencia epistémica y el problema de la invención del otro. In E. Lander, ed. *La colonialidad del saber: eurocentrismo y ciencias socia*, 145–62. Buenos Aires: CLACSO-UNESCO.

Esteva, G., et al. 2008. *Cuando hasta las piedras se levantan. Oaxaca, México, 2006*. Buenos Aires: Editorial Antropofagia.

Liempe, Ch. 2008. Resistirse a la desaparición. La experiencia del pueblo mapuche. In N. *Giarracca and G. Massuh, eds., El trabajo por venir*, 124–35. Buenos Aires: Ed. Antropofagia.

Mignolo, W. 2008. El vuelco de la razón: sobre las revoluciones, independencias y rebeliones de fines del XVIII y principios del XIX. *Otros Bicentenarios*, www.otrosbicentenarios.blogspot.com.

Ocampo, B. 2004. *La Nación Interior*. Buenos Aires: Ed. Antropofagia.

Prada, R. 2005. Sobre la caracterización de la formación social-cultural-territorial. Conferencia en el Instituto Goethe-Buenos Aires (Inédito).

Quijano, A. 2000. Colonialidad del poder, eurocentrismo y América Latina. In E. Lander, *La colonialidad del saber: eurocentrismo y ciencias sociales*, 201–46. Buenos Aires: CLACSO-UNESCO.

NOTES

1. The "Argentine phenomenological ethnological" school, begun by an anthropologist of Italian origin, Marcelo Bórmida, who was trained in the natural sciences in Europe, had obvious racist biological characteristics and left its mark on the discipline, both at the University of Buenos Aires and in the National Council of Scientific and Technical Research (CONICET). For twenty-five years it was a hegemonic school, virtually the only one in existence during the military dictatorship period when it reached its peak. With Bórmida's death in 1979, his wife continued his line of work. Since 1983, it shares the academic field with schools having North American, European, and postmodern influences.

2. During the twentieth century, the intellectual Osvaldo Bayer, along with the writ-

er David Viñas, took on the task of denouncing the dark beginnings of the "white-washed" nation-state in their essays and novels. Viñas writes about ethnocide "as the hidden cadaver in the back room" (cited by Ocampo 2004).

3. See Gustavo Esteva et al., 2008. For more on this topic, see Benjamín Maldonado (this volume and *Autonomía y comunalidad india*, 2002; *Los indios en las aulas*, 2002, both available in the library of CSEIIO www.cseiio.edu.mx). Also, Jaime Martínez Luna (this volume and in http://espora.org/biblioweb/Comunalidad/).

4. The African descendents represented 30 percent of the population in 1810. They were decimated by epidemics during the nineteenth century, due to the oppressive conditions in which they lived and the many wars in which they were made to fight.

5. In his novel *Facundo*, one of the best literary works of his time, Sarmiento vilifies and warns about the dangers of a Riojan Creole, a very courageous leader to whom he attributes ominous traits which he relates to the ecological conditions of the "desert" (Andean fields). Facundo Quiroga is remembered today by these peoples who are faced with expansion of open-pit mining, as the first one who defended their hills from European greed at the beginning of the nineteenth century.

6. For example, Antonio Berni's pictorial works: "La huelga," "Juanito Laguna," "Ramona Montiel"; also "Martín Fierro" by José Hernández from the middle of the nineteenth century, and the works of Roberto Arlt, Leopoldo Marechal, Germán Rozenmacher ("Cabecita negra"), and of course, Viñas and Bayer.

7. Maybe it was first Peronism, the government of General Juan Perón of 1945–1955, which noticed this situation, granted political value to and inspired dignity in those proletariat sectors, "the little black heads," "the shirtless ones" ("los descamisados"), as well as in the various sectors at the interior of the country. According to Beatriz Ocampo (2004), in this way Peronism went from being a political movement to being a cultural-political one, which in part explains its persistence later on the Argentine political scene.

8. Radical Orientation Force of Argentine Youth, FORJA, was a political association founded in 1935, that acted within the sphere of influence of the Radical Civic Union, and which was dissolved in 1945, when Peronism took charge.

9. Though the second Peronist government lasted from 1973 to 1976, when the coup-d'etat occurred with the death of Juan Perón in 1974, all the transformative possibilities of that era ended.

10. I am grateful to the sociologist Pedro Krotsch, National Director of Agricultural Education during those years, for helping me remember those times and for corroborating the information that is presented here.

11. Simultaneously, "Popular High School" experiences were emerging in several factories taken over by the workers, both in the federal capital and in suburbs of Buenos Aires.

12. George Soros and Luciano Benneton are multimillionaires with important land investments in southern Argentina.

13. *Qullamarka*: territorial demand by various Kolla communities that have joined together to demand 1,500,000 hectares of land in the north of the country in order to reconstitute the traditional territory that existed during the Inca Empire.
14. In the sociological literature, clientelism refers to the exchange of goods required by the poor for political favors.

20.

The Complex Decolonization of the School

By Raúl Zibechi, Uruguay

Uruguayan activist, researcher, journalist, and writer for the Semanario Brecha in Montevideo. Email: raulzibechi@gmail.com

FOR A LONG TIME we have known that school is one of the most serious problems facing peoples striving to overcome the condition of submission and dependence. However, we are not very clear how collective learning processes, either libertarian or liberating, could be put into practice. Even concepts of liberatory education or emancipatory pedagogy ring hollow whenever either of these is consigned to spaces or times created for the purposes of cultural homogenization and the formation of a dependent citizenry. As with the state, school is not a neutral instrument to be modeled on a whim by whoever takes control.

In this sense, the questions Lois Meyer poses to Noam Chomsky zealously seek to open the doors of this tortuous maze, from which we will not exit affirming the school as a central space in the education of youth nor, as Chomsky clearly notes, with general answers that become new traps capable of disempowering and restricting liberatory energies. For some time we have had precise and convincing analyses of the disciplinary and homogenizing role of the school and its vocation to engender passive and dependent citizens, as Chomsky indicates. It is more difficult to find ways to overcome this situation.

"School can become more dangerous than education," Ivan Illich warns us. His scathing critique of institutionalized schooling leads him to conclude that the school system annuls the capacity to learn, while the teacher, converted into custodian, moralist and therapist, contributes to the child's deformation. The school deforms with the goal of creating citizens intended for the market and the state, not human beings as they themselves and their communities want them to be.

As a parallel, Jacques Rancière analyzes the hegemony of what he calls the "stupefying teacher," stressing the difference between teaching and learning. While teaching pretends to be a science with rules and objectives, means and ends, learning is an uncertain art that cannot be planned. The teacher who teaches is one who explains and whose work consists of demonstrating to the students that they are not able to learn without being told how. On the other hand, the emancipatory teacher is capable of inducing or inciting ("obliging" says Ranciére) students to use their own intelligence, that is, to learn. From there he maintains that "one who teaches without freeing stupefies. And one who liberates needn't worry about what the liberated should learn" (Ranciére 2002, 28).

We could enumerate a long list of fairly accurate criticisms of the school and the education system as we know it in our societies. Until now, the overwhelming majority of reform efforts have tried to improve the school, create adequate pedagogies, and discover those teachers who is capable of overcoming widespread discontent through their teaching. These efforts, in turn, have proven to be relatively permeable to change, especially those that are formulated from above, usually in response to timely proposals from the ever-attentive World Bank. Until now, the changes introduced by the system have not achieved their goals, and widespread discontent continues.

Fewer are those who propose to "tear down the schools," following in the footsteps of those in the 1960s who proposed to tear down the walls of psychiatric hospitals. However, society still has a need to transmit knowledge to its children, to teach them to learn, even though usually this leads to new and more subtle forms of discipline.

Moving away from school as it "actually exists," I propose to address three aspects that are closely tied to the historical experience of Latin American social movements. To the degree that they embody those born in the basement of our societies, to use a phrase coined by the Zapatistas, they are most concerned about removing the flaws in a school system that has contributed to maintaining their domination. I am referring to those "without," the nonexistent, the invisible; the Indians, the peasants without land, those without a roof over their heads, those without work, those without rights.

I will address myself to three aspects: a) the school created and administered by the community; b) the "dislocated" school that is in movement; and, c) the creation of an environment that promotes the art of learning. In the first case, I will use the experience of the community (*ayllu*) school in Warisata, Bolivia; in the second, the reflections and school practices of the Movimiento Sin Tierra—Landless Workers Movement (MST)—in Brazil; and finally, I will share a reflection having to do with how the Kichwas learn to weave. These three cases are about collectives that fight to break down colonial and classist domination and, to do so, they need to construct forms and ways to collectivize the arts of learning in their social sectors.

I. The school-community of Warisata was built beginning in 1931, as part of the long process of fighting for indigenous schools. Since the beginning of the twentieth century, the Aymaras of the Bolivian Highlands sought to learn to read and write Spanish, in order to defend themselves from large landowners who were trying to expropriate their ancestral lands by taking advantage of their illiteracy. In collusion with lawyers and judges, the landowners managed to mock the legal attempts made by hundreds of communities to regain their lands, which after the failure of several revolutionary attempts was their only realistic recourse. The battle for the school was part of the battle for land (Claure 1989).

The construction of Warisata, located very near to Lake Titicaca in the foothills of the snowy peaks of the Royal Mountain Range, began thanks to the fortunate encounter of two educators: Avelino Siñani, an Aymara who founded several clandestine schools, for which he was imprisoned and tortured,[1] and Elizardo Pérez,[2] a teacher committed to indigenous self-education.

The principle characteristic of the Warisata school was the central role played by the communities, who built the school (an immense two-story building) working in shifts, providing materials and labor. Community members in communal assemblies decided on the building design, organized school activities including the curriculum, and administered the school. Teaching took place inside classrooms and outdoors; children learned by working in the enormous gardens surrounding the school, participating in clean-up, in decision-making, and in everything related to the school's daily functioning.

The school replicated the community and contributed to strengthening it, both materially and spiritually, by recreating indigenous identity and validating community culture. One of the effects of the community's mobilization to create the school was the early revitalization soon afterwards of the Amauta Parliament, which made fundamental decisions. In other words, everything communal was concentrated in the school and the school replicated the community, which had contributed the land and labor to make the school possible. A good example: the markets are usually located far away from the communities, in the municipal centers where Indians are exploited because they are compensated poorly by the merchants for their products. The Amauta Parliament decided to circumvent this problem by opening a market every Thursday in the plaza of Warisata, where the school could take its excess produce and community members could trade fairly (Pérez 1992, 109). "In this way, the communal social group found another way to reproduce itself: by controlling trade" (Claure 1989, 106). By the same logic, a

Commission of Justice was created to address the internal issues of the community.

Before long, communities and community members from around the country began to replicate the Warisata experience. In this way, the school, though hounded by landowners, was able to expand and thereby guarantee its survival, since all were clear that only by generating a wide social movement would they be able to move forward. However, towards the beginning of 1940, the government decided to put an end to the school community, the institution was closed down, the teachers were persecuted, and the site was ransacked by powerful leaders from neighboring municipalities. However, the movement to recover indigenous identity and communal organization that initiated the Warisata school was decisive in the 1952 revolution that ended the feudal regime in Bolivia.

The Warisata educational experience unleashed a broad movement throughout the country, through the founding of dozens of nuclear schooling centers in the Highlands, the valleys, and the jungles. By 1938, there were already twelve centers from the Chilean border to the jungles of Santa Cruz, passing through Oruro and Cochabamba. In 1937, Pérez was named the national director of indigenous education, a position he took advantage of by traveling throughout the country, founding new schools inspired by Warisata. In 1947, in the midst of a growing and potent workers' and peasants' movement, he was elected deputy, and in 1948, due to public pressure, he was named the minister of education, a position he resigned just two months later. The educational movement integrated itself into the great popular movement that overthrew the landowner and mining oligarchy during the insurrection of 1952, driven by hundreds of youth educated in the spirit of Warisata.

As indicated by Felix Patzi, former minister of education for the government of Evo Morales, Warisata inspired a pedagogy contrary to modern pedagogies. Modern pedagogy drills the alphabet within a confined space where teachers wield power and where their authority imposes itself even over the wider community. Warisata was "an active school, full of light, sun, oxygen and wind" (Patzi 2001, 55). It was a *textless* education that combined work with learning, like the Andean pedagogy based on "learning by doing" and on ancestral communal organization, very different from modern instrumental and scientific rationality. The teachers were familiar with the rural environment; their main activity wasn't the classroom, but rather gardening, cultivating, building, brick making, etc.

Educational authorities and their advisors were elected by direct vote and by rotation; the Amauta Parliament determined the educational policies, which then were approved by the communal and regional assemblies. Education was incorporated into everyday life and collective control, and in this way the school lost its "autonomy" from the rest of society. Warisata was a communal way of organizing education. The school didn't place itself above society and against majority interests.

II. Rural workers without land, from Brazil, have come up with their own way of setting up their schools. They have about five thousand settlements with two million inhabitants, in which there are 2,000 schools with 4,000 teachers, who attempt to implement their own unique pedagogy.

They have discovered that those without land only have a place in school if they find ways to transform the school, because "traditional schools don't have room for people like those without land, either because the formal structure doesn't permit their enrollment, or because their pedagogy doesn't respect or recognize their reality, their knowledge, the way they learn and teach" (Salete 2001, 46).

In the beginning, they only proposed to transform the school, without a model to follow. They started with the idea that the school should be open to social and historical movements. Soon they formulated a central thesis that gave priority to movement[3] over pedagogy: "The primary educational principle of this pedagogy is movement itself" (Salete 2001, 49). They began to implement a kind of pedagogy that couldn't be restricted to the time and space of the school because it involved life as a whole. It dealt with a pedagogy of movement that can be summed up in the idea that "we change ourselves by changing." "Instead of signing on to or affiliating with any one existing pedagogy, the Landless Workers Movement (MST) tries to put them all in motion, and to let each specific educational circumstance show which ones need to be emphasized from one moment to another" (Salete 2001, 52).

In MST schools, education occurs through the new social relations produced and reproduced by the movement, which modify behaviors, propose values, and deconstruct and construct concepts, customs, and ideas, says the pedagogue Roseli Salete Caldart. In this sense, work and social relations are the key aspects of the umbrella of educational processes that the movement defends. This proposal suggests that pedagogy is never ending, that social relations cannot crystallize in something fixed and permanent, since this inertia would lead to the reproduction of forms of oppression. This has led the MST to propose the "school in movement."

For those without land, the objective is that those in society who conquered the land should take responsibility for the school. In other words, there is no separation between school and social movement, because in the process of their liberation, individuals should take responsibility for their own education; they should learn about and know thoroughly and rigorously the reality that surrounds them.

Here a contradiction appears that is hard to resolve, one that goes to the very essence of schooling:

> The social movement needs to fill up, to inhabit the school, and the school needs to watch over the social movement. School is, in general terms, a conservative institution and is resistant to the idea of movement and direct connection to

social struggles. Typically, the ways in which it historically has served to maintain social relations of domination were concealed under the guise of autonomy and political neutrality. For this reason, the school alone cannot contribute to educating agents of change. On the contrary, the social movement needs to occupy and look after the school, building a new education project together with the educators already there. (Salete 2001, 76)

Now, if education consists of social relationships, these should be the central axis of the education process. Ultimately, social relationships are what teach, what form, not teachers or even movement conceived of as a structure. "Social relationships are the foundation of the educational environment of a school. They are what put pedagogies in movement" (Salete 2001, 78). It is the ordinary life experience of new social and interpersonal relationships that is capable of initiating change in people. By educational environment, the author, who is an advisor to the MST in the area of education, means "the intentional process of organizing and reorganizing the social relationships that constitute the style of being, of functioning, of the school, so that this style can be more educational, more humanizing of its participants."

The peculiar thing is that the educational environment *is* movement. From there we deduce that it is not about constructing models of schooling or pedagogy, but rather unchaining processes, propelled by values and principles that are lasting referents for the movement itself. A school in movement creates and recreates educational actions in its daily routines, thereby combating all inertia.

The pedagogy of movement doesn't fit in school. But school fits in it, not like a closed pedagogical model, a method or a structure, but like a style, a way of being a school, a stand confronting the task of educating, a pedagogical process, an educational environment. When a school in movement crystallizes into a model, a rigid form, movement is no longer the educator, because movement is a process, it is continuous action and reflection, it is a production of new syntheses in every moment of its history and its accelerated time.

The construction of social movement as an educational environment supposes that every act, every activity, every space of action will have an educational purpose. By "educational environment" we mean the conditions that make a specific activity educational, emphasizing the relationships and processes among people, objects, times and spaces, more than the material structures or the organization. Historically, MST was built as "an educational professional development environment for 'those without land'" (Salette 2002, 251).

As a consequence, the teacher stops being "Mr. Pedagogy" and is replaced by a collective environment, one that educates everyone, with all the tensions and contradictions of life itself; an environment-movement, or an environment in movement, a form of self-education in transformation for a new world.

In some schools without land, I remember especially one in southern Brazil, the students move toward a collective and rotating self-evaluation, though they don't call it that. This is a school for young people and adults, I don't know if the experience is also applied with children, in which at the end of the course of study when they proceed with the evaluation, they all form a circle, which includes also the coordinator (their term for the "teacher"). The evaluation of each individual is conducted by three persons, one of whom is standing beside the person being evaluated. Then the circle begins to turn, and the next person in the circle is evaluated by three persons, one of whom is new, and the previously evaluated person becomes the last one to participate as an evaluator. In this way, there are always three evaluators and one who is being evaluated, while the rest of the class listens. At the end of each evaluation, the other students can participate, asking questions and asking for clarifications.

The student being evaluated also can participate, contributing to his or her own evaluation.

In Zapatista schools the students do not receive grades. Rather, at the end of the year they publicly display to their parents what they have learned. Those whose learning has not been sufficient usually are accompanied by the coordinators who expand and enrich the student's participation. Also, in these schools children are not encouraged to solve problems individually. The teacher tells the class that everyone must participate in solving the problem, in order to motivate a collective and communal spirit.

In this way, the role and power of the teacher as evaluator is diffused in the collective, at the same time that passive students become active evaluators. The subject-object relationship tends to dissolve in a plurality of subjects (Lenkersdorf 1996). Of course, it can be argued that this kind of evaluation is problematic in terms of rigor, which would be a limitation of the experience, especially in the case that the majority of students opt for "light" or minimally demanding evaluations. Even so, I believe it can be interesting to try out other open and participatory forms of evaluation. In this way, "social movement" as a theoretical concept is no longer an organizational structure, but becomes an affirmation of "movement" in a literal sense: changing places, materially and symbolically, since one of the pillars of the traditional school (the active role of the teacher and the passive role of students) has been "moved" through the slippage of traditional roles and the creation of others that are new.

III. Learning in the Andean indigenous world is an integral and collective-collaborative process in which human beings, nature, and the gods and deities intervene. The words "teach" and "teaching" are rarely used, and everything centers on learning. This is not based on a binary or hierarchical teacher-learner relationship, nor is it mediated through orality, but rather through the unfolding of a visual, tactile pedagogy (Castillo 2005). One way of approaching an awareness of this type of learning is to consider the way Andean weaving is transmitted and learned.

In indigenous cultures, objects and subjects don't exist, or if you prefer, they only exist in an integrated way, neither separately nor as opposites. Based on an analysis of the structure of the Tojolabal language, Carlos Lenkersdorf finds that in the Tojolabal cosmovision the subject/object relationship doesn't exist, instead there is a plurality of subjects (Lenkersdorf 1996). This simple observation has enormous repercussions regarding the question of teaching and learning. Strictly speaking, there aren't those who teach or those who learn, but only a type of collective learning.

To this, we would have to add that studies by various indigenous researchers coincide in the prominent role that observation and visualization play in learning, which indicates that in order to learn you have to be a good observer or cultivate that ability, though in reality we learn with our whole body. Martin Castillo points out that "learning Andean weaving is characterized by learning more than 'teaching,' a 'self-teaching' in which verbal interaction is not always necessary" (Castillo 2005, 73). In summary, there can be learning without teaching, or a "pedagogy of implicit learning."

Along this path toward autonomy in learning about teaching, we can come to new discoveries. How do we learn? And, above all, why should we learn?

In the Andean world, people who learn to weave do it with all the same intentionality that they learn any skill: to live, to fulfill themselves as "someone who knows that s/he knows, knows how to be, and knows how to live within their culture, that is, a harmonic and integrated person" (Castillo 2005, 101–2). In the process of personal fulfillment, the heart plays a fundamental role, or, as the weavers say, "the heart drives and the eye watches." For this reason, learning doesn't necessarily require the intervention of another person.

The intervention of the heart in learning connects directly to the role of desire and will, that is, the commitment of individuals to themselves and to those around them. We learn because we want to learn, not because we have to. Children in the communities don't ask permission to learn; they look for opportunities and thus generate their own spaces and ways of learning. Regarding weaving, it is said that girls learn their first skills in secret "so that after they are capable and sure of themselves, they demonstrate their skills in public" (Castillo 2005, 160).

However, learners often need help, but this is provided by "the network of communal inter-learning." On the one hand, there are people who spontaneously offer support to their neighbors or friends. On the other, there is guided learning, but not in the traditional sense. Even in this case, the learner takes the initiative to "be guided," a strategy called "guided participation." This involves a cluster of strategies characterized by the lack of the subject-object relationship, as well as by the active participation of the learner, which converts him or her into the subject of their own learning. In synthesis, "observation, corporality, discretion, autonomy, collaboration, integrated learning, and the natural gradation of learning are put into play" (Castillo 2005, 172).

In Zapatista schools, students create their own school textbooks in some subjects, such as history. Their work consists in knowing and transmitting the history of their own community. To do this, they consult with elders, and based on these consultations they write a brief local history. In this way, they become the subjects (or authors) of a school text (very basic to be sure), they sharpen their research skills, and they create a text in which their community has actively participated. This methodology seeks to break down the barrier that exists between school and society-community.

Finally, indigenous teachers who are part of the Coalition of Indigenous Teachers and Promoters of Oaxaca (CMPIO) adopted an experience that was developed by the Maoris of New Zealand (a model which now receives governmental support in that country), to educate children in the indigenous language in communities where this language has been lost or is at risk. This model is called the "language nest" and it involves total immersion of children from one to six years old in the indigenous language, with the goal of creating a space and environment where the language is still spoken, that is, with the participation in the nest of adults and elders who still speak the local indigenous language. The coordinator of alternative projects of the CMPIO, Fernando Soberanes, explained in a lengthy interview that

> we are not talking about children learning the language as if it were a school subject, but rather that babies from 0 to 3 years old acquire the indigenous language as a FIRST language, and then learn Spanish. In the case of the preschool, primary and middle school students who are adapting the model for the revitalization of their language, they acquire the knowledge not only by paper and pencil, but by living the language, learning the culture and the cosmovision from the wisdom of the indigenous language itself.[4]

This is a non-scholastic communal project, in which the local community participates and guides the learning outside of the school after agreeing in communal assembly to do so.

It is interesting to me to highlight two modes or strategies at work: in the first, the learning space is a family environment, which assumes that a primary importance is given to the affect of the facilitators of learning; and in the second, the community "takes over" the learning space, that is, it appropriates the learning environment in order to transmit certain learnings that can no longer be learned in society. Both aspects, which cannot be cut off from learning "in" nature, permit one to "live the learning," which seems to be one of various ways to appropriate what is learned.

The previous examples show that there are ways of learning that differ from Western ways, and that every social sector, every people, every community, and every person has their own ways of learning. These ways should be considered valid strategies and they should be supported, in order to diversify our forms of learning as one of the ways to contribute to emancipation. "Dislocating" our culture centered on *logos*[5] can only enrich everything connected with learning and teaching. This supposes, inevitably, calling into question the role of both the teacher and the state, which are both anchored in the text-centered logic that is incompatible with orality and corporality. Therefore, only indigenous peoples and popular sectors, that is to say, the dominated upon whom text-centeredness has been imposed, are the most interested in putting into practice holistic forms of learning.

I have the impression, one I cannot prove, that the text-centered logic, in which the literal word reigns supreme, finds its natural space and time within the classroom, where children are seated and the teacher wields power. The experiences mentioned above, in which the community exercises power in the school, in which the school is dislocated and put into motion and where "other pedagogies" are practiced, are not in any sense established models to be followed or imitated. I feel they are experiences in harmony with the concerns and preoccupations that Noam Chomsky has manifested during his prolific life.

In any case, we can take these as points of reference, more or less successful, more or less applicable in other spaces and places, which can help us in the arduous and difficult task of de-alienating and decolonizing education. For such a purpose, we can count on nothing other than our own experiences, we can guide ourselves only with the precarious compasses and astrolabes that we have been building during our five centuries of resistance to the powers of the powerful.

The Complex Decolonization of the School

REFERENCES

Castillo Collado, M. 2005. *Aprendiendo con el corazón. El tejido andino en la educación quechua*. La Paz: Plural.

Claure, K. 1989. *Las escuelas indigenales: Otra forma de resistencia comunitaria*. La Paz: Hisbol.

Illich, I. 2006. *La sociedad desescolarizada*. Buenos Aires: Tierra del Sur.

Lenkersdorf, C. 1996. *Los hombres verdaderos. Voces y testimonios tojolabales*. México: Siglo XXI.

Patzi, F. 2001. *Etnofagia estatal. Análisis de las reformas educativas en Bolivia*. La Paz: IIS.

Pérez, E. 1992. *Warisata. La escuela-ayllu*. La Paz: Hibol-Ceres.

Rancière, J. 2002. *El maestro ignorante*. Barcelona: Alertes.

Salete Caldart, R. 2001. *A escola do campo em movimento*. Brasilia: Articulaçao Nacional por uma Educaçao Básica do Campo.

———. 2002. *Pedagogia do Movimento Sem Terra*. Petrópolis: Vozes.

NOTES

1. Alvelino Siñani was an Aymara amauta (wisman) who already in 1917 had a small clandestine school for Indians in the Warisata region, even though he was illiterate. He died in January 1941, shortly after the school was destroyed.

2. Elizardo Pérez was a mestizo teacher of indigenous students who served as an administrator at various levels in the official education system. He published a book (*Warisata, the Ayllu School*) that gives an account of the process of creating the school. He died in September of 1980 in exile in Quilmes, Argentina. In 1983, Uruguay's president, Hernán Siles Zuazo, repatriated his remains and honored him with the title "Precursor of Indian Liberation."

3. Note from the author: "'Motion' would not be a good translation here. The correct translation is 'movement,' education in movement, but with a double meaning: movement as in a social movement, but not like an institution, because then there is the other meaning of an education that moves, something that is never fixed or quiet."

4. Fernando Soberanes Bojórquez, interview by the author, January 12, 2009, in Oaxaca, Mexico.

5. Author's note: "I think the logos is a part of the body, but not 'all' the body. And I believe that we learn with the logos, with our hands, our feet, our head and skin, with our senses, etc. Our Western culture is logocentric at least since the Enlightenment. And this is something that I believe limits growth and learning."

21.

U.S. Imperialism and the Declaration on the Rights of Indigenous Peoples

By *Glenabah Martinez, United States*

Active member of Taos Pueblo, New Mexico, and associate professor of education at the University of New Mexico in Albuquerque. Email: glenie@unm.edu

ON SEPTEMBER 13, 2007, the General Assembly of the United Nations adopted the Declaration on the Rights of Indigenous Peoples. The declaration outlines the rights of an estimated 370 million indigenous peoples throughout the world. A majority (143) of the member states voted in favor of adopting the declaration and eleven abstained from the vote. Four member states voted against approval of the text. The states voting against the declaration were Australia, Canada, New Zealand, and the United States. Robert Hagen, U.S. advisor, explained why the U.S. voted against the adoption of the declaration. He identified three core provisions of the declaration that the U.S. could not support: 1) the nature of the declaration; 2) the right of self-determination; and 3), the provisions on lands, resources, and redress. Hagen writes: "The declaration on the rights of indigenous peoples, if it were to encourage harmonious and constructive relations, should have been written in terms that are transparent and capable of implementation" (Hagan 2007, para. 2). Shortly after the vote, all four nations were criticized by the general public and by entities directly engaged in work with indigenous peoples. Noam Chomsky was one of several scholars who expressed disappointment with the four nations, yet he recognized the potential of the declaration to aid indigenous peoples to achieve self-determination. In the interview conducted by Lois Meyer in fall 2007, he stated:

> Once the declaration is in words, it can be used as a means of organizing and education, so it does mean something. And it's taking place. It's not coming out of the blue. It's taking place against a background in which somebody like [Evo] Morales would be elected by the Indian majority. There are even calls for an Indian nation in South America controlling their own resources. And the same thing is happening elsewhere in the world.

Chomsky recognizes and acknowledges the importance of history in mobilizing people at multiple sites in their unified struggle for justice.

As I read the declaration and the interview with Chomsky, I am reminded of the struggle for land, religious freedom, and justice that many indigenous peoples have been engaged in since 1492. In particular, I recall the ways that my people at Taos Pueblo resisted the U.S. government's assault on our culture in the twentieth century.

In 1906, Taos Blue Lake and the land surrounding it (48,000 plus acres) was appropriated by U.S. President Theodore Roosevelt for the Carson National Forest. The lake and surrounding land is sacred to the indigenous people of Taos. By proclaiming this land as part of the U.S. National Forest system, the Taos people lost exclusive use of the land. Not only was religious life threatened, but so was the purity of the lakes and streams which were and continue to be the main sources of water for ceremonial life, drinking, cooking, irrigation, fishing, and stock raising. This shameful act taken by the U.S. government was met with strong opposition by the Taos people through an intensive campaign to gain support at the popular, legal, and governmental levels for the return of the sacred lake and surrounding land.

Other shameful acts occurred throughout this tumultuous

period in the early twentieth century. On February 24, 1923, Commissioner of Indian Affairs Charles Burke sent a circular addressed "To All Indians" (Department of Interior, Office of Indian Affairs, 1923). Burke ordered that all Indians refrain from taking time off from school and work to participate in dances and other elements of religious ceremonial life. To emphasize this point, Burke traveled to Taos Pueblo in early April 1923, to deliver his message directly to the Taos Pueblo Council. Referencing a letter dated "Easter Sunday" from an anonymous source, written to Elsa Clews Parsons (anthropologist), Zumwalt described the event: "Commissioner Burke, accompanied by Interior Secretary Hubert Work had 'invaded the Taos Pueblo's Council' and accused the Indians of being 'half-animals' by virtue of their 'pagan worship'" (Zumwalt 2006, 264). Council members refused to comply with Burke's orders forbidding the withdrawal of a select group of Taos Pueblo boys from school for religious instruction. The office of Indian Affairs ordered the arrest and incarceration of the leadership of Taos Pueblo. Later, they were released from the Santa Fe jail by order of District Court Judge Colin Neblett.

A year later, on May 5, 1924, the Council of the New Mexico Pueblos responded to Burke's letter in a statement, "Declaration to all Indians and the People of the United States" (Council of All the New Mexico Pueblos 1924), in which they argued for their right to exercise freedom of religion. The Council spoke directly to Burke's denunciation of the religious practices at Taos Pueblo.

> Commissioner Burke went to Taos Pueblo and there he gave an order which will destroy the ancient good Indian religion of Taos if the order is enforced. He ordered from this time on the boys could no longer be withdrawn temporarily from the government school to be given their religious instruction. These boys would stay longer in school to make up for the time lost, and there is no issue about the Indians not wanting their children to be educated in the

Government schools. But if the right to withdraw the children for religious instruction be withdrawn, then the Indian religion will die. The two or three boys taken out of school each year are the boys who will learn all the religious system of the tribe, and they in turn will pass on this knowledge to the generations to come. (Sando 1989, 79)

The attack on the traditional spiritual form of educating our youth at Taos Pueblo was one element of the larger struggle of the Taos people to exercise our rights as cultured people. Our sacred land, religious life, and youth were victims of a larger agenda to eradicate our identities and claims to sovereignty. Like the struggle to regain the sacred Blue Lake that started in the early twentieth century, the Taos people continued to educate our youth in our traditional ways. This was kept from the public eye. The struggle to regain title to the sacred lake and land, however, became increasingly public with the progression of each decade.

The campaign to restore the sacred lake to the Taos people drew interest from national press organizations. *New York Times* journalist Donald Janson traveled to Taos to interview John J. Reyna, Taos elder and governor of Taos Pueblo, and reported his findings in an article published on April 25, 1966. Governor Reyna explained in Tiwa, language of the Taos people, the significance of the sacred site to the Taos people. Mr. Paul Bernal, council official, translated for Governor Reyna:

The lake is as blue as turquoise. It is surrounded by evergreens. In the summer there are millions of wild flowers. Springs are all around. We have no buildings there, no steeples. There is nothing the human hand has made. The lake is our church. The mountain is our tabernacle. The evergreen trees are our living saints. They are with us perpetually. We pray to the water, the sun, the clouds, the sky, the deer. Without them we could not exist. They give us food, drink, physical power, knowledge and understanding. (Janson 1966, 33, 44)

In early July of 1970, a delegation of Taos leaders—Juan de Jesus Romero, Querino Romero, John Reyna, and Paul Bernal—traveled to Washington, D.C., to testify in support of H.R. 471, which would transfer 48,000 acres of land back to the Taos people. On the first day of the hearings before the Subcommittee on Indian Affairs of the Committee on Interior and Insular Affairs, our spiritual leader (cacique), the late Juan de Jesus Romero, stated the following in Tiwa (and was translated by Paul Bernal):

> I came here to deliver this, my spiritual message to you American people and our Indian fellows who are present here with us in the room of justice. . . . I came here because I recognize the dispute and the struggle and the torture that I have experienced with my people done by the U.S. Government . . . I came here to tell you that we are supposed to be in a good relationship. . . . We are supposed to act like one, not like an enemy. . . . My people are living poor, and that is the way of our nature. But we believe in worship. We believe in prayers. . . . I am the leader of the tribe of Taos Pueblo and I am the spiritual leader. . . . I am 90-years-old. I have a lot of responsibility. I go and fast and pray, and that is my daily chore and that is my duty, because I love the human being. I have no discrimination in thinking. I include everyone, the white, the black, the Indians, and what-have-you in this world. God put this ecology in this country and I have responsibility for that ecology in this country, the great sun, the moon and the good air. (107)

The message delivered by our cacique emphasized the nature of our Taos religion and culture as one that is rooted in the land and water, and the universality of his prayers for all human kind.

Immediately following the opening statement by our cacique,

governor of Taos Pueblo, the late Querino Romero addressed the senators:

> We have six underground chambers, properly located just east of the Taos pueblo village. These are homes where we talk about the religious principles. We need the Blue Lake area. . . . In these places we select our Indian youth at the age from 8 to 12, put them into the indoctrinations [schooling], for some 8 months. . . . This is the Indian education ground. The ecology of the different kinds of nature—the water, and the springs and the lake, the evergreens, the pine tree, the spruce—from the lowest altitude to the highest above the timberline. . . . We don't play with this religious land. We are not going to play with it. We don't want monetary judgment. We don't want economic benefit. We want to keep this [site] forever wild like nature gave it to us. (108)

The hearings ended on July 10, 1970, and the delegation of Taos elders returned to Taos. The sixty-four-year struggle continued only for a few more months because on December 15, 1970, U.S. President Richard Nixon signed the bill that restored Taos Blue Lake and the surrounding land to the Taos people.

The oratory of leadership throughout the twentieth century is filled with power. Even now as I read the transcripts of speeches made by our leadership at various stages of the battle to regain our lake and land, I can hear their words in our native language. I can visualize the flowers, the lake, and the mountains. I can see and respect the deep meanings of nature and our culture. The oratories represent wisdom, beauty, and purity unblemished by colonization. They are expressions of intellectualism at its best.

In 2001, Chomsky was asked to comment on imperialism, the media, and the role of intellectuals. V. K. Ramachandran asked Chomsky if he had to rewrite "The Responsibility of Intellectuals" (originally written in 1967), what would he have to say? Chomsky responded:

In retrospect, it seems to me there were unclarities and omissions. One has to do with the category of intellectuals. Who are they? Suppose that we take the term "intellectual" to refer to people who think seriously about issues of general human concern, seek and evaluate evidence, and try to articulate their judgments and conclusions clearly and honestly. Then some of the most impressive intellectuals I have known had little formal education, and many of those who are granted great respect as leading intellectuals do not deserve the name. If we adopt this conception, there is no special "responsibility of intellectuals" other than the responsibility of people generally to act with integrity and decency, but there is a responsibility of all of us to work for a society in which everyone is encouraged and helped to become an intellectual, in this sense. (14)

As I review the historical records of the twentieth century, the "responsibility of intellectuals" was exactly the responsibility taken by our elders. They were acutely aware of the importance of exercising sovereignty and self-determination through the maintenance of cultural integrity. Cultural integrity was at the center of resistance and at the core of cultural survival. Or as aptly stated by Chomsky in 2007, developments in the present, like the Declaration on the Rights of Indigenous Peoples, are "not coming out of the blue."

On September 13, 2007, the votes against the approval of the U.N. Declaration on the Rights of Indigenous Peoples by Australia, Canada, New Zealand, and the United States did not occur out of the blue, either. The U.S. vote against the adoption of the declaration is a patterned response to the exercise of sovereignty and expressions of self-determination. I was not surprised to learn that the United States voted against the approval of the declaration, for three major reasons.

One, the behavior exhibited by the United States from the

beginning of nationhood has not been positive in its relations with nations that do not serve mainstream U.S. economic and political interests. The evidence to support this assertion can be found in a review of U.S. "Indian" policy since the Washington administration. Consider the response of U.S. President Andrew Jackson upon hearing the ruling of *Worcester v. Georgia* in 1832. The Court ruled that the Cherokee Nation was entitled to federal protection if the state of Georgia infringed on Cherokee sovereignty. According to Satz, Jackson stated that "the decision of the Supreme Court has fell still born, and they find they cannot coerce Georgia to yield to its mandate" (Satz 2002, 49). Within the same decade, a majority of the Cherokee Nation and other southeastern nations faced forced removal from their aboriginal homelands to "Indian Territory" (present-day Oklahoma) west of the Mississippi River.

Two, my discussion of the decades-long struggle by Taos peoples to regain ownership of Taos Blue Lake and surrounding sacred sites, coupled with the struggle to maintain our cultural forms of education in the 1920s, provides additional evidence of the imperialistic nature of the United States.

Finally, the record of non-cooperation of the United States in venues of international negotiations *prior* to the vote on September 13, 2007, did not indicate any possibility for a radical change in the disposition of this nation. For example, the International Court of Justice (ICJ) heard the case of *The Republic of Nicaragua v. The United States of America* in 1986. The International Court of Justice ruled in favor of Nicaragua on June 27, 1986. The ICJ ruled that the United States had violated international law by supporting Contra guerrillas in their war against the Nicaraguan government and by mining Nicaragua's harbors. At a U.N. Security Council meeting on October 28, 1986, a resolution that called on all states to observe international law was on the agenda. U.S. Ambassador to the U.N. Vernon Walters asserted the position of the U.S. on the ICJ ruling: "No court, not even the International Court of Justice, has the legal power to assert jurisdiction where no basis exists for that jurisdiction" (46). The Security Council voted on the resolution, and of the fifteen states, the United States vetoed the resolution, three abstained, and eleven voted in favor of the resolution.

Given the historical record of U.S. international and domestic relations throughout the past 500-plus years, there are no surprises. However, there certainly is an opportunity for the current administration of the United States to change the course of history. Perhaps the Obama administration will take a step in a different direction and join two of the original four dissenting nations by supporting endorsement of the Declaration on the Rights of Indigenous Peoples. On April 3, 2009, Australia announced its support of the declaration, and five days later on April 8, Canada's House of Commons passed a resolution to endorse the declaration. Entities within the United States, including the National Congress of American Indians and the State of Maine's General Assembly, passed resolutions in support of the declaration in 2008 and 2009, respectively. For too long the United States has exercised power to the detriment of indigenous peoples of both hemispheres. It is time for all entities—indigenous and non-indigenous—to critically examine the past as a means of guiding political work now and in the future.

REFERENCES

Burke, C. 1923. *Message to all Indians*. Retrieved February 24, 2009, from National Archives and Records Administration. Web site: http://www.iwchildren.org/redholocaust/1665message.htm.

Janson, D. New Mexico's Taos ask restoration of shrine area title. *New York Times* (April 25, 1966): 33, 44.

Office of Press and Public Diplomacy United States Mission to the United Nations. *Explanation of vote by Robert Hagen, U.S. Advisor, on the Declaration on the Human Rights of Indigenous Peoples, to the UN General Assembly* (September 13, 2007). Retrieved January 20, 2009, from http://www.usunnewyork.usmission.gov/press_releases.

Ramachandran, V. K. Chomsky in first person. *Frontline* 18 (December 21, 2001) 8–14.

Sando, J. S. 1982. *The Pueblo Indians*. San Francisco: Indian Historian Press.

Satz, R. N. 2002. *American Indian policy in the Jacksonian era*. Norman: University of Oklahoma Press,

Taos Indians—Blue Lake Amendments: Hearings before the Subcommittee on Indian Affairs of the Committee on Interior and Insular Affairs, United States Senate, 91st Cong., 2nd sess. (1970).

United Nations. 1986. Security Council meeting 2718. Retrieved May 1, 2009 from http://www.undemocracy.com/S-Pv.2718.

Zumwalt, R. L. 1992. *Wealth and rebellion: Elsie Clews Parsons, anthropologist and folklorist*. Urbana: University of Illinois Press.

III.
FOLLOW-UP INTERVIEW WITH
NOAM CHOMSKY

Reflections on a Hemispheric Conversation among Equals

Interview with Noam Chomsky by Lois Meyer, June 17, 2009

BEFORE I RAISE SPECIFIC topics, are there things you found in the commentaries you read that you would be interested in commenting on?

I found things that are interesting for me to think about, but I do not know if I have much that I can say about them. Like the emphasis on community, on learning through doing, which is part of progressive education, as one of them mentioned, on reshaping our notion of knowledge to respond to the life of the community, and to study and restore the communitarian tradition that had been developed and that somehow survived the colonial and capitalist onslaught. I find it so interesting to read about the differences between Oaxaca and other parts of Mexico, the reasons for these differences, and how lucky Oaxacans are that their topography was considered less desirable for colonization!

The fact that the Oaxacans retained the traditions and want to revive them and find value in them is certainly worth pondering. Some of the notions I am sort of familiar with. I went to a progressive school myself that did have somewhat of the character of some of the things they are describing. There were classrooms and teachers and so on, but student initiative was encouraged, cooperative work was encouraged, competition was downplayed, students could initiate topics that, if the class was interested, they could pursue. But in Latin America it obviously goes much further.

And I do not entirely understand how it works. Now, it is fine when you want to reproduce the community, so you have a brick-layer, a farmer, and so on. But there is a lot of value in the outside world. How do you get that? There is science, the arts, the history of the rest of the world, and so on. I think that a community that simply tries to reproduce itself is going to lose its young people. It is not the Amish,[1] where they are basically insulated from the world.

The commentary by Gunther Dietz, who is one of the best known and most prolific writers about this construct of *interculturalidad*, speaks to that. Speaking particularly about Mexico, he says that there is a new phenomenon that makes indigenous communities dynamic. Since the government re-scinded its commitment to the revolution and to being ac-tively involved as a protagonist in social issues, since they have pulled back on that, communities have joined together to develop inter-community organizations. One of the conse-quences has been the appearance of relatively young people who are a hybrid, he says. They display a renewed commit-ment to community, but because they are functioning more regionally now, they also have a sense of supra-community involvements. And he describes this phenomenon as being extremely dynamic and positive in the way that you are con-cerned about. It no longer means just reproducing what the community has been, but indeed opens the community to other kinds of what he calls hybrid ideas.

Dietz's views on *interculturalidad* are much more posi-tive than those of some other commentators, who tend to see this whole direction as a political manipulation of the issue of diversity for governmental purposes. Do you have a comment on this concern that the promotion of intercultural education in Mexico and beyond is really a political ploy?

To undermine the communitarian aspect.

That is exactly it, and to retain state control.

Well, whether it is intended that way or not, you can easily imagine how it would turn out that way. The outside forces are pretty powerful. There is everything from state power to just the appeal of television, which shows young people the mostly fraudulent aspects of an outside world that you can imagine easily appealing to them. And resisting that is not so simple. In our own society, you may want your children to grow up not being part of the consumer culture, but it is not easy. There are a lot of temptations that draw them into the isolating, individualist consumer culture. And how to protect yourself against that is a huge dilemma. I have seen it erode in many places, even in places which were created as an effort to withstand it. For example, the Israeli kibbutzim were created as an effort to build communities that would be separate from the individualistic, capitalist society. I think that some of them, at least, were very egalitarian, based in women's rights, cooperative work, common eating, everything. And over time they just drifted into becoming pretty much wealthy suburbs where people have some collective interactions, but life became highly individualistic and interconnected with the outside world. It is just hard to resist.

Why do you think that happens in communities like the kibbutzim and others that have a strong spiritual base, as well as political commitment? How does that happen that their commitments, or at least their communal practices, erode and they become suburban and individualistic? Is it just human nature?

There are many values in life: serenity, friendship, community, and so on. But there is also the appeal, especially to young people, of the excitement of an imagined outside world, an assortment of commodities, iPods, pop music, and whatever else. In fact, another kind of community which is drawing them outside is Internet communities. The question is whether the local community itself can create enough of a living dynamic, a character, so that it especially appeals to young people who would then want to be part of it enough to resist the outside forces that are attracting them. And it is going to be harder still if they decide they want to go to universities and have professions where they are immersed in the outside society. It is difficult to just stay in isolated, Amish-style communities, which still live in the eighteenth century.

Some of the commentators suggest that the concept of community is being reinterpreted in the face of trans-nationalism and the phenomenon of migration out of these communities. Territoriality, the base in land, is changing. One of the commentators, Stéfano Varese, talks about seeing this in California, for example, in the way that migrant communities from Oaxaca and other parts are actually creating organizations to reclaim their culture and language in the place where they now have relocated. Elsie Rockwell describes a kind of phenomenon in urban centers in Latin America where the idea of land is being reinterpreted in new, urbanized ways. Instead of the Landless Workers Movement from rural Brazil, it becomes the Movement without a Roof, thereby accommodating the concept of land to the urban scene.

What are the implications of global migration, "diaspora" as it is being called, for these claims of the right to land? This strikes me as something very interesting that the authors did not go into deeply, but looking across the commentaries, there are various references to the issue of what land means today and what the right to territorial claims means in a globalized world.

You see many manifestations of this in the rich, developed countries, too. For example, there is a rather striking development in the community that I come from, the American Jewish community. In the past twenty or thirty years, there has been a very substantial turn of young people toward their conception of seventeenth-century Jewish life in the Eastern European *shtetl* (town): the Hasidic movement,[2] the religious commitments, the clothing. It involves hundreds of thousands of people, and they go and live in separate communities in New York state. It draws kids who feel alienated and isolated in our kind of atomized society. This gives them a kind of community.

Take another place where I have seen it. When Franco's totalitarian dictatorship in Spain broke down, lots of things sprang up that were there but had been suppressed. There was a revival of languages and cultures in communities that, under the dead hand of dictatorship, had languished. And some regions, such as the Basque country, are virtually reviving the language. I remember once I happened to be in Barcelona for a weekend and I was in a hotel that overlooked the central square. On a Sunday morning in this big cathedral on the square, people were trooping in from all over, young and old. There were musicians sitting on the steps of the cathedral, playing traditional folk music. There was dancing to traditional folk songs, very lively and enthusiastic. They were reviving a whole way of life that one had thought had disappeared a long time ago. And this, right in the middle of the urban center, with all the temptations and outside attractions you can imagine. How deep it goes, I do not know, but there definitely are things like this happening. In fact, one of the reactions to the concentration of power in the European Union's centralization of power has been regionalization and the growth of what some call a "Europe of the Regions," where particular regions are reviving cultural autonomy and traditional customs and languages right in the middle of advanced industrial economies. These same people use information technology and other conveniences.

I do not think you can predict how human society is going to go. But this need for community is very widely felt in Western societies, more so in the United States than in Europe. In Europe, there is a greater tendency to stay where you grew up. In the United States, people move all over the place, so it is highly atomized. I saw an example of this with my wife.[3] We live in a suburb of Boston. You sort of know people in a suburb, but there is nobody you can even turn to in a time of need. I found myself calling 9ll, the telephone number for emergency assistance, when there was something really simple that I just could not do. If a neighbor had come over, we could have done it.

A friend of mine just visited who lives part-time in an Italian village. She was telling me that there is no such thing there as home care for the elderly. She said that it is a village responsibility. The children are used to it. The elderly parents or grandparents get sick and die, so you take care of them. It is a communal activity. The idea that there should be something like professional health care, like a medical specialty for the aging or something, is not a concept. Here, it is necessary because the communities are gone and families are scattered.

When I lived in the Mission District of San Francisco for many years, especially during the years of the Salvadoran civil war, I watched as my Central American friends who were displaced from their families because they were refugees, or political organizers, or whatever brought them to San Francisco, would create virtual families and communities. They would reconstruct, as best they could, what they had left behind and what they could not go back to. And it was a blessing to me that I was included as part of their reconstructed family and community. It taught me a great deal, in fact, it certainly expanded if not planted my hunger to understand this thing called *comunalidad* as it is experienced in Latin America. I am not going to say there are not such places in

the United States, but intense communal experiences certainly are not a part of most people's lives.

I think this is a source of a lot of serious problems. I am sure you know that in the wealthy suburbs of a city like Boston, there are a lot of teenage problems which, if they existed in the past, were not so visible. I am talking about such things as drinking, drunk driving, crazy parties, doing drugs, any kind of reaction to the meaninglessness of life. For them it's as if life does not mean anything. They have everything, every commodity they could want, but it does not mean anything, so they go lose themselves in something. A huge number of kids in the suburbs are seeing therapists in the absence of functioning families.

I would like us to look at this from the other side of the hemisphere. Several of the indigenous commentators wrote that their whole conception of life, everything about indigenous life ways—the epistemology, the spiritual commitments that pervade everything—all this is completely different, 180 degrees different, from Western life, from Western thought. Yet, despite the obvious and insidious sicknesses that are consuming Western societies, the hegemony of Western ways over indigenous ways is projected in our world as though this were a David and Goliath[4] battle, as though indigenous *comunalidad* had no chance to survive.

That is right.

Still, in the voices of these commentators, the indigenous movement is committed to taking on that fight, and they are engaged in it. Given the way you have just described what you see in suburban Boston, the phenomenon in the United States, is this really a David and Goliath fight? What are the

opportunities, the cracks in Western hegemony, which would suggest that this struggle could really begin to turn around?

First of all, it already has an appeal. The drifting of young, wealthy, suburban kids to what from many points of view are cultish communities, like Hasidic groups, or the Moonies,[5] or an ashram,[6] or something like that, is a clear attempt to find meaningful communities that you do not have in an atomized existence geared to personal self-interest. So I do not think it is necessarily a losing struggle. In fact, it is quite an appealing picture of a possible future, when integrated somehow into an advanced, industrial, highly technological society, which you are not going to get out of, because it is already here.

But it does not have to work this way. In fact, it could take other directions altogether. Take something concrete. There are some very surreal aspects to the current economic crisis in the West. Sooner or later, I think, or at least I hope, it may dawn on people that they can do something about this. It is very closely related to what we are talking about. For example, right now in the United States, a huge amount of money is going into rescuing banks. At the same time, the industrial system is being essentially dismantled. Now, it is not entirely dismantled, because it has just shifted to cheap production abroad under multinationals. But the domestic part of it is being dismantled. And that means that skilled workers, the major workforce, are losing their existence. And that is the basis for every aspect of their lives. I mean, families will collapse, their communities will collapse and become wastelands, rust belts, and so on.

At the same time that this is happening, what is being done right now by the current economic plan? At the same time that the Obama administration is dismantling U.S. industrial capacity, it is sending its transportation secretary to Spain to arrange with Spanish companies to build high-speed rail systems for the United States, using stimulus money that is paid for by the American taxpayer. So the American taxpayer is sitting here watching their lives disappear. Their taxes are going to import from Spain, which is not the highest technology society in the world, the kind of equipment that could be built in their very own factories, the ones in their towns. But this is not going to be done by the bank that owns the factories, or by the corporate managers, or by the government.

But *they*, the workers, could do it! That is, there is really nothing to stop them from taking over the factories. That is a community activity, of course, taking over the factories. Now, you might need some outside funding, but it is going to be a fraction of what is being poured into the bankers' pockets. Take over the industries, reconstruct them, convert them. It has been done before. During World War II, for example, a huge part of American industry was radically converted. It led to the most rapid industrial growth in economic history. Industrial production virtually quadrupled in four years. So, it is economically feasible. It is even legally feasible. I mean, economics professional textbooks will tell you there is no reason in economic theory or law or anything else why, in their terminology, a corporation has to be responsible to shareholders rather than stakeholders. Stakeholders are the workforce and the community. It could be *their* corporation, meaning drop the corporate terminology and framework, and just take it over and run it. Do with it what ought to be done for the benefit, not only of themselves, but the population, in fact, the world. We have to get away from a fossil-fuel-based economy. It is all feasible.

And the contradictions are so close to the surface. As I say, there is something just surreal about the administration sending its representatives to Spain to get their corporations to take our stimulus money to provide to us what we are dismantling. If these things can somehow come to people's attention, it could lead to a major reconstruction of the economy along highly democratic lines.

And this is not so far below the surface and the consciousness of people. If you go back to the nineteenth century, industrial workers in the rising industrial plants took it for granted that they should own the plants. Those who work in the mills should own them. Wage labor was just an attack on personal dignity and personal rights; it is no different from slavery except that it is less permanent.

That was such a popular notion that it was even a slogan of the Republican Party under Abraham Lincoln. The critique of slavery, if you look at it, is that it is permanent; otherwise, it is just like wage labor, working under the control of someone else. Wage labor is a form of slavery. And it goes right back to the enlightenment. So this idea is nothing exotic or out of basic tradition. Of course, it is outside the tradition that has been crafted to produce a society of subordinate working people following the orders of management. But I think that is probably a thin layer, and with the proper forms of activism and engagement it could be overcome. Here ideas like the communitarian values that have been preserved in places like Oaxaca fit in pretty naturally.

As I was reading and pondering these commentaries, one that I found very interesting, given what you have just said, was written by Jaime Martínez Luna, one of the major theorists and analysts of *comunalidad* in Oaxaca. He and some others spoke about the distinct differences between, for example, Marxist thought and *comunalidad*. One of these differences had to do with how land and work are conceptualized. So, in one sense, the idea of taking over factories because they belong to the community seems similar to the commitments of indigenous *comunalidad*. But on the other hand, Martínez Luna spoke deeply about the fact that the commitment in *comunalidad* is not to improve individual salaries or benefits. He stressed that the land does not belong to those who work

it, that is not the conception. Instead, it is a spiritual relationship with the land, a relationship of caring. That spirituality kept hitting me in the face as I read the commentaries, from South America all the way north to the comments of my colleague Glenabah Martinez from Taos Pueblo. Many of our commentators spoke about the spiritual basis of indigenous claims. Has this spirituality been part of the communitarian history in the United States, for example, or is it a fairly unique and new phenomenon within these indigenous political movements?

I think that is what the workers' movement was always about.

Spirituality?

Well, people like Rosa Luxemburg,[7] a revolutionary socialist, said that we are never going to have socialism until there is a spiritual transformation among the population to recognize a different array of values. So, of course, you are not going to worship the factory. But if the factory is yours, you are running and managing it, you are deciding what happens in it, you are deciding how work should be organized and who should do what work, there is a kind of a spiritual dimension to that. In fact, even the slogan of the union movement has always been solidarity, meaning that is our value, we are working together, for each other, not just for ourselves.

In fact, if you look at different industrial countries, depending on the extent to which they were business run, solidarity had different meanings. So take, say, the United States and Canada, which are pretty similar societies in many ways. But the United States is more business-run than Canada is. Canada is somewhat more diverse, with less concentrated capital. And that shows up strikingly in the notion of solidarity.

So a major issue right now in the United States is health care.

It is privatized and it is a total disaster. This is the only industrial society where health care is essentially rationed by wealth, not by need. You are not cared for because you need care, but because you can pay for it. That is a very inhuman sort of value. And it is unusual, unique to the people of the United States.

Now, let's consider solidarity in these cases. In both Canada and the United States, the health care systems were kind of spearheaded by the unions, but in a way which is interestingly different and which reflects the character of the two societies. In the United States, the United Auto Workers formed one of the most powerful and progressive unions and got a good health care system and other benefits for themselves. They made a sort of compact with the company by saying something like, "Let's keep peace, but to do so you are going to give us decent health care and benefits and a decent life style." Of course, a compact with the company is suicidal, because they are involved in a class war. You may think it is a compact, but they do not. In fact, we are now seeing the results, when they decide that the next stage in a class war is you lose what you have gained. And, of course, it meant that, in the United States, there is no national health care. I mean, there is some, but not much.

In Canada the same unions fought for national health care, not just for themselves, so there was solidarity with the country. And they managed to put through a national health care system. It is not the best in the world, but it is much more efficient than in the United States, and it satisfies needs at a much lower cost. In both cases, there was solidarity, but with a different kind of moral dimension to it: are we more responsible to ourselves or to the people in other parts of the country?

And there is a kind of internationalism that did not show itself here. Now, every union is called an international because there is at least a conception that we are really struggling for the working people of the world. It does not mean much in practice, but it is there in the background of consciousness. That is why they are called internationals. So there is no sharp contradiction between these various notions of solidarity and internationalism. They can be realized in a variety of ways.

Right now, for example, it is a matter of critical importance for international solidarity of working people to move high on their agenda. The World Trade Organization, and other institutions created by the rich and powerful, are in large measure designed to set working people around the world in competition with one another, thus driving down wages and living conditions, while professionals are protected by a variety of means and the top managerial and ownership class enjoys wealth beyond the dreams of avarice. These devices are masked with highly misleading terms such as "globalization" and outright falsifications like "free trade agreements." As long as this process remains a one-sided, bitter class war, which in many ways it is, the vast majority will suffer. But international solidarity could overcome this increasing tragedy, and in some ways is taking place. Via Campesina, the international peasant organization, is one example. The United Steel Workers (in the U.S.) have offered support for union organizers in U.S. ally Colombia, which holds world records for violent repression of labor activists. And there are other signs of developments that should and could take off in ways that would provide some real meaning to the term "international" in the union movement.

And regarding interculturality, it would make sense that it would be realized in a variety of ways. It is a richer society, a richer world, if there are varying cultures, languages, traditions, and so on. So, there can be different ways of working out what may be common notions within an overall framework of solidarity with one another.

In our earlier conversations you spoke at length about the bloody process of state formation, and many of the commentators address this topic. In regard to what you are saying

now, they speak about the difficult challenge of creating a broader concept of indigenousness, given that their communities have been forced to participate in what Stefano Varese calls the "fictional ethnicity" of nationhood. That is, they have been split into different supposed national communities. Yet there is the effort to see themselves as Aymaras, or Zapotecs, or whatever united indigenous people they might be, apart from the various nation-states into which they have been chopped up and dissected. It seems like this is another one of those expressions of what solidarity could mean.

Humans have many different kinds of associations, or they should. Solidarity of the workforce across national borders in one kind of association. One example is your connection to working people in Bangladesh, let us say—you are on the same side in the struggle for taking over your own work, controlling it and managing it. So there is solidarity with others. On the other hand, you may be part of a religious community, which gives you a different form of association. And you may have other forms, too. Maybe you like music. Okay, that is another international association, the international music culture. And in a civilized world, these things would all go on side by side. Each individual would be a member of many communities. The next individual would share some and not others.

This would involve a breakdown of the nation-state system, which I think is probably coming because it is extremely artificial and hard to keep together. In fact, you take a look around the world. Almost every major conflict, maybe every one, is the result of the artificial drawing of lines by expanding European imperialism. Take, for example, Afghanistan and Pakistan. This region is now called AfPak because the conflicts are so interrelated. What divides Afghanistan and Pakistan is a line that was drawn by British imperialists to try to expand India as far as possible. It is called the Durand Line.[8] It happens to cut right through a major tribal area, the Pashtun area. In fact, most of the fighting that is going on that is called terrorism is right around there. Now, the Pashtun have never accepted that line. We may say terrorists are crossing from Pakistan to Afghanistan, but they may be saying, "I'm going over to visit my grandmother." And the state of Afghanistan, as long as it was viable, never accepted it, either.

And that is the kind of thing that is happening all over the world. The struggles in Africa have to do with the fact that the lines that were drawn by the imperial conquerors divided areas of essentially the same people and tried to separate them, and then integrate each of them into an artificially developed system of domination and control, even language, and so on. Of course, this leads to endless conflict. In fact, the same thing is true of the United States and Mexico. We talked about this last time. It used to be a porous border until NAFTA came along.

Given this, how do nation-states serve neoliberal, transnational purposes? Why are they being maintained if nobody wants them?

Well, some people want them. Any corporation wants them.

Why?

Every corporation relies on some state. They may call themselves multinationals, but if you look at the multinational corporations, they are based in a particular state, and the citizens of that state provide them with subsidy, protection, ability to function internationally, and so on. None of them are international, they are all state-based. And that has not changed with so-called globalization.

And that serves a purpose?

It serves their purpose. And, of course, there is a kind of spiritual dimension to this, an ugly spiritual dimension. The fostering of hyper-nationalist loyalty is a kind of spirituality as well. It is kind of like attending a soccer game where you go crazy about your own team. There is sort of a spiritual connection there, if you like. It is very anti-human and antisocial, but it is certainly there. It is very meaningful to people. For many people, it is the most meaningful thing in their lives. So if your team loses, you attack the other team's fans or threaten to kill the coach, or something like that. Nationalism is a very similar phenomenon. In fact, it has been pointed out by political scientists in the United States that what are called Democrats and Republicans—which at the moment happen to differ a little bit but usually they don't differ very much—they are like competing football teams. You have a loyalty to your own team and you want your team to win, even if it means using players that were just bought from the other team. These things are definitely real. In a sense, there is a spiritual dimension to them, just a very negative one. In this sense, spirituality is always part of people's lives. We do not want to knock it out. We should not. The idea is to turn it into something constructive instead of something murderous and destructive.

And how would that process work?

It works by trying to develop in a community some authentic systems of solidarity that fulfill people's needs without excluding and hating and antagonizing the other—the outsider. Any community has the problem that it is separating itself from something else. We would like to direct that so that it is not a source of antagonism, but just an appreciation of differences in interaction. So, there is something about the way that sports, say, are conducted which is highly conducive to arousing dangerous passions. And that starts with children. Children's sports are organized not to have fun, but to win. That is actually something quite new, at least in the United States.

Listening to you now, I am thinking of one of the commentators, Elsie Rockwell, who has collaborated with the Zapatista autonomous educational movement. She begins her commentary with a quote from Zapatista Subcomandante Marcos, in which he describes what is going on today as a Fourth World War, the financial centers against everybody else. She talks about how this warfare is there to turn differences among peoples into relationships of domination and subjugation, and the tremendous effort being expended not just to find differences but to demean and even demonize them.

The demeaning of others translates into subordination internal to the community. So war is the extreme case. You demean and demonize the enemy to the point where you want to destroy him, but you also accept that you are totally controlled at home. You subordinate yourself to your own state to try to destroy the enemy state, while they are subordinating themselves to their state. But the people should be on the same side! In fact, the antiwar movements that developed after the major European wars were striking in this respect. One of the main themes of the great antiwar novels after the First World War was the idiocy of essentially the same people in the trenches on both sides slaughtering each other, each committed to a power system that was oppressing them and that had nothing to do with them, when they had a lot in common with the people in the trenches right across the border. It takes effort to overcome these manipulated divisions, but I hope it is not impossible, or else the species is in trouble.

Many of the commentators speak to the fact that indigenous understandings and values expressed as *comunalidad* are almost the last resort for humanity.

This has to be done for a very simple reason: we are destroying the environment. There is no way to overcome the environmental problems which are very dangerous and imminent, without meaningful solidarity.

And it translates into very simple things; you do not have to make it very abstract or put it in polysyllables. Take a simple, concrete case. When you leave today, I am going to go home. Well, how do I get home? We have a market, it is sort of a market, not total but partial, and the market permits certain choices. For example, it permits me to choose between a Ford and a Toyota. It does not permit me to choose between a car and what I would like, a public transportation system. That is just not an option offered by the market. Markets are designed to prevent cooperative solutions. A subway system would be a cooperative enterprise in a democratic society. We get together and pay our taxes to provide for a subway system. Now, it may turn out that everybody in a town where I live would like to have a subway system instead of fighting traffic for two hours a day. But there is no way for them to get what they want because the system is designed so that it is virtually unavailable. You have to fight for it. You have to fight against the market and in favor of democracy. And there are tremendous pressures trying to drive you in the other direction. So everybody suffers.

It is the same in other respects. And now this is a matter of life or death. I mean, if we do not convert from heavy, irrational use of a fossil–fuel intense economy, there is not going to be any world for our grandchildren. So these are urgent problems.

In fact, it is kind of interesting to see that the urgency is finally beginning to be understood even by the people who basically own the world. So take the *Wall Street Journal*, which is the premiere business journal of the world, very reactionary, responsive to business and corporate elites. They have been on the forefront of denying and ridiculing the idea that there is an environmental crisis, global warming, and so on. Just this past week, one of the daily issues had a separate section about the environmental crisis which was quite extreme in its perspective. I mean, they just took for granted that we have got to terminate the use of fossil fuels, and said that we have to go to some sort of a rational, sustainable economy, and that we even have to geo-engineer the earth so that we can cool it off. So they even went beyond the environmentalists. It is a very radical shift. I think it is a sign of the recognition by the people who unfortunately own the world that they do not want to lose what they own. It also means that there are opportunities for developing popular, constructive approaches to democratizing, or taking over, these systems.

In bringing this conversation to a close, there are a few political issues that I thought were very interesting in the commentaries. Jaime Martínez Luna in Oaxaca stated that some theorists "continue to be obsessed with democracy, a topic in need of debate in light of current realities."

What do we mean by democracy? There is a very thin version of democracy that prevails in Western, capitalist society. Democracy means you show up once every couple of years and you push a button and you pick one or another representative of a very narrow sector of power. Then you go home and forget about it. That is what is called political democracy, you know, free elections, which are free in that you do not have a gun pointed at your head.

But another form of democracy which is quite deeply rooted is that you should have democratic control of every institution, control of your workplace, control of your community, control of the means of communication. Everything should be popularly controlled, with direct participation in management. That is another sense of democracy.

That sounds like *comunalidad.*

Well, that was the view of the major social philosopher of the twentieth century, John Dewey, who is as American as apple pie, straight out of mainstream America. And it was the view, as I mentioned, of industrial workers in the nineteenth century. It is not exotic. It can be revived.

The second thing, and something Benjamín Maldonado specifically asked me to ask you, is what sense you make of Felipe Quispe's criticisms of Evo Morales in Bolivia (in this volume), and of the Bolivian scene. Is there anything you want to say about those particular criticisms?

Well, I read some of the criticisms and I can sense their emotional content, but I did not really understand the basis for them. I did not see the evidence for them. If there was evidence, I did not see it. I was quite surprised by the virulence. I do not doubt that there are grounds for criticism. Still, from where I look, it looks like a pretty important—maybe the most important—effort in the world to create a popular-run society. I do not know of anything else that comes close.

And finally, please comment on Barack Obama. Glenabah Martinez from Taos Pueblo in New Mexico ended her commentary by saying that maybe this is a moment when the tragic history of the United States toward its indigenous peoples will change. Maybe, finally, there is hope for change, though past history in the United States would not indicate that change is likely. But Felipe Quispe, Aymara from Bolivia, said that all the U.S. presidents from James Madison to Barack Obama have come out of the same elite schools that prepared them to rule. Do you have a sense of Obama?

Not only that. The president does not rule in a vacuum. Presidents are put into office by coalitions of investors who finance the campaigns. Elections are basically bought. There has to be a concentration of capital that coalesces to buy the campaign, and they set the parameters within which the president operates. In the case of Obama, it happens to be the financial institutions. I mean, it should not surprise anyone familiar with history that Obama's main commitment has been to reconstitute the financial institutions, essentially without change. That is what they are pouring all this money into. In fact, mainstream economists are pointing this out. It is common knowledge. Yeah, that is what they are doing. Those are the people who financed him, and those are the ones who hold the commanding heights of the economy, and so they set the conditions within which policy is set. Now, there are deviations, but it is probably one of the best-established observations about Western industrial democracies.

So, is there hope that there will be a change of direction, in your mind?

There can be a change if there are popular movements, and that is always the struggle. The only reason we have freedom of speech, women's rights, minority rights, and anything else, is that there was a wave of popular struggle that brought them about. These rights do not come as gifts from above, they are achieved at a price. And they have to be defended, or else they are taken away.

Is there anything you would like to end with?

Just that I would like to understand better, get a better grasp of, the concept of restoring communal values in education and other aspects of life. I hope to see it develop in a way which will not be David and Goliath, but rather Goliath and David, that is, where communalism prevails.

NOTES

1. Christian religious denomination in the United States known for its simple living, plain dress, and resistance to adopting many modern conveniences, such as telephones and automobiles.

2. Conservative movement within Judaism that adheres strictly to the commandments of the Torah in terms of distinctive dress, the wearing of side curls, communication in Yiddish, and prohibition against mingling between the sexes. They tend to live as separatists, avoiding contamination by outside influences such as television and the media.

3. Dr. Chomsky suffered the loss of his wife, Carol Chomsky, in December 2008, after a long illness.

4. Biblical Old Testament story about a young Jewish boy, David, who defended the people of Israel by single-handedly battling a well-armed Philistine giant named Goliath, killing him with nothing more than a slingshot. The reference now implies that right can conquer might.

5. Members of the Unification Church, founded in 1954 in Seoul, Korea, by Sun Myung Moon.

6. Originally, "ashram" referred to a hermitage in ancient India where sages lived in peace and tranquility amidst nature. Today, the term is also used to refer to other spiritually-based intentional communities, often headed by a religious leader.

7. Rosa Luxemburg was a Jewish-German Marxist theorist, socialist philosopher, and revolutionary for the Social Democracy of the Kingdom of Poland (her birthplace) and Lithuania, the Sparticist League, and the Communist Party of Germany. She was killed in 1919, during a revolt against the Weimar regime in Germany.

8. Established in 1893 by the British Empire to mark the border between Afghanistan and what was then British India (now provinces of Pakistan), the Durand Line artificially separates territories inhabited by the Pashtun people and has never been accepted by them as a legitimate national boundary.

IV.
A FINAL COMMENTARY

22.

Comunalidad and the Education of Indigenous Peoples

By Benjamín Maldonado Alvarado

Mexican anthropologist specializing in indigenous education, who has lived in Oaxaca for thirty years, collaborating with various indigenous organizations and carrying out ethnographic studies among the Mixe, Mazateco, and Chatino peoples. Email: benjaoax@yahoo.com.mx

I HAVE THE UNIQUE privilege of commenting on the third interview. Other commentators in this volume were familiar only with the first two interviews, since the third took place while most of their commentaries were still being written and translated.[1]

IN CONVERSATION WITH INDIGENOUS *COMUNALIDAD*
Throughout the third interview with Lois Meyer, Noam Chomsky expresses once again his appreciation for the revival of community life through various strategies, and he celebrates the fact that there survives the will to live communally, and therefore to strengthen and recover *comunalidad* among original peoples. "The fact that they retained the traditions and want to revive them and find value in them is certainly worth pondering," he comments. Chomsky mentions several examples of experiences in his personal life in which community-based practices were valued. While these were positive, he recognizes that they also were limited, and that "in Latin America it obviously goes much further." It is apparent to him that *comunalidad* as described by these Indo-American commentators is lived out with greater strength and depth.

Nevertheless, like many people in Oaxaca, Mexico, or

throughout the hemisphere, Chomsky holds the erroneous view that *comunalidad* inevitably reduces or seeks to reduce itself to that which is local, or even worse, that it excludes anything from the outside, or anything global, regardless how valuable, useful and necessary it might be. This view holds that those who appreciate communal ways and fight to strengthen them want to isolate their people from the world, and lock themselves up in a nonexistent world free of evil. According to that logic, when Chomsky asks how one would propose to integrate communal and global perspectives, he inevitably arrives at an important conclusion, "a community that simply tries to reproduce itself is going to lose its young people." This is very true, and communal education attempts to create a solution—to reproduce *comunalidad* without losing (or continuing to lose) the young people. Isolation or purism is not at all what the communalists have in mind. Rather, they focus on the need to equip their people to circulate in the world, confident of their identity and with a strong sense of belonging to their community. In other words, they strive to overcome the vulnerability and dependence generated by postmodern nomadism.

The community of origin becomes the reference point in the opening up of new territories, that is, in the experience of a wider and more encompassing territoriality. It is clear that the migration of original peoples throughout the world does not cut them off from their community of origin or from the hope to rebuild that contact, except in those cases where the rupture with the community is due to political motives or cultural rejection derived from acculturation. The community is not only their place of birth or where their families live. It is a historical territorial place to which they are linked by a way of life which has allowed original peoples to sustain a self-managed existence. Only by continued connection with the community can they intensely live *comunalidad*.[2]

To remake communal life means to revive the joy of living,

and this, of necessity, is a political attitude: if one no longer holds the control of communal life in one's hands, this is because someone or something impedes it, and that something is the state. The act of revitalization has a name—autonomy.[3] Autonomy is not needed by original peoples so that they can begin to think about and attempt to create a new and different model of society. Rather, autonomy is needed to strengthen what is and has been their own way of life for centuries and—from that historical experience which has nurtured their children and youth for many generations—to be able to promote a radical transformation of the Mexican nation-state.[4] This leaves crystal clear that regaining that which is autochthonous inevitably implies retaking ground from the state, contesting and displacing state power. This is a reality that Chomsky himself indicates that he has witnessed in other parts of the world.

The community has been the incubator of indigenous resistance, under the powerful protective cover of communal life and communal ways of thinking. But resistance is not an end, it is a means; in other words, the point is not to live permanently in resistance—it would be absurd to resist only to enable oneself to live forever under colonialism. Rather, the intent in resisting is to achieve a people's own forms of liberation. The community is not the appropriate site for the liberation of original peoples in their struggle against colonialist domination by nation-states. Instead, it is the greater community, the collective of communities belonging to the same culture which together form a people. Communal thinking must be able to conceptualize and demonstrate how to project the single community outward to encompass a greater people, in order to ground autonomy in that intra-cultural concept that is an original people.[5]

Regaining cultural and political autonomy is both a prerequisite and a challenge of *interculturalidad*, given the inevitable attraction that modernity holds, mainly for those brought up in it or in the desire for it, that is, youth and children. The problem with such an attraction, as Chomsky points out, is not only in the types of activities that it generates in the population. Above all, the ideology that undergirds the various technological elements of modernity is problematic—an individualistic ideology of consumption, guided by the state. This suggests problems and challenges: problems derived from the irrational use of information and communication technologies (ICTs), and challenges like attempting to rationalize their use, which implies trying to fit them into a different rationality than the one that created them and to which they respond. The school is the principal battleground for this challenge, where students are liberated from the ICT grip only poorly, if at all. Absorbing ideas and instruments such as *interculturalidad* and ICTs without reflection means entering modernity in a subordinate and uncontrolled manner, without the possibility of taking control of the process. In many respects, this works to the advantage of continued state domination. "Resistance is always difficult," Chomsky says, but that has discouraged only a few.

I agree with Chomsky when he acknowledges the importance of a community base: "The question is whether the local community itself can create enough of a living dynamic, a character, so that it itself strongly appeals to young people who would want to be part of it enough to resist the outside forces that are attracting them." Yet he seems somewhat skeptical when he points out that the mere fact of attending a university will make this communal goal more difficult, knowing that the students "are immersed in the outside society." The immersion of indigenous individuals in the outside society is neither frightening nor worrisome. To the contrary, knowing that they will be immersed in the outside society, community-based education seeks to prepare them to do this efficiently, with the most resources possible, but without sacrificing their sense of belonging to the community or their communal identity, to be able to walk on this earth without losing their footing.

Comunalidad *and the Education of Indigenous Peoples*

The massive movement of indigenous migrants throughout the world has meant a restructuring of community life and a redefinition of territoriality, which is no longer reduced to the community's physical borders. The migrant's life takes place in an expanded territory, which some authors have called trans-territorial community. In my perspective, this effectively implies a symbolic expansion-in-movement of the community borders, which nevertheless are always linked to their original territory. There is no trans-territorial community if the migrant does not maintain an organic relationship with the communal life of his or her community of origin, if he or she does not maintain their right to the land and to be considered a community citizen through the fulfillment of their communal obligations. We must remember that among original peoples, citizen rights are only for those who fulfill their obligations to the community.[6]

The lack of community life is not only characteristic of an individualistic form of social organization, it also characterizes the social structure: community life cannot be built if there is no basis for it, that is, if there is no foundation upon which to build the structure. Collectivist lifestyle and a communal, non-individualistic structure are two intimately associated aspects, as one cannot occur without the other. Just as, logically, there cannot be community life in an individualistic society, neither can there be a communal structure, a community, where there is no communal life. This would make no sense. Communal life within a community comprises a complex experience that in no sense implies keeping everything local. Instead, it implies the ability to extend the experience, to take it into the world and reproduce it wherever necessary, as Lois Meyer pointed out in respect to her experience with families in the Salvadoran refugee community in San Francisco.

The regenerative power of *comunalidad* is evident when Chomsky brilliantly suggests one of the great options for reorganizing the world: *take back its control*. He bases himself in historical examples to argue the viability of workers taking control of production, or of society assuming control of its life. The sustenance of these ideas exists in the people, Chomsky says. For example, ever since the beginning of the Industrial Revolution, workers (and campaigning politicians, like Abraham Lincoln) thought of wage labor as a form of slavery, different from formal slavery only in that it is less permanent. Obviously, they rebelled against its imposition. Significantly, the existence of this popular idea condemning wage labor and the attitudes it generates resides, according to Chomsky, in the historical memory of the public, and not too far from active memory. For this reason, the state has concerned itself with manipulating those ideas, and ideologizing that memory. Therefore, the domestication of this memory seems, without doubt, to be one of the tasks that most preoccupy nation-states. Precisely for this reason, decolonization and autonomy necessarily involve the recovery of memory and of autonomous thought processes, and the liberation of the imagination in order to be able, with a clarity that is not manipulated, to envision the horizon that one hopes to achieve in order to live freely. The people must be thinking about, and acting toward, the real possibility of retaking social control. This is what Chomsky proposes when he talks about production and the community-based character of autonomy: "But *they*, the workers, could do it! That is, there is nothing to stop them, really, from taking over the factories. That is a community activity, of course, taking over the factories."

In order to achieve this, Chomsky puts forward the transcendental and also historical role of solidarity, which on occasion is present, at least in the professed international commitment of workers and others who are oppressed. Solidarity is one of the most elevated moral values of Western society; it is perhaps the primary ethical principle, the one that distinguishes people of worth from the rest of the population, from the masses. And here we could propose a very interesting difference with regard to the ethical principles of communal societies, that is, with the moral values of original peoples. For them, the important ethical principle is reciprocity, which differs from solidarity basically in three aspects.[7]

1. Solidarity is a unidirectional relation, a one-way street. It is about giving without expecting to receive, wanting to support without wanting or demanding support in return, an act of kindness without knowing for whom. On the other hand, reciprocity is a two-way relationship. It is giving in order to receive, knowing that society morally sanctions an unequal restitution of goods. In other words, person A must receive from person B exactly what he or she gave, at the moment it is needed, or there will be consequences.[8]

2. Solidarity is always selective. One can only be in solidarity with one person in a family, not with all, just as one cannot be in solidarity with all the organizations in a city or country. In contrast, reciprocity must be rigorously inclusive of all members of the community. It is unthinkable that it could be selective.

3. Solidarity is temporary. It should not be permanent, since its raison d'être is mainly to support someone in difficult moments, but almost never for life, as that would become a somewhat perverted relationship. On the other hand, reciprocity is obligated to be permanent.

These three characteristics of reciprocity have their social consequences. Unlike solidarity, reciprocity powerfully contributes to creating a solid social fabric, very tight, just like the threads of a weaving, while solidarity creates less communitarian relationships, like a net. I do not mean to say that solidarity is not valued by original peoples, but it has a different value than reciprocity. Solidarity between peoples, and between persons, is experienced more intensely if it has the communal characteristics of reciprocity.

The future of *comunalidad* is closely tied to the question of the future of the nation-state. Chomsky places himself among those who augur the collapse of this sociopolitical model by virtue of the fact that it is difficult to maintain both the state and the nation at the same time. But the incongruity of the nation-state model and its lack of future do not imply its disappearance, but perhaps its evolution into something even more deformed and absurd in order to keep it alive. That is, what could occur is something similar to what I think happens to a political system that is based on a contest of power exclusively between political parties. Such an absurd and incongruous political system, besides being onerous, does not seem to be viable, and in Mexico it is increasingly despised by society. But this does not lead to its disappearance; rather, it retreats and energizes itself within the possibilities available, producing even worse incongruencies, such as inter-party alliances, as a means to defeat the popular will and keep in power people from different political bands.

At the end of the third interview, Chomsky refers to the many educational efforts that have been discussed at various moments by the commentators in this conversation. He characterizes such efforts as part of a struggle to restore communal values through education. I would like to put forward two ideas on this topic, concerning the context in which these efforts are debated and what they hope to restore.

The context of education is the very context in which original peoples live today, and it is inherently colonial. There is no postcolonial context in the hemisphere because colonialism did not end with the independence movements. The nation-states that emerged in the Americas when classical colonialism (one nation dominating another) was eliminated have generated since the nineteenth century a merciless and expanding internal colonialism (one nation dominating its original peoples). Defined by material plundering and by ethnocide, this internal domination has been accomplished through the institutions that intervene in communal life. Currently, the most aggressive of these are four: the school, the Protestant Church, political parties, and the courts. These instruments of domination are weapons used against original peoples. However, in various ways these peoples have tried to appropriate these dominating institutions and strip them of their ethnocidal content, in order to function within them and incorporate them into their lives, as they did in their time with two other institutions of domination, the Catholic Church and the municipality.

In the Mexican case, the colonial aggression perpetrated by Mexicans against original peoples has been much more aggressive, intense and permanent than that of the Spaniards. I believe something similar has occurred in other countries. Today's national governments have struck out against original peoples, battering them with an ethnocidal vengence that was not so totalitarian during the Spanish viceroyal era. The school has had a central role in these attempts to create monocultural nations, despite the presence during centuries of a great diversity of original peoples. The political function of the school is ethnocidal domination, the eradication of languages and customs of indigenous peoples by means of an interventionist army—teachers and schools. This is what teachers and organizations fight against when they seek what Chomsky calls the restoration of communal values. Those communal values, which for five centuries have been attacked and corrupted by colonial pressures, are still alive, and they are focused on their own restoration. Communal education, both official and unofficial, tries to deactivate that culture-killing weapon that is the school. Its goal is to convert the school into a space where respect and coexistence can be generated, in other words, where the intercultural utopia can and must be built.

The restoration of communal values through education implies an understanding of the values that the school usually disrupts. In an interesting conversation held in Oaxaca in March 2003, the renowned thinker and Andean activist Grimaldo Rengifo (who is a commentator in this book) pointed out that the school tends to disrupt three kinds of conversations that are fundamental for original peoples.

The first is the parent-child dialogue. School de-communalizes the lives of indigenous peoples by opening up the obvious gap between the knowledge and customs of the parents and the new knowledge and new customs of their schooled offspring.

The second is the conversation between individuals and nature. School de-naturalizes the lives of original peoples by imposing scientific reasoning and excluding indigenous knowledge. This leads to a distancing of the student from all that is in the natural world, the wealth of knowledge which is cultivated in the cosmovision of those who are not schooled.

The third is the conversation between individuals and deities. School desacralizes the lives of original peoples by questioning and mocking the beliefs and rituals through which the community traditionally relates to the sacred supernatural.

By intervening in or interrupting these three conversations in the classroom, the school justifies and promotes in students attitudes of disrespect toward the knowledge, attitudes, and reasoning of adults. These ruptures are also reflected in part in the hidden academic curriculum which underlies the obvious, aggressively scientistic curriculum. Grimaldo expounds on this topic in his beautiful text, "Why is school unfriendly to the knowledge of peasant children?" [9]

The knowledge of the community is questioned daily as obsolete, backwards, and without rational base, and in this way it is considered an obstacle which impedes one from freely exploring the world as one chooses. These statements, constantly repeated in different ways inside the classroom, tend to loosen the child from the mental ties that keep her linked to the traditions of the community, thereby gradually educating her as a free individual.

When the option for progress takes root in the students and succeeds in becoming their personal, willful choice, the signs of respect erode; students no longer greet adults and elders on roads and streets, and they often question the technical decisions that the elderly peasants make in their communal assemblies, based on their cosmovision. If the alienation persists as a product of the colonization of their minds, the community's young generation becomes hostile toward the traditions the people live. The school is not alone in this role, since we also have to consider the roles played by the mass media, such as radio and television, and modernizing institutions.

Additionally, beyond the knowledge that is transmitted or excluded in the school curriculum, these ruptures generate, as basic components of the hidden curriculum, an attitude and also a new mentality:

> School teaches the child to play with representations and to mentally construct with them new realities and a different life order. In this way, the child learns to develop ideas that, although they may not have a concrete referent in the present reality of his community, perhaps tomorrow [he] will, on the condition that the present reality changes. And this change is based on a utopia promoted by the idea of progress. In this way, too, the child is inculcated with the tendency to modify his community beyond what the traditions teach.

> But school also teaches one to experiment, to handle nature with questions so that it responds to the orders that the researching student gives. Thus the child is learning to control and dominate the world, inclined toward a change that is not regenerative or true to the universe as she lives and experiences it, but one derived from knowledge of the laws of nature. In possession of these skills, her community and everything that happens within it begins to be seen as

a reflection of a passive attitude toward nature, a product of the ignorance of her parents. The child does not follow the conversation when her parents practice their rituals. Instead, whenever the opportunity arises, she intervenes and criticizes what the community does, proposing instead transformations that she considers appropriate. The myth that is inculcated by the school is that only by controlled manipulation of nature can one come to know the world. Other forms of knowledge derived from respectful dialogue with nature are forgotten.[10]

To hear wise, coherent, and radical voices, and to recognize their coincidences with the brilliant and entirely free thought of Noam Chomsky regarding the perspectives of original peoples in this ancient New World, allows us to feel the heartbeat of history present today in our experiences of life and struggle. In this way, we regain both enthusiasm for the struggle and also control of the reins for engaging the future.

NOTES

1. It is important to keep in mind that the third interview was a discussion based on brief summaries of only those commentaries that had been received and translated into English at an early stage of the manuscript development process; many of the commentaries had not yet been completed or translated.

2. The presence of self-management in original peoples' communal life is more than evident throughout history. By "self-managed" we mean that these communities have functioned without external intervention, much less intervention from dominant governments. A very clear example is traditional medicine, which always is a complex and impressive self-managed health system by means of which indigenous communities have treated the illnesses of their children, youth, adults, and elders.

   All original peoples have relied on four basic elements for their healing: medicine men (wise persons who, in addition to healing, are also priests and astronomers); healing knowledge (profound knowledge about body functions and the causes of health and disease—much of this knowledge is shared among members of the community); medicines (plants and other natural elements of animal

Comunalidad *and the Education of Indigenous Peoples*

or mineral origin); and healing places (the house of the medicine man or the sick person, or a hill or other supernaturalized geographical space).

3. The autonomy of indigenous communities is an historic experience based in *comunalidad*; therefore, *comunalidad* is the basis for developing new forms of struggle to transform the nation-state in order to achieve life with autonomy. However, this is not an imposed, vertical, and authoritarian autonomy, such as that found in Marxist ideology. An example is the so-called autonomy of thinkers such as Héctor Díaz-Polanco, advisor to the Sandinista government with obvious consequences in the life of the Miskitos, who then wanted to impose an authoritarian autonomy in Mexico with the Zapatista uprising, through the so-called Pluriethnic Autonomous Regions. A more in-depth discussion of this topic can be found in chapter 5 of B. Maldonado (2002), *Autonomía y comunalidad india*, available at: http://www.cseiio.edu.mx/biblioteca/humanidades.php.

4. Interestingly, Mexico has antecedents of this perspective of social change based on the historical communal experience. A century ago, the Mexican (Oaxacan) anarchist and revolutionary Ricardo Flores Magón found in indigenous communal life the historical precedent to assure that communities and the country in general could reorganize themselves, based in *comunalidad*, once the armed columns got rid of the local bourgeoisie and socialized the means of production and the stores. Such was the Mexican concept, or the Magonist version, of the revolutionary struggle for *tierra y libertad*—land and liberty. The characteristics of Indian socio-political organization (he does not call it *comunalidad*) that Flores Magón was interested in highlighting are three: 1) common ownership of the land and free access by all its inhabitants to natural resources (forests, water, deposits); 2) communal work, referring to collective agriculture, as well as forms of inter-familial mutual assistance; and, 3) hatred toward external authority and its uselessness. Flores Magón's ideas esteeming the way of life of original peoples appear in his article "The Mexican people are capable of communism" (*Regeneración*, September 2, 1911). Other articles on the topic published by *Regeneración*, are: "The right to property" (March 18, 1911), "The social question in México" (February 10, 1912), "Without government" (February 24, 1912) and "Without bosses" (March 21, 1914). These are available at www.antorcha.net or www.archivomagon.net. There is a recent anthology in English: Bufe, C. & Verter, M. (eds.) (2005) *Dreams of freedom: A Ricardo Flores Magón reader.* Oakland CA: AK Press. Concerning the Indian in Magonist anarchism, see Maldonado, B. (2003). "El indio y lo indio en el movimiento magonista," at: http://www.antorcha.net/biblioteca_virtual/politica/indio/lo_indio.html.

5. A constant topic of reflection by several commentators in this volume has been *interculturalidad*, questioned due to its characterization as a political response, principally by imperial states, to their emergent and recent diversity. Outside the boundaries of this discussion, I think that it is more important to discover ways to have intracultural dialogue, that is, dialogue among communities of the same cultural group, so that they begin to function as a people, to form connections

in order to make collective decisions, in a general assembly of communities that belong to the same culture. By solidifying themselves as original peoples through intra-communal dialogue, they will be able to fight for the transformation of the nation-state into an *intercultural* society, which obviously does not exist today.

6. Communities that are created for purposes of self-protection by those exiled abroad (at times migration has been compared to a kind of economic or labor exile) develop notable forms of communal life. But most common is the situation where thousands of native migrants who live outside of their territory (as is clearly the case with Oaxacans) create communities in their new places of residence where they reproduce cultural activities, strengthen their original language, and create organizations through which they maintain formal relations with their community of origin, their authorities and the communal assembly.

7. Reciprocity is the ethical foundation of communal organization, which is why all members of the community must contribute, and failure to comply is sanctioned with social rejection. Solidarity, on the other hand, is a virtue displayed by some and never demanded, though it is desired.

8. For example, if person A is asked to sponsor a communal or private fiesta, person B (as well as many other persons) could take person A 100 loaves of bread to help him out. In this way, Person A takes on the commitment that when person B has to sponsor a fiesta, he or she has to provide him 100 loaves of bread in return. If person A does not do this, the community considers it a grave moral fault and Person A is punished by being disparaged by the entire community.

9. Available at Proyecto Andino de Tecnologias Campesinas (PRATEC), www. pratec.org.pe.

10. In the same text, Grimaldo Rengifo bluntly states that "only in colonial contexts does learning one piece of knowledge involve canceling out others. In human life, there is no biological, psychological or any other basis for justifying that learning one piece of knowledge implies disparaging another. A child can learn one or more languages without positioning them hierarchically. We find no reason, other than that derived from a systematic exercise of cultural domination, to support the idea that promoting the notions of progress, modernity or development that are engraved into the modern ideal, demands that practices that constitute the millenarian life of a People must be forgotten and rejected."

V
CONCLUSION

AN OPEN-ENDED CLOSING

By Lois Meyer, Julianna Kirwin, and Erin Tooher

Lois Meyer is an applied linguist, associate professor in the Department of Language, Literacy & Sociocultural Studies at the University of New Mexico (UNM) in Albuquerque, U.S.A., and close collaborator with the Coalition of Indigenous Teachers and Promoters of Oaxaca (CMPIO). Email: lsmeyer@unm.edu

Julianna Kirwin has an MA in Language, Literacy & Sociocultural Studies at UNM, and has been a practicing artist for twenty years and an elementary school art teacher at Santo Domingo and San Felipe Pueblos, NM, for six years. Email: juliannakirwin@gmail.com

Erin Tooher is currently a doctoral student in linguistic anthropology at UNM with a focus on Mayan-language bilingual education in Guatemala, high school teacher for five years in rural New York public schools, and presently core writing instructor in the English Department at UNM. Email: etooher@unm.edu

THIS TEXT OFFERS AN open-ended closing, for the time being, to this hemispheric conversation among equals. It is not a small or uncomplicated question to ask what we have learned from this exchange of texts and thoughts among Noam Chomsky and indigenous activists and scholars from across the Americas.

We are three bilingual white women, thirty to sixty years old, all born in the United States and presently residing in the U.S. Southwest. One of us is a professor while the other two are graduate students at a large state research university, where we have spent the fall of 2009 together reading and reflecting on this book. All of us have been immersed in different ways in the political, linguistic, educational, and cultural issues and realities of Latin America for some time. Cumulatively, we have lived outside the United States for twenty-three years, more than twenty of these in Latin America; together we number more than forty-five years living and teaching in New Mexico, with its pervasive Native American and Hispanic presence.

Despite our backgrounds, all three of us acknowledge that we are part of what Evans, Evans, and Kennedy (1987) call the "non-poor," defined as "the middle class who as a group have low infant-mortality, high life-expectancy, and enough sustenance to be above the 'poverty line.'"[1] For Evans, Evans, and Kennedy, the "non-poor" are "the privileged and protected like [our]selves" for whom a transformative education must be one "which not only raises consciousness but also develops actions to change oppressive structures." Paulo Freire, in dialogue with these authors, repeatedly pointed to ideology as a major barrier to the transformation needed by the "non-poor" (like ourselves), who "do not customarily want to be transformed or to give up the privileges which they have enjoyed." "Ideology" is a very abstract and alienating term, hard to connect with on a passionate, personal level. As we studied this manuscript, one of our first learnings was a painful one: hegemony, the "ideological captivity of persons in North American society,"[2] pervades our daily lives, the books we read, the thoughts we think, and the disciplines we study. We are far from exempt or exemplary; instead, we tend to go along, tend to sleep along with the others, and for the non-poor, as Freire adds, it is quite a comfortable slumber.

Reading commentary after commentary in this volume, we came to realize how inexperienced we are even at *listening in* on a hemispheric exchange of views such as this. Our familiarity with Latin American indigenous voices and perspectives is more limited than we had suspected, and we are entirely unaccustomed to accessing Latin American indigenous insights as the source of our "learnings." Listening to these voices has been, for us, a rude awakening, jolting us to consciousness and forcing us to acknowledge and interrogate our own beliefs and experiences, in the light of *comunalidad* and indigenous resistance. We now see that Dr. Martin Luther King Jr.'s warning to the American people in 1965 about the tragedy of "sleeping through a great revolution"[3] could have been directed specifically at us in 2009. Ours has not been a comfortable process of learning, but we are grateful for the awakening that has begun.

At the most basic level, we are humbled and awed, and also angered, to encounter so many indigenous voices, perspectives, cultural practices, and resilient resistance movements in the Americas, about which we previously knew little or nothing. The dominant presence of English-language publications worldwide explains, at least in part, why these authors, renowned as writers and activists in their own countries and continents, are quite invisible to readers elsewhere, especially here in the United States. A yawning "language divide" is faced by speakers and writers of other languages, whose voices are largely unknown by an English-speaking readership. Tillie Olsen, in her classic feminist book *Silences* from 1978, wrote about the profound silences in society and within the publishing industry that traditionally have been imposed upon women, "the unnatural thwarting of what struggles to come into being, but cannot." Olsen focused her gaze on those writers, especially women, who struggled to make ends meet, raise children, survive, "their art . . . anonymous; refused respect, recognition, lost."[4] In this hemispheric conversation we encounter a form of editorial silencing Olsen did not contemplate—the international anonymity of writers and thinkers from the New World whose perspectives, written in Spanish or indigenous languages, are unrecognized in the West, even by English-speaking indigenous peoples, due to the dominance of the English-language press and the general bilingual incompetence of U.S. readers.

In order for the commentators in this book to speak directly with Noam Chomsky, intensive effort was invested to break this journalistic silence. Without the "insider" knowledge and collaboration of our Mexican co-author from the "other side" of the language divide, Benjamin Maldonado, and the technical support of the Internet, identifying and contacting these commentators to propose and confirm their participation would have been impossible. Noam Chomsky, too, willingly agreed to participate in this unusual virtual conversation with intellectual colleagues who nevertheless were complete strangers to him. Once the interviews and commentaries were in hand, detailed translation work on three levels—that of text, subtext, and context—was necessary so that Western readers, ourselves included, could comprehend the varied cultural contexts the authors referenced. In this volume, commentators repeatedly point out that language has been and remains a weapon of domination, one that has been used for centuries to marginalize and silence the views and voices of their peoples. Here the commentators' words were translated into English with great care and attention to contextual detail and local meanings, and City Lights willingly agreed to publish the resulting exchange. In this way, the weapon of domination, language, has been recast and transformed into a powerful sound system that amplifies and projects their views to a global audience.

Silences in conversation are not just empty spaces, we are told by conversation analysts; they "belong" to someone. That is, where there is silence, there too is meaning; someone who was "expected" to say something, or to express some reaction, to agree or disagree with what was said, or to respond in some way, didn't. Very few native English-language speakers participated in this hemispheric conversation. The silencing of our native-speaker voices in the body of this conversation serves two purposes. First, our silence has been a conscious decision, in order to enable traditionally muted indigenous-language speakers and Spanish-language speakers to express themselves powerfully and without interruption about their own indigenous struggles of resistance. By our silence, conversational spaces are opened up, inviting others to fill them. Secondly, our silence has given us time to figure out what to say, that is how to talk about or even think about what we have heard here. Only now at the end of this hemispheric conversation, do we feel prepared, though tentatively, to offer something to the exchange from our own perspectives. Here we will attempt to identify some elements of what we as English-speaking readers committed to breaking the comfortable middle-class hold on our thoughts and daily practices, take away from this hemispheric conversation.

COMUNALIDAD

It has been, and continues to be, hard for us to wrap our minds around the Oaxacan concept of *comunalidad*, or the Aymara's *ayllu*. While these concepts may have somewhat distinct meanings for those who participate in them, it is clear that both extend far beyond the friendly neighborliness we hope to experience in our local communities or the civic involvement promoted in U.S. towns and cities. The complex intertwining of history, morality, spirituality, kinship, and communal practices that compose the cosmovision of *comunalidad* is unparalleled, we suspect, in our contemporary, Western, "atomized" (as Chomsky phrased it) society. Rengifo starkly differentiates "the living world of indigenous peoples, in which everything is experienced as alive and imbued with personhood; and a mechanical world, a world of objects which is the one lived and projected by modernity."

We have begun to grasp that what counts as knowledge and its legitimate sources in universities and other so-called modern institutions is incommensurate with the knowledge produced and preserved in *comunalidad* The contrast between knowledge-in-books and knowledge-in-practice is palpable and sobering in this conversation. In the 2004 interview, Chomsky stresses both the antiquity of the indigenous knowledge system and its fragility, as well as the Machiavellian corporate efforts to steal this knowledge in order to control and exploit its use. In our comments below, we refer to indigenous knowledge as a knowledge-practice system in order to keep this fundamental characteristic of the cosmovision of *comunalidad*, so different from our own book learning, prominent in our minds.

The theme of a world that is alive, responsive, nurturing, holistic, and spiritualized weaves in and out of these commentaries, challenging our ingrained conceptions of logic, objectivity, and scientific rigor. Martinez Luna's words, also quoted in the introduction, ring like a refrain through our thoughts:

> *Comunalidad* is a way of understanding life as being permeated with spirituality, symbolism, and a greater integration with nature. It is one way of understanding that Man is not the center, but simply a part of this great natural world. It is here that we can distinguish the enormous difference between Western and indigenous thought. Who is at the center—only one, or all? The individual, or everyone?

Spirituality and integration with nature are themes that are named repeatedly by these commentators, especially those who are indigenous. These authors decry that Western modernization has elevated, even idolized, the individual and dismissed as superstition or mythology any suggestion of a sacred and animate world, thereby "de-communalizing, de-naturalizing, and de-sacralizing" our lives.[5] They urge us to consider that it is we who are schooled in false ideology and myth. Individualism is a myth, they suggest, for despite our protestations, we are not, have never been, and cannot possibly be, in this world alone, either as individuals or as a nation. The supposed objectivity and supremacy of our scientific knowledge is equally an ideological invention: "The myth that is inculcated by the school is that only by controlled manipulation of nature can one come to know the world. Other forms of knowledge derived from respectful dialogue with nature are forgotten" (Rengifo).

We are left to ponder in amazement what this "learning" could mean for us in our modern, technological, and atomatized lives. Interestingly, Chomsky reminds us that spirituality dedicated to the sacredness of life in community is a part, though often overlooked, of who we are as a nation. One of his examples is the international solidarity movement, "something new in the history of imperialism." It began in the 1980s when thousands of ordinary U.S. citizens, many from "evangelical churches in places like Kansas and Arizona and rural Maryland," went to Latin America to labor alongside the poor and to use their faith and their bodies as shields against repression and state violence. From these simple but profound beginnings, worldwide solidarity today has become crucial to the survival of resistance movements, for it "can really make a difference, inside the imperial state, inside the suppressed communities" (2007). However, the "dangerous memories" of these and other actions of personal conviction and global solidarity carried out by U.S. citizens against acts of state power and oppression that are supported, even exported, by our own government, are rarely, if ever, taught in our schools.

The power and omnipresence of our cultural myth of individualism lead some commentators to question even our Western understanding of the concepts of community and solidarity. Rengifo is guarded about Chomsky's description (2004) of community, influenced greatly by Dewey. Chomsky's description, he says, "to my way of thinking centers on the individual and his/her relationships," causing Regifo to distance this view from the Andean understanding of *ayllu*. And in a particularly vivid passage for us, Maldonado differentiates solidarity from reciprocity, "the important ethical principle of indigenous peoples," doing so on moral grounds. He contrasts the two concepts on three defining features:

1. Solidarity is a unidirectional and unequal relation, a one-way street, while reciprocity is a two-way relationship, requiring that one make an equivalent response;

2. Solidarity is always selective and individuated, while reciprocity must be rigorously inclusive of all members of the community;
3. Solidarity is temporary, while reciprocity is obligated to be permanent.

We understand that Maldonado's intent is not to discourage our acts of solidarity, but rather to forcefully communicate that we have the capacity and the obligation in global *comunalidad* to go even deeper, to reach out more inclusively, to let ourselves receive as well as give, and to never, ever turn our back and walk away.

These commitments of *comunalidad* on a global scale seem overwhelming to us, and we admit that we often felt overwhelmed as we listened in and reflected on this hemispheric conversation. Global *comunalidad* brings up more questions than it answers, in our minds. Is it possible that *comunalidad* can only be achieved in small-scale, rural, land-based communities, making it difficult if not impossible or even anachronistic in our urban, anonymous, consumerist, and bureaucratized lives? Martinez Luna rejects such an idea: "Comunalidad is an historical experience *and* a vibrant present-day set of behaviors which is constantly renovated in the face of the social and economic contradictions generated by capitalist individualism."

We are left, then, with profound questions: what would *comunalidad* look like if it were a vibrant present-day reality in *our* communities and nation and world? What transformations would occur in our representative democracy, in our capitalist economy, and in our bureaucratized institutions, if these were "constantly renovated" by a set of behaviors that might characterize global *comunalidad?* Close on the heels of these questions follow others, much more uncomfortable in their self-inquiry: is each of us, individually, invested enough and courageous enough to take on the reciprocal commitments and obligations of global *comunalidad*, regardless of the impacts on our daily life, our family, and our community? Or in King's terms, is each of us individually willing, first, to wake up to a great revolution that is roiling our world, and then "to work passionately and unrelentingly to get rid of injustice in all its dimensions," and collectively to "develop a coalition of conscience?"[6]

ALTERNATIVE EDUCATION

Is it possible for schools to *actualize* communal teaching-learning processes and indigenous notions of nurture and equality among all entities of the cosmos? If so, how could this be done?

The answers for indigenous Latin America, we have learned, are far from straightforward. Views among these commentators vary greatly; consensus is hard to locate in this exchange. Esteva, citing Illich, contends that learning has never been either a goal or a descriptor of schools, and that schools must be circumvented so that learning can be returned to the community. Martinez Luna seems to concur, relating the concept of *comunalidad* to the "liberation of knowledge" and a "new pedagogy," a discourse that takes place *outside* of the "cubicle, classroom or laboratory." According to Maldonado, the political function of schools is "ethnocidal domination, the eradication of languages and customs of indigenous peoples by means of an interventionist army—teachers and schools." Chomsky, it seems to us, would concur with this view, and also with the sole hope Maldonado holds out: communal education, which "tries to deactivate that culture-killing weapon that is the school . . . to convert the school into a space where respect and coexistence can be generated." Still, Zibechi provides an important reality check: "We are not very clear how collective learning processes, either libertarian or liberating, could be put into practice. Even concepts of libratory education or emancipatory pedagogy ring hollow whenever either of these is consigned to spaces or times created for the purposes of cultural homogenization and the formation of a dependent citizenry."

The experimental models of alternative education described in several of the commentaries provide hope. These alternative schools represent profoundly altered conceptions of teaching-learning and serve as provocative critiques of mainstream Western schooling. From our perspective in the United States, it is easy to dismiss as remote and exotic the schools described by Soberanes, Chen, Mamani, Zibechi, and others. Language nests in Oaxaca, educational codices in the re-created schools of Guatemala, and Brazilian schools in movement without roofs, seem a far cry from our test-driven schools that seek uniform, so-called world-class academic outcomes through imposed education standards and scripted curricula. We must remind ourselves: these *comunalidad*-inspired schools exist in the world as models-in-development of educational autonomy and emancipation from what American author bell hooks describes as the "dominator culture,"[7] pervasive in our society as well as in Latin America. The examples provided by these Latin American indigenous schools lead us to question the larger political context of *our* school system and its broader societal context: what significant social movements, if any, can we point to in the United States since the 1960s? Do our public schools reflect any noticeable alternative educational efforts, other than drop-outs, push-outs, and stay-outs? What forms of subjugated knowledge exist in our educational settings? In other words, where are the silences among our students, and in U.S. society as a whole? Are these being addressed at all?

Rockwell discusses the "highly codified and fragmented knowledge, alien to local experience," which is reified in schools and which organizes their bureaucratic educational practices and structures, contributing to "the actual or mental desertion of students on all levels." We ask ourselves: when will U.S. parents and educators, and especially legislators, consider the possibility that achievement gaps and desertion rates in our public schools reflect not unsupportive parents or inadequate teachers, as is widely asserted, but rather the "actual or mental desertion" of alienated

An Open-Ended Closing

students who find what they are learning, or rejecting, at school to have little relevance or meaning in their lives?

As educators listening in to this hemispheric conversation, we cringe at the blanket recriminations that are lobbed at the education system and its practitioners. How many of these critics have been responsible for the learning of a classroom of students, we wonder, or agonized during a sleepless night over their curriculum, their progress, or their futures? Still, we are inspired by the powerful history and tenacious persistence of the indigenous movement across the hemisphere and its activism as "the new actor on the social stage" in the twenty-first century, as López states. The indigenous movement has been an increasingly vocal presence in many countries, countering whenever it can the educational ethnocide described by Maldonado. Still, despite progress, the indigenous movement and these voices continue to be profoundly silenced in educational textbooks and the popular media.

The theme of *interculturalidad*, especially in education, is a topic mentioned by many of the commentators, yet we are still unsure what it means, what it looks like, and how it is accomplished in practice, either in Latin America, or by extrapolation, in our own communities and schools. We are quite certain that its vision far surpasses our national and local versions of community- and place-based education, or bilingual education, even where the latter has not been restricted by law, as has occurred in California, Arizona, and Massachusetts. Rockwell and Bertely describe schooling for a new model of citizenship. This new model is constructed from below and is based on territorial and educational control, self-sustainable development, care of the environment, reciprocity and solidarity, and the strengthening of communal organizations, languages, and cultures. We will eagerly listen in on this hemispheric conversation in the future, in the hope of understanding how such an educational model, inspired and grounded in *comunalidad*, can be concretely brought to life.

LANGUAGE AND MEMORY

The commentators in this volume provide an important critical lens on ideas of globalization that suggest that the world is becoming homogenized and interconnected through one-way, top-down processes (Friedman 2005, 2009;[8] Gray 1998, 2000, 2009[9]). They suggest that *comunalidad* and indigenous languages are pushing back at globalization and its language homogenization from the "bottom up" and from the "inside out." Migration is extending the geographic boundaries of communities, and languages and knowledge-practice systems like *comunalidad* are migrating as well, introducing alternate ways of speaking, thinking, and behaving into multinational corporations and local communities and schools worldwide. As a knowledge-practice system, *comunalidad* refutes linguistic homogenization, giving witness to the importance of language variation and the multilingual person, referred to by María Yolanda Terán and others. Speaking as an indigenous Kichwa person from Ecuador, Terán demonstrates the linguistic complexities of globalization and the significant power that multilingualism possesses. Globalization is not a one-way street that allows dominant languages to roll over and suffocate original languages across the globe. The commentaries clearly show that while globalization and language homogenization may be on the move worldwide, so too are bottom-up resistance efforts and the linguistic reciprocity of multilingualism.

Still, from all parts of the hemisphere, these commentators grieve the fragility and loss of their original languages, even as they celebrate the presence in multiple sites of local resistance and language revitalization efforts. "Language loss" is a strange term, we have come to believe. Why not just admit that these languages have been intentionally suffocated or shamed out of existence, and thereby acknowledge the physical and psychological violence committed against their speakers by colonizers and nation-states alike? Centuries of language domination have instilled in indigenous peoples fear, distain, even hatred, of their own languages, stifling their desire to speak their own tongues or pass these on to their children. The cultural suffocation of these languages has caused great personal and collective trauma. Parents insist that their children learn the dominant language and forget their own, to spare them, they say, the suffering and shame they themselves have endured. An indigenous language, Chen reminds us, "preserves in every word the essence of the community" and is a repository of its historical memory. It is no wonder, then, that indigenous languages and the memories they contain have been manipulated, ideologized, and domesticated by nation-states, in recent decades more than during colonial times, Maldonado reports. The revitalization of indigenous languages, he continues, is intimately linked to the "recovery of [communal] memory and autonomous thought processes."

There are a few powerful examples of memory recovery documented in these commentaries. Chen, Soberanes, Martínez, Zibechi, Bertely, and the Oráns come to mind. They inspire us with what might be called "positive" memory recovery, where community healers, elders, educators contracted by the community, and others, return their knowledge-in-practice back to the community, its schools, and its children. We wish this volume included more such cases.

There is an unmistakeable lesson here for the non-poor. The recovery of memory, specifically dangerous memories about violent colonization and the annihilation of cultures and languages, is, like *comunalidad*, reciprocal, not unilateral. Complex accounts of violence, shaming, manipulation, and domestication, are concealed parts of *our* history, they did not just "happen" to indigenous "others." We have come to the conviction that *comunalidad* morally compels us to recover these memories, to begin locally to examine our own history of English-language domination within the borders of our own community and state and nation. Fortunately, we are not alone in this conviction; others, especially Noam Chomsky, have led the way. In his prolific writings and in these interviews, Chomsky unsparingly documents the dangerous memories of both overt and covert U.S. violence and oppression. He reminds us, "if you look at [the U.S.] before it was colonized, there were hundreds of languages, radically different cultures, all sorts of diversity. The United States is institutionally homogenous now because of conquest and extermination" (2004). He continues, "the U.S. sits on half of Mexico . . . not only did they take the riches of Mexico, they also took the culture" (2007).

Other dangerous memories, deeply relevant but barely alluded to by these commentators, fester outside our national borders: our nation's long history of infiltrations, collusions, subversions, and manipulations of governments, economies, and military regimes in Latin America and elsewhere. We ask ourselves: do we, as educators in U.S. schools, have the courage to follow Chomsky's example? Are we willing to put at risk our professional and personal futures in order to recover these memories, or will they remain part of what school teaches us we should not talk about, Chomsky says, to more expeditiously erase them from memory? Recovery of these dangerous memories can be traumatic for us as U.S. citizens and for those whose lives have been scarred by our insidious and violent actions. But if we hope for the clarity and autonomy of thought of which Maldonado speaks, and the reciprocal caring promised by global *comunalidad*, the recovery of these difficult memories, it seems, must be a first step.

AN OPEN-ENDED CLOSING

Like the schools begun by the Movement without Land in Brazil (Zibechi), merely listening in on this hemispheric conversation has perturbed us, dislodged us from our ordinary patterns and activities, and propelled us into movement. At least, we hope that this is so. This conversation has taught us one lesson clearly: that we must listen intently, and open our minds to ideas that are new and surprising, even shocking, such as global *comunalidad* and its reciprocal and inclusive commitments. If we stop listening, how can we possibly stay awake? How can we learn differently? Listening in has heightened our social awareness. For us, this means awareness of the Western hegemony in which we are deeply entrenched and also awareness of the plethora of ways of living, thinking, and behaving beyond those so pervasively familiar to us that they lull us into our sleepy complacency.

But listening, and even learning, are still insufficient. We find our thoughts returning again and again to the admonition Freire directed to the non-poor, that is, to us: greater consciousness is not enough; we must take actions to change oppressive structures. Chomsky tells us in his first interview that the opportunities are greater today than ever before for global *comunalidad* to impact world policies and actions because of the existence and future activism of the international solidarity movement. Here we come face to face with *our* unique role and responsibility as collaborators with the New World of indigenous resistance: what can *we* do—or more importantly, what *are we doing*—to dismantle oppressive structures in our own communities and elsewhere, in order to permit an array of alternative possibilities to flourish locally and globally? That is, how are we *acting* in our daily lives, in and for global *comunalidad*, so that the opportunities for action which Chomsky believes exist today are transformed into concrete active resistance?

We must not lose sight of the fact that our activism must be embedded within, and never separate itself from, the multivoiced hemispheric conversation on resistance, hope, and renewal. There are unique sources of inspiration and guidance for our actions of solidarity that must come to us from elsewhere. We remember Mamani's assertion of the growing moral authority of indigenous peoples for the preservation of human values, biodiversity, and the defense of Mother Earth from devastation. "The efforts invested by indigenous peoples in the education of their children and youth, as well as in the recovery of cultural values, have no other end than this: the free determination by indigenous peoples, in opposition to the old processes of nation-state formation, to pursue the path toward reestablishment of universal values and the recognition of Earth as the big home for us all."

We have chosen to title this final comment "An Open-Ended Closing" in order to signal, as does Chomsky, that while this book must end, we are committed to continuing the hemispheric conversation itself. This conversation has only just begun, and it is crucial that it continue. Without a doubt, we, the non-poor, need to keep engaging in conversations such as this, so that we continue listening and chipping away at our preconceived and rigid notions of knowledge, ways of being, and ways of teaching and learning. It seems imperative that we continue learning about and from indigenous efforts of resistance across the Americas in order to rouse ourselves time and again from sleep into action. And if the reciprocity of global *comunalidad* is to have any meaning, we too must resist, acting courageously to change the oppressive structures which oppress others as well as ourselves, and which, in the end, can destroy us all and the planet we live on. Our hope is that this book will be one small contribution toward conscious, concerted activism, carried out in global *comunalidad*, which will set our collective course toward a different and hopeful future.

NOTES

1. Alice Frazer Evans, Robert A. Evans, and William Bean Kennedy, *Pedagogies for the Non-Poor* (Maryknoll, NY: Orbis Books, 1987). In this unusual and powerful book, Evans, Evans, and Kennedy document the reflections of "a multiracial group of women and men with birthplaces and/or former vocational assignments on six continents: Nicaragua, South Africa, Lebanon, Korea, Switzerland, the USSR, and the United States." This group met at a December 1982 meeting of the International Advisory Council of Plowshares Institute, drawn together by their shared commitment to "transformative education especially for the 'non-poor'," among whom they included themselves. The book includes an interview with Paulo Freire about "pedagogies for the non-poor."
2. William Bean Kennedy, ibid., 239.

An Open-Ended Closing

3. Martin Luther King, Jr., "Remaining Awake Through a Great Revolution." Commencement Address for Oberlin College, Oberlin OH, June 1965, downloaded on Jan. 5, 2010, at http://www.oberlin.edu/external/EOG/BlackHistoryMonth/MLK/CommAddress.html.

4. Tillie Olsen, *Silences* (New York: Feminist Press, 2003), xiv.

5. Rengifo, quoted in Maldonado in this volume.

6. Ibid.

7. bell hooks, *Teaching Community: A Pedagogy of Hope* (New York: Routledge, 2003).

8. Thomas Friedman, *The World is Flat: A Brief History of the 21st Century* (Farrar, Straus & Giroux, 2005); *Hot, Flat and Crowded 2.0* (Farrar, Straus & Giroux, 2009).

9. John Gray, *False Dawn: The Delusions of Global Capitalism* (New Press, 1998); *Two Faces of Liberalism* (New Press, 2002); *Gray's Anatomy: Selected Writings* (Anchor Canada, 2009).

Index

Balibar, Etienne, 260
Barbados I–III (anthropologists'
meetings), 265–67
Barcelona, 67
Basque language, 80, 347
Bayer, Osvaldo, 301, 312–13n2
Benetton, Luciano, 311
Bergese, Ivanna, 36n20
Bernal, 334, 335
Bertely Busquets, María, 29, 141–59,
393, 395
Bible, 57
bilingual education, 47, 60, 120, 221,
248–49
Argentina, 308, 310
Bolivia, 200–12 passim
Guatemala, 201–212 passim, 220,
226–30
Mexico, 103, 107, 111, 159n15
Panama, 235–36
restricted by law, 393
Bill of Indigenous Rights (Mexico), 145,
158
Blue Lake, 332, 334–35, 336
boarding schools, 181
Bolivia, 18, 51, 72–73, 74, 286, 287,
291–300 passim
Argentina and, 310, 311
Chile and, 80, 298
education in, 200–12 passim, 221
revolution of 1952, 319
Bonfil Batalla, Guillermo, 117, 172, 266,
273, 274
book burning, 266
books. See literature; teacher-made
books; textbooks
borders, international. See international
borders
Bórmida, Marcelo, 312n1
Brazil, 61, 73–74, 208, 273
ethanol production, 76
See also Landless Workers
Movement (MST)
Britain
Chile and, 80
Durand Line and, 356
See also England; Scotland; Wales

Burke, Charles, 333

CCIODH, 15, 16
CMPIO. See Coalition of Indigenous
Teachers and Promoters of Oaxaca
CNEII. See National Congress of
Indigenous and Intercultural
Education (CNEII)
CO_2 sales, 223
"cabecitas negras," 305
caciques, 156n3
California, 271, 393
Canada, 78, 81, 331, 337, 339
national health care and, 353–54
capitalism, 123, 213–16 passim, 240, 264,
265, 272, 293
Amazonian peoples and, 222–23
Argentina, 310
See also debt crisis; market tyranny;
unemployment; wage slavery
Caracoles, 158n12
Cárdenas Condori, Victor Hugo, 297
Cárdenas, Lázaro, 92, 98n5
cargos, 94–95
Carson National Forest, 332
Carter, Jimmy. See Carter
administration.
Carter administration, 17-18, 70
Casa de la Cultura del Maestro
Mexicano, 107
casinos, 81
Castillo, Martin, 325
Castro Gómez, S., 303
Catalan, 57, 67
Catalonia, 42, 57, 67
Catholic Church, 253, 294, 375
caudillos, 156n3
censorship, 47. See also book burning
censuses, 201–2
Central America solidarity movement,
77, 389
Chatino people, 104
Chen Morales, Guillermo, 25, 225–31,
392, 395
Cherokee Nation, 338
Chiapas, 174, 267. See also Acteal
Massacre; Zapatistas

childcare givers, 110–11
children
labelled "migrants" before they've
migrated, 166
See also teenagers
Chile, 80, 208, 285, 298, 311
Chinanteco people, 108, 271
Chol people, 141, 267
Chomsky, Carol, 35n10
Chomsky, Noam
2004 interview, 10–13, 41-62, 387
2007 interview, 13–19, 65-82
2009 interview, 32–34, 343–364
and dangerous memories, 395-96
on community, 59, 345–51 passim
on education, 53, 56–57, 67–69
on indigenous people, 49, 63–64
"The Responsibility of
Intellectuals," 336–37
on September 11, 2001, terrorist
attacks, 133–34
on solidarity, 13, 56, 76–77, 353–60
passim, 397
on sports, 358–59
churches
solidarity movement and, 77
See also Catholic Church;
Protestant Church
citizenship, 147, 149, 171, 179–80, 259,
260, 264, 371
education and, 200, 203
clandestine schools, 318
class, 168. *See also* "non-poor"
class war, 355
Coalition of Indigenous Teachers and
Promoters of Oaxaca (CMPIO),
101, 106–7, 109–11, 326–27
cochineal insects, 96
codices. *See* educational codices
coercion, 59, 60, 120, 121
collective authority, 164
collective land. See *ejidos*
collective learning, 325
collective ownership. *See* communal
ownership
colleges and universities, 148, 166, 246.
See also Ivy League schools
Colom, Álvaro, 225

Colombia, 51, 58, 208, 221, 249, 355
colonialism, 52, 122, 203, 243, 369,
374–75
colonists and colonizers, 86, 149
English, 44
Spanish, 94, 261, 285, 302
colonization, 89, 122, 129, 243, 284–87
passim, 292–97 passim, 377. *See also*
decolonization
Columbus, Christopher, 261
Columbus Day, 70
Comisión Civil Internacional de
Observación por los Derechos
Humanos. *See* CCIODH
Commission of Concord and
Pacification, 158n11
commodification, 94
of cultural diversity, 163
of education, 128
of nature, 269
communal education, 391
communal labor, 95–96, 379n4
communal ownership, 87, 97, 379n4
communalism, 88, 93. See also
comunalidad
"communalism" (word), 97
community, 277–81, 368–72 passim
Chomsky on, 59, 345–51 passim
education and, 111–12, 318, 327,
328, 370
as family, 94
knowledge and, 139
migrants and, 368, 371, 380n6
traditional medicine and, 380n5
See also *ayllus*; *comunalidad*
community collaboration, 254
Community Middle Schools for Original
Peoples, 108
community police, 95
compulsory schooling, 171
comunalidad, 13, 23–24, 33, 85–99, 121,
191–97 passim, 222, 352, 367–80
passim, 387 98 passim
and globalization, 394
global *comunalidad*, 390-91, 396-98
in education, 108, 110–11
methodology of, 9–26 passim
"*comunalidad*" (word) 10, 30–31

INDEX

Gramsci, Antonio, 81, 169–70, 272, 281
Gray, John, 394, 399
graduate students, 48–49, 79–80
Great Britain. *See* Britain
Guadalupe Llano de Avispa, Oaxaca, 111–12
Guatemala, 201–212 passim, 219–20, 225–31, 271
guerrilla movements, 265
"guided learning," 326
Gutiérrez Luís, Beatríz, 36n20

hacienda system, 278, 281n2
Hale, Kenneth, 48, 79
Harvard University, 46
Hawaiians, 271
health care, 348, 353–54. *See also* traditional medicine
hegemony, 81, 88, 272, 384
culture and, 169
language and, 21–22
See also Western ideological hegemony
Hernández Díaz, Andrés, 152–54
heteronomy, 121
Hidalgo Guzmán, Juan Luis, 107
high schools, 309, 313n11
higher education, 116–17, 249, 296, 297, 370. *See also* colleges and universities
history teaching
Mexico, 177n14, 185, 326
Hobsbawm, Eric, 146
Holt, John, 126, 127–28
Los hombres y las mujeres del maíz (Bertely), 152
homogenization, 13, 47, 216, 286
Argentina, 303, 304
Guatemala, 205
See also cultural homogenization; educational homogenization; institutional homogenization
hooks, bell, 392
Human Terrain System, 169
hybridity, 344

ICTs. *See* information and communication technologies (ICTs)

ILO. *See* International Labor Organization (ILO)
IMF. *See* International Monetary Fund
identity distortion, 305
ideology, 9, 10, 292, 370, 384
capitalist, 272
Marxist, 379n3
Illich, Ivan, 123, 131n6, 315–16, 391
immigrants, European. *See* European immigrants
immigrants, Irish. *See* Irish immigrants
immigrants, Jewish. *See* Jewish immigrants
imperialism, 43, 53, 296, 356–57, 389
in Mexico, 146
U.S., 271, 272, 331–40 passim
See also anti-imperialist movement
Incas, 300n2, 300n5
independence movements, 214
independent candidates for office, 157n8
India, 52, 356
"indigenous education" (term), 122
indigenous languages, 25, 57, 218, 221, 251, 287
in education, 201, 205
Kenneth Hale and, 48, 49
"language divide" and, 21–22, 385
Mexico, 103, 111–12
Panamanian constitution and, 236
prohibited in Argentine schools, 304
in U.N. proceedings, 256–57
See also Aymaya language; bilingual education; Kichwa language; Maya Achi language; Mixtec language; Tiwa language; Tojolabal language; Wampanoag language; Zapotec language
indigenous medicine. *See* traditional medicine
indigenous nation (proposed), 79, 81
indigenous peoples
alternative vision of work (and life), 152–54
Barbados meetings and, 266
Bolivia population, 201
Chomsky on, 49, 63–64

Makarenko, Anton, 90
Maldonado, Benjamín Alvarado, 31,
    37n22, 108, 367–80, 386, 389-91
    passim, 393, 395-396
Malinowksi, Bronislaw, 29–30
Mamani Condori, Carlos, 25-26, 36n19,
    283–89, 392, 397-98
mandatory testing, 82n1
Manta Air Base, 73
Maoris, 111, 326
Mapuche people, 310–11
Mariátegui, José Carlos, 306
Marcos, Subcomandante, 162–63
MAREZ. See Municipios Autónomos
    Rebeldes Zapatistas (MAREZ)
market tyranny, 360
Martínez Delia, Paulino, 104
Martinez, Glenabah, 22, 27, 331–39, 395
Martínez Luna, Jaime, 23-24, 25, 31,
    85–99, 352, 388, 390, 391
Martínez Vásquez, Victor, 35n7
Marx, Karl, 88, 97, 123
    on communalism, 93, 94
    productivity and, 95
Marxism, 88, 379n3
mass media, 168, 242, 377. See also
    television
Massachusetts, 124, 393
    Ayn Rand curricula in, 68
massacres, 230–31n1, 302. See also Acteal
    massacre; Bagua massacre
materialism, 93
Maya Achi language, 225, 228, 230
Mayan education, 205
Mayan teachers, 158n15
Mayans, 201, 219–20, 266, 267
    in the U.S., 271
McCarty, Teresa, 34–35n4
medicine, traditional. See traditional
    medicine
"melting pot," 118
memory, 372, 394–96
"men and women of corn," 150–51
mental desertion, 392
mestizaje, 105, 173, 195, 196, 202
    Ecuador, 252, 253
Methodological Re-Creation of

Intercultural Bilingual Education
    Achi/Spanish (REMEBI). See
    REMEMBI
methodology of comunalidad. See
    comunalidad: methodology of
Mexican Teachers' Cultural Center. See
    Casa de la Cultura del Maestro
    Mexicano
Mexico, 141–59, 191–97
    Agrarian Law, 154
    Autonomous Department of
        Indigenous Matters (DAAI),
        157n5
    Constitution, 102, 106, 154,
        158n11
        Article 27, 144, 268
    Constitution of 1824, 115
    Constitution of 1857, 86
    Department of Basic Education,
        136
    economic conditions, 74–76
        NAFTA and, 17, 43, 75, 102,
            104, 267
    education policy, 18, 41, 85, 147,
        166, 167
        General Education Act, 106
        "intercultural education," 103,
            107, 149, 162, 183–88
            passim
        State Education Act, 85, 106
    "indigenist" policy, 156n4, 157n5–
        6, 194
    indigenous education, 101–13,
        115–24 passim, 159n15,
        180–90 passim, 208
    indigenous peoples' rights, 142–45
        passim
        General Law of Linguistic
            Rights of Indigenous
            Peoples, 200
        Law for Indigenous Rights,
            177n6
    "Pluriethnic Autonomous
        Regions," 379n3
    political parties, 145, 374
    Revolution, 87, 143, 273
    schools' imposition of Spanish, 57

Rengifo Vásquez, Grimaldo, 24-25,
    32, 277–81, 376, 377–78, 380n10,
    387-89
reparations, 269
repression, 201
    Argentina, 306–7, 308–9
    Colombia, 355
    Mexico, 14, 48, 105, 109, 268, 375
    Peru, 289n1
    South America, 72
    Turkey, 49–50
    See also massacres; state terrorism
resource exploitation. See natural
    resource exploitation
respect, 94, 95, 108, 144, 249, 279, 280,
    375. See also disrespect
restitution, 269
Reyna, John J., 334–35
Ribeiro, Darcy, 273–74
rights, 156n1–2, 208–9, 219, 220, 247,
    268
    Argentina, 310
    Barbados I and, 266
    citizenship and, 371
    Guatemala, 225
    ILO Convention 69 and, 157n9,
        158n11
    Mexico, 142–49 passim, 181, 196
    norms and, 155
    struggle and, 363
    See also Bill of Indigenous Rights
        (Mexico); language rights;
        seeds: human rights and
riots, tortilla. See tortilla riots
Rockwell, Elsie, 161–77, 392, 393
Romero, Guerino, 335, 336
Romero, Juan de Jesus. See de Jesus
    Romero, Juan
Roosevelt, Theodore, 332
roots, 119
Rozat, Guy Dupeyront, 190n12
Ruíz Ortiz, Ulises, 14
rural out-migration, 102, 104, 166

"salad bowl" concept, 118
Salete Caldart, R., 321
Salinas de Gortari, Carlos, 116
Salvadorans, 371

San Andrés Accords, 144, 145, 154,
    157n6–7, 158n11, 158n15, 162, 164
San Cristóbal de las Casas, 267
San Francisco, 348, 371
San José del Progreso, Oaxaca, 103
San Juan Bautista Tuxtepec. See Tuxtepec
San Miguel, Walker, 297
Sandoval Cruz, Fausto, 133-139
Santa Cruz y Calahumana, Andrés de,
    297
Sarayaku people, 222–23
Sarmiento, Domingo F., 303–6 passim,
    313n5
Satz, R. N., 338
school decolonization, 315–30
school inspectors, 307
schooling. See education
schooling, compulsory. See compulsory
    schooling
schools. See boarding schools;
        clandestine schools; colleges and
        universities; high schools; middle
        schools
scientism, 376
Scotland, 42
secret schools. See clandestine schools
secret societies, 46, 48, 72, 148
seed banks, 13, 76
seeds, 13, 19, 35n5, 55, 280
    human rights and, 55, 62n6, 151–52
    See also genetically modified seeds
self-censorship, 47
self-determination. See autonomy
self-evaluation, 323–24
Sem Techo, 165
separatist movements, 144
September 11, 2001, terrorist attacks,
    133–34
seventies (decade), 264–66 passim
shame, 219, 230
silence, 385-86, 392
Silences (Olsen), 385
Siles Zuazo, Hernán, 329n2
Sinañi, Avelino, 318
Sindicato Nacional de Trabajadores de la
    Educación (SNTE). See National
    Syndicate of Education Workers
    (SNTE)